Philosophy and Politics - Critical Explorations

Volume 35

The purpose of Philosophy and Politics - Critical Explorations is to publish high quality volumes that reflect original research pursued at the juncture of philosophy and politics. Over the past 20 years new important areas of inquiry at the crossroads of philosophy and politics have undergone impressive developments or have emerged anew. Among these, new approaches to human rights, transitional justice, religion and politics and especially the challenges of a post-secular society, global justice, public reason, global constitutionalism, multiple democracies, political liberalism and deliberative democracy can be included. Philosophy and Politics - Critical Explorations addresses each and any of these interrelated yet distinct fields as valuable manuscripts and proposal become available, with the aim of both being the forum where single breakthrough studies in one specific subject can be published and at the same time the areas of overlap and the intersecting themes across the various areas can be composed in the coherent image of a highly dynamic disciplinary continent. Some of the studies published are bold theoretical explorations of one specific theme, and thus primarily addressed to specialists, whereas others are suitable for a broader readership and possibly for wide adoption in graduate courses. The series includes monographs focusing on a specific topic, as well as collections of articles covering a theme or collections of articles by one author. Contributions to this series come from scholars on every continent and from a variety of scholarly orientations.

Zhuoyao Li

Pluralism, Confucianism, and Artificial Intelligence

Toward A Pluralistic Political Theory

Springer

Zhuoyao Li
St. John Hall B30 #16
St. John's University
Queens, NY, USA

ISSN 2352-8370 ISSN 2352-8389 (electronic)
Philosophy and Politics - Critical Explorations
ISBN 978-3-032-25604-1 ISBN 978-3-032-25605-8 (eBook)
https://doi.org/10.1007/978-3-032-25605-8

This Springer imprint is published by the registered company Springer Nature Switzerland AG
The registered company address is: Gewerbestrasse 11, 6330 Cham, Switzerland

Introduction

The crisis of modernity has never been the absence of reason but the proliferation of its forms. From the Enlightenment's confidence in universal rationality to the post-metaphysical humility of contemporary political theory, the modern project has been defined by its oscillation between the aspiration to moral unity and the reality of ethical diversity. The question that animates this book—how the universal claims of reason can coexist with the plural forms of human life—emerges not as a merely academic problem but as the deepest condition of modern legitimacy. Every effort to ground political authority, moral obligation, or social integration has, in one way or another, confronted the same aporia: how can coercive power be justified to all without erasing the diversity that constitutes the human world?

In the classical city-state, the unity of moral and civic life was achieved only at the cost of exclusion; in the Christian and early modern imagination, universal salvation required the suppression of rival beliefs; and in the liberal modernity that succeeded them, the rational individual replaced the citizen of the good as the bearer of universal moral law, only to find oneself estranged in a world of competing reasons. What was once experienced as the collapse of divine or metaphysical authority has become a permanent feature of the human condition: pluralism is no longer an aberration but the horizon of all political and moral thought.

The central question of this book is: *how can political legitimacy be sustained under conditions of deep reasonable pluralism?* The book argues that the task of modern political philosophy is not to overcome the tension between universality and particularity, but to articulate a framework within which their coexistence can be both legitimate and productive. Rather than seeking a synthesis, we must learn to inhabit the space of their difference. Specifically, this book argues that John Rawls's *proviso*, often treated as a procedural side note in *Political Liberalism*, in fact articulates a deeper logic of pluralistic justification that extends far beyond liberal democracy. The *proviso*'s modest rule—that comprehensive doctrines may enter public discourse provided they are later expressed in terms of and eventually strengthen public reason—captures the fragile equilibrium between freedom and justification that defines modern legitimacy.

This thesis can be demonstrated from three interrelated aspects of modernity. Part I of this book undertakes a reconstruction that leads to a reinterpretation of the *proviso*. Chapter 1 reconstructs the distinction between morality and ethics and sets up the perennial conflict between the universal and the particular. Chapter 2 focuses on justification as the bridge between universal morality and particular ethics and reinterprets the *proviso* as the foundation for a pluralistic political theory.

If Part I reconstructs the philosophical core of the *proviso*, Part II of the book tests its resilience against a different moral ontology. In Confucian ethics, the person is defined not by autonomy but by relational roles. Authority arises from moral exemplarity rather than procedural agreement. To many liberal theorists, such hierarchy appears incompatible with equality. Yet, Confucianism's emphasis on moral self-rectification and harmonious reciprocity offers resources for reimagining the motivational dimension that procedural liberalism lacks. The Confucian challenge to the *proviso* is twofold. First, can a tradition grounded in filial piety and ritual propriety recognize moral equality? Second, can its hierarchical conception of virtue coexist with the *proviso*'s egalitarianism? This book contends that both questions can be answered affirmatively if Confucian ethics is interpreted through the lens of reciprocal justification. Part II thus interprets Confucianism not as an alternative to liberalism but as its interlocutor. Chapter 3 introduces the idea of deep reasonable pluralism and argues that a modified version of the *proviso* can be utilized to construct a pluralistic Confucian theory of liberal democracy. Chapter 4 applies the pluralistic perspective to argue against Confucian meritocracy and for a pluralistic view of legitimacy. Chapter 5 examines the dualist constitutionalism in South Korea between the liberal Constitution and the Confucian constitution as a case study. Chapter 6 extends the pluralistic theory to political Confucianism in the context of global justice.

Part III of the book transposes the logic of the *proviso* into the technological domain. The rise of algorithmic governance confronts humanity with a new kind of pluralism: systems of artificial reason that participate in decision-making without the capacity for moral understanding. Machine learning models, trained on vast datasets, generate outcomes that shape human lives yet their inner workings often resist explanation. In such contexts, the classical liberal premise that legitimacy rests on reciprocal justification seems to falter. How can citizens demand reasons from systems that cannot speak? How can the *proviso* survive when its interlocutors include non-rational agents? The answer, this book argues, lies in extending the *proviso*'s procedural structure to the design and governance of AI systems. Just as citizens in a plural democracy must translate their private reasons into publicly accessible justifications, so must algorithmic systems be designed to render their decision processes intelligible to those affected. Transparency, contestability, and participatory oversight become the technological analogues of public reason. Chapter 7 outlines the basics of artificial intelligence and its social, moral, and political challenges, and ends with a speculative model of Confucian artificial intelligence and its discontents. Chapter 8 applies the pluralistic political theory by constructing an extended version of the *proviso* to guide artificial intelligence adoption, policy, and regulation.

Across its three parts, the book argues that the *proviso*, far from being a parochial device of liberal etiquette, articulates a general logic of justification that can ground a pluralistic political theory. To appreciate the *proviso* is to recognize the dignity of others as beings who must be addressed with reasons rather than coerced by force. In a world where pluralism has ceased to be a merely theoretical problem and has become the empirical condition of political life, the *proviso* functions not as a definitive solution but as a normative discipline—a mode of discourse that sustains the possibility of universality within the persistence of difference. The task of political philosophy, therefore, is not to foreclose the space of justification through definitive resolutions, but to preserve and renew it through ongoing acts of reason-giving. This book undertakes precisely that task: to trace the logic of the *proviso* from its foundation in liberal political theory to its prospective transformation within a global and technologically mediated order, and to argue that the right to justification remains the most profound and radical articulation of human freedom.

Acknowledgment

This book continues the line of inquiry I began in *Political Liberalism, Confucianism, and the Future of Democracy in East Asia* (2020). While my thinking has evolved in significant ways over the past few years, the central narrative and philosophical concerns of that earlier project remain integral to the present volume. In many respects, this work both deepens and extends my earlier arguments while addressing new and urgent questions that have emerged in our rapidly changing world. We are living through an extraordinary historical moment, and I hope that this book makes some modest contribution to understanding where we stand and where we might be headed.

Several chapters of this book were first presented at conferences and workshops, where I benefited from generous feedback and critical engagement. Chapter 3 was presented at the 2025 Annual Meeting of the American Philosophical Association (Central Division). An earlier version of Chap. 4 was delivered at the 2022 Conference of the Northern New England Philosophical Association (NNEPA). Chapter 5 was discussed in a workshop at the Institute of Korean Philosophy and Culture (IKPC) at Sungkyunkwan University, and an earlier version of Chap. 8 was presented at the 2025 Meeting of the Long Island Philosophical Society.

Different versions of several chapters have appeared elsewhere. A slightly different version of Chap. 3 was previously published at *Comparative Political Theory*, 2: 2 (2022), pp. 148–164. Chapter 4 was published under the same title at *Philosophy & Social Criticism*, 46: 9 (2020), pp. 1076–1092. Chapter 6 appeared as a contribution in Janusz Salamon and Hsin-Wen Lee (eds.), *The Bloomsbury Handbook of Global Justice and East Asian Philosophy (Bloomsbury Publishing, 2024).* I thank the respective publishers for kindly granting permission to reproduce portions of those works here.

In the course of writing this book, I have incurred many intellectual and personal debts. My colleagues in the Department of Philosophy at St. John's University have offered invaluable feedback, encouragement, and collegial support. I am especially grateful to David Rasmussen, Alessandro Ferrara, and Sungmoon Kim for insightful conversations that helped shape key chapters of this work. Their intellectual generosity has left a lasting mark on the arguments developed in the pages that follow.

Competing Interests The author has no competing interests to declare that are relevant to the content of this manuscript.

Contents

Part I
Pluralism

Chapter 1
Between Morality and Ethics

Abstract This chapter reconstructs the perennial tension between universal morality and particular ethics in modern political philosophy, drawing on Habermas, Forst, and Rawls to argue that morality, grounded in the human capacity for reciprocal justification, serves as a freestanding framework prior to ethical diversity. It critiques traditional approaches for failing to reconcile these domains without authoritarianism or formalism, showing how Habermas's discourse ethics achieves separation but exacerbates a motivation problem in pluralistic societies. This chapter lays the foundation for the book's pluralistic *proviso* as the bridge enabling legitimate coexistence of universality and particularity under deep reasonable pluralism.

Keywords Morality · Ethics · Justification · Habermas · Forst · Reasonable pluralism

1.1 Introduction

At the center of pluralism is the ever-changing relationship between the universal and the particular, which has never been harmonious. How do people's particular and diverse beliefs be properly reconciled to support a universal and commanding system that not only functions but also respects said beliefs? From the Greek *polis* to the modern liberal democracy, the political affair between the universal and the particular has never truly come to sustainable fruition that equally reflects both aspects of reality. In the seemingly homogeneous Greek ethical order, the coherence came at the cost of its short-lived blossom rooted in a deep tension between the family and the state. Once the homogeneity broke down, later political theorists have been "at once satisfied and stupefied"—stupefied because reality, like Messer Remirro de Orco, is cruelly cut in half, and satisfied because now they are able to

Z. Li, *Pluralism, Confucianism, and Artificial Intelligence*, Philosophy and Politics - Critical Explorations 35, https://doi.org/10.1007/978-3-032-25605-8_1

renew the task and reshape the political reality.[1] Whenever the two forces come close to be unified, tension breaks out and ruins the system. Thomas Hobbes' universal sovereignty overpowers its particular citizens with fear, Jean-Jacques Rousseau's general will suffocates the particular interest of its *citoyen*, Immanuel Kant's categorical imperative and self-legislative subject are too formalistic to be effective, G. W. F. Hegel's recognition-based constitutional monarchy bears of the risk of justifying totalitarianism, just to name a few examples. It would appear that the traditional approaches are running out of power, and the universal and the particular can never be fully reconciled. How to maintain a legitimate political system that is not simultaneously at the cost of its citizens' individual liberty and equality remains the perennial question.

The advent of modernity and pluralism only add to the complexity of the problem. The tension between the universal and the particular further manifests itself in such issues as multiculturalism and global justice, making the problem ever so urgent. Jürgen Habermas' unique approach based on his ingenious discourse ethics represents both a re-examination of and a distinct attempt to solve the problem. According to Habermas, one of the crucial reasons for the failures of traditional political theories is that they were under the spell of the teleological and metaphysical point of view—such as the philosophy of the consciousness and the philosophy of history—that is no longer applicable in the pluralistic and post-metaphysical world of modernity. A modern problem requires a modern solution. Therefore, Habermas, like Hegel, draws a fundamental distinction between morality (*Moralität*) and ethics (*Sittlichkeit*): the former refers to the universal and transcendent aspect, and the latter refers to the particular and contextual aspect. Habermas' approach, in a way, is contingent upon a focus and sublimation of the moral and the universal, and the avoidance and transformation of the ethical and the particular. In order not to follow the overburdened footsteps of his predecessors in trying to maintain both aspects in a teleological and metaphysical manner, Habermas rebuilds the foundation of his new approach almost entirely on the universalizability of his discourse principle. In a nutshell, Habermas creates a fundamental separation to deal with the fundamental tension.

In this chapter, I will show that Habermas' discourse ethics *does* represent a break from traditional approaches and hence is able to open up brand new possibilities in dealing with the universal-particular problem and in turn the issue of pluralism. In order to maintain his discourse principle in the moral and political sphere, Habermas abstracts norms and principles, and restricts himself in dealing only with the question of the just. However, the separation of the question of the just from that of the good does not mean that the two are not interrelated. Instead, the separation Habermas creates gives birth to a twofold motivation problem that is by no means easy to solve. By "motivation problem" I mean the perennial problem of how to motivate people to become a member of a certain community and participate in its

[1] Niccolò Machiavelli, *The Prince*, 2nd, trans. Harvey C. Mansfield (The University of Chicago Press, 1998), 30.

political function. More importantly, the motivation problem shows that the more abstract and simple discourse ethics makes the moral and political sphere, the more substantial and complex the ethical and civil sphere becomes. In the context of pluralism, there is then a trade-off between the moral pluralism of the just and the ethical pluralism of the good, and Habermas' solution is able to deal with the former only at the cost of exacerbating the latter, which leads to what I will refer to as "deep reasonable pluralism" in later chapters. In conclusion, I will argue that the moral question of the just cannot be sufficiently answered without at least creating the condition for answering the ethical question of the good. The condition, as we will see in Chap. 2, is a justificatory framework that reconciles the universal with the particular and properly accommodates pluralism.

1.2 The Moral and the Ethical

We tend to disagree with one another on virtually every issue, ranging from what kind of sugary soda the government should ban to what kind of life one ought to live. Often, we are left with diverse claims that are so different and perhaps even incommensurable that moral claims inevitably imply small-scale authoritarianism when addressed among free and equal persons.[2] There are two possible scenarios when people argue and disagree with one another about a moral issue. In one scenario, the argument is between a moralist and an amoralist, and the primary disagreement occurs in terms of the question "why be moral?" because the amoralist simply does not take morality into consideration. In the other scenario, the argument is between two moral persons, and disagreements occur in terms of which moral standpoint ought to be adopted, since they each holds a different moral view.[3] According to Rainer Forst, the first scenario, or the fact that some philosophers are still trying to convince amoralists or "moral skeptics" why they need to be moral is, to borrow Heidegger's remark, "a scandal of philosophy."[4] The question of "Why be moral?" does not even arise for a moral person; and someone who does not understand herself morally simply cannot be brought to see the point of morality.[5] In other words, for the most of us, although we might disagree in terms of *how* morality is grounded, *that* morality exists and has a foundation is shared by moral beings; otherwise moral appraisals and reproaches will make no sense in everyday language. If morality is the shared basis on top of which we form our different points

---

[2] Gerald Gaus, *The Order of Public Reason: A Theory of Freedom and Morality in a Diverse and Bounded World* (Cambridge University Press, 2011), xvi.

[3] The third scenario, in which two amoralists disagree with each other on a moral issue is inconceivable, because both are outside morality and hence can neither agree nor disagree on a moral issue.

[4] Rainer Forst, *The Right to Justification: Elements of a Constructivist Theory of Justice*, trans. Jeffery Flynn (New York: Columbia University Press, 2011), 58.

[5] Ibid., 58.

of view, then what is the source of moral disagreements? In this book, I mean by morality the most fundamental framework that every human being possesses that makes meaningful social communication and the sense of "ought" possible. By ethics I mean particular points of view that each one of us forms on the basis of the general and reciprocal moral framework under the influence of such social factors as culture, religion, philosophy, and so on. Morality and ethics share an intimate relationship. On the one hand, ethical views are impossible without morality, because the former derive the sense and power of "ought" from the latter. On the other hand, how we understand and ground morality is also shaped by our ethical views, which is why utilitarianists would ground morality on different concepts of the good and Christian theologians might offer a religious foundation for morality. Nonetheless, morality as defined in this narrow sense is something sharable among every person and on the basis of which all ethical views develop.

In light of this distinction, moral disagreements become two-dimensional. First and foremost there is the shared basis of morality, without which no disagreement can be formed, and we confront a Kierkegaardian "absolute paradox."[6] Again, we might disagree on *how* morality is grounded, but *that* morality exists is the shared foundation among all human beings. Only secondly are there actual disagreements, which is again twofold. On the one hand, two moral persons can disagree in terms of their different ethical views (within a shared moral framework), in which case their disagreement is a purely ethical one. On the other hand, a moral person might accuse the other of not carrying out the latter's moral duty, and the disagreement is in terms of what *ought* to be done. The latter case is tricky, because ethical views reshape our understanding of morality too, and this apparent moral disagreement might be reduced to an ethical one as a matter of interpretation. For instance, a conditional religious (and hence ethical) duty is easily misunderstood as an unconditional (and hence moral) duty when the accuser fails to see the difference between the two, which often leads to an authoritarian demand that infringes upon the status of the accused as free and equal person.[7] If the disagreement is indeed an ethical one, there is probably nothing we can do to fully resolve it, because the disagreement ranges across two possibly incommensurable ethical views. Consequently, the ethical "ought" becomes equally valid and hence equally powerless to function as a moral criterion. On an individual level, the claim that one ethical person "ought" to do something simply because certain ethical view says so is indeed what Gaus calls small-scale authoritarianism.[8] On a political level, the history of war of religions fully demonstrates how devastating the world could become without a principle of toleration. Hence, to avoid the totalitarian implication, the only solution is to exclude the ethical and focus only on the moral, which crosses the boundaries of different

---

[6] Søren Kierkegaard, *Philosophical Fragments*, trans. Edna Hong and Howard Hong (Princeton University Press, 1985).

[7] This is also a common criticism made against the Kantian and abstract morality culminating in the Categorical Imperative.

[8] Gerald Gaus, *The Order of Public Reason: A Theory of Freedom and Morality in a Diverse and Bounded World* (Cambridge University Press, 2011), xvi.

ethical views and maintain a general and reciprocal coverage among *every* moral person. The success of a theory of justice thus depends on how well it accomplishes this goal.

Forst's central message in *The Right to Justification* is that justification is behind everything, and the right to reasonable justification is the ground on which we develop a viable theory of justice.[9] Specifically, Forst argues that a variety of definitions of human beings, such as *animal rationale* and *animal sociale*, essentially characterize humans as justifying and reason-giving beings: "they not only have the ability to justify or take responsibility for their beliefs and actions by giving reasons to others, but in certain contexts they see this as a duty and expect that others will do the same."[10] *Gründe*, the German word for reason, implies that reasons establish a supportive ground (*Grund*), which point Forst takes to mean that the ground created by reasons "must therefore be a shared, common basis for justified, well-founded thought and action."[11] In other words, this reason-giving and reason-demanding property of human beings is a good candidate to ground something as general and reciprocal as the Kantian morality without resorting to a metaphysical "must."

Moreover, Forst draws a distinction between "rational grounding" and "reasonable justification," which echoes Rawls' similar distinction according to which the rational refers only to one's self-interest, whereas the reasonable must include considerations of others.[12] To illustrate, Forst argues that the moral and the ethical try to answer differently the question "What should I do?" A moral answer requires "considering the legitimate claims of all morally affected persons," where as an ethical answer, on the other hand, is concerned with "the values, ideals, and 'final ends' that constitute a good life and how this is then to be realized," none of which needs to take into consideration competing ethical views.[13] Since justification is behind everything, we now have two manifestations of justification. Ethical justification, which corresponds to rational grounding, should be viewed in three dimensions: that of the individual ethical person, that of those who share particular ethical views, and that of the ethical community. Regardless of which dimension one is in, ethical views can be justified on rational grounds, that is, whether the views are in conformity to particular ethical standards. Moral justification is simpler in depth but more complicated in scope, because in the end a moral view must "in a strict sense be normatively justifiable equally in relation to *every* affected person, and that a *categorically* binding force inheres in moral norms because no reasonable moral ground can be brought to bear against them."[14] Sufficient moral justification must include

---

[9] Rainer Forst, *The Right to Justification: Elements of a Constructivist Theory of Justice*, trans. Jeffery Flynn (New York: Columbia University Press, 2011), 1.

[10] Ibid., 1.

[11] Ibid., 13.

[12] John Rawls, *Political Liberalism* (New York: Columbia University Press, 2005), 49.

[13] Ibid., 15.

[14] Ibid., 17.

every moral being, rather than only the particular beings belonging to a particular ethical community in the case of ethical justification.

Now we can put these concepts together and line them up in two general groups. The first and moral group includes the concept of the reasonable, a single moral community that includes every moral being, and the right and demand of moral justification that is the same for everyone. The second and ethical group includes the concept of the rational, different ethical communities based on different ethical views, and the demand of ethical justification that differs among ethical community. This distinction between the moral and the ethical has two implications. First, the ethical cannot ground the moral. To use Forst's metaphor here, there is a moral being behind every ethical being, moral justification is logically prior to any ethical justification.[15] If a claim cannot be morally justified, it will not be accepted even if it can be ethically justified.[16] Although ethical views can conflict, morality cannot, because it is the framework that makes ethical disagreements possible. Secondly, the ethical cannot justify the moral. The foundation of morality is not about the vision and the realization of the ethical good "but rather a concern for others within the space of what is reciprocally and generally owed."[17] Thus, no ethical and secondary justification qualifies for a moral and primary justification. As Forst puts it, "a theory of the good, however formally and universally it may be laid out, cannot provide the criteria for the moral ought. For the good, which should be protected and enabled by moral norms, is determined, on the one hand, by individuals themselves in an ethically autonomous way, and on the other hand, with the help of the criteria of reciprocity and generality, for which no objective theory of the good is required."[18] Once again, morality takes priority over ethics.

If the ethical cannot ground and justify the moral, then how should morality be grounded and justified? To answer this question, Forst accepts the Kantian formulation of duty but offers his version with a twist. Combining cognition with recognition, Forst argues that morality is closely linked with the simple *fact* of "being human."[19] To unwrap this fact, it means that "the moral person does not first see a human being and then, on the basis of further consideration, come to the conclusion that the other is a moral person. Rather, cognition and recognition are here so interwoven that an 'evaluative perception' takes pace."[20] This "evaluative perception" is the knowledge and mutual recognition of a moral authority that Kant would label as respect. If this were correct, then the so-called Prichard's dilemma loses its

[15] Rainer Forst, *The Right to Justification: Elements of a Constructivist Theory of Justice*, trans. Jeffery Flynn (New York: Columbia University Press, 2011), 18.

[16] This implication is important for two reasons. First, it is also found in Habermas' works and his deep fear of the ethical that became Nazism in the twentieth century. Second, it paves the road for a negative approach to justice, which I will discuss later.

[17] Ibid., 33.

[18] Ibid., 93.

[19] Ibid., 59.

[20] Ibid., 59.

paradoxical nature.[21] The confusion instead lies in the lack of awareness that the normativity of morality is "a normativity sui generis"; in other words, the sense of "ought" that defines morality owes its existence to the fundamental nature of human beings as justificatory beings, and morality is "merely the form of this 'justifying' existence in a particular practical context."[22] Moreover, the recognition of a moral "ought" is "part of our nature as *animalia rationalia*, as justifying beings," and as reason-giving beings we owe each other generally and reciprocally such justifications. To make it even more Kantian, Forst concludes that "[the] kingdom of ends is of this world"—morality justifies itself in virtue of its own existence and is grounded on the duty of general and reciprocal (or reasonable) justification.[23]

This conclusion is crucial. Like Thomas Scanlon, Forst's conception of morality is narrower than it is broadly conceived, and it includes what we, as human beings in this world, owe to each other on the most fundamental and universal level.[24] Under the influence of Axel Honneth's theory of recognition, Forst's theory of justification is, as he puts it, both reciprocal and general. Reciprocity means that "no one may refuse the particular demands of others that one raises for oneself (reciprocity of content), and that no one may simply assume that others have the same values and interests as oneself or make recourse to "higher truths" that are not shared (reciprocity of reasons)."[25] Generality means that "reasons for generally valid basic norms must be sharable by all those affected."[26] Because of the reciprocal and general structure of justification, Forst argues that "we can call a social context 'political' when human beings find themselves in an 'order of justification,' which consists of norms and institutions that are to govern their lives together—in cooperation as well as in conflict—in a justified or justifiable way."[27] This "order of justification" is none other than the order of justice.[28]

Second, given the priority of the moral over the ethical, there are two senses of "ought." The ethical "ought," which is contingent upon rational grounding of ethical views, loses its general and reciprocal justificatory power; hence, "a theory of the good, however formally and universally it may be laid out, cannot provide the criteria for [a sufficient] ought." The moral "ought" on the other hand is grounded on the

---

[21] Prichard's dilemma argues that morality cannot be justified. On the one hand, it is circular to appeal to anything moral to justify morality, like saying "you ought to do this because it is moral." On the other hand, it defeats the whole purpose of justifying morality if one appeals to anything other than morality, such as utility and other goods, because a person ceases to be moral if something other than morality actually motivates her.

[22] Rainer Forst, *The Right to Justification: Elements of a Constructivist Theory of Justice*, trans. Jeffery Flynn (New York: Columbia University Press, 2011), 61.

[23] Ibid.

[24] Thomas Scanlon, *What We Owe to Each Other* (Harvard University Press, 1998).

[25] Rainer Forst, *The Right to Justification: Elements of a Constructivist Theory of Justice*, trans. Jeffery Flynn (New York: Columbia University Press, 2011), 6.

[26] Ibid., 6.

[27] Ibid., 2.

[28] The later John Rawls, as we will soon see, adopts a very similar understanding of the political.

duty of reasonable justification that is in essence general and reciprocal, which maintains its justificatory power despite a variety of different ethical views. With this insight, what we call reasonable pluralism is rather ethical than moral, because our disagreements are primarily or even exclusively ethical, since morality is generally and reciprocally shared in the first place. Forst's reconstruction of the Kantian moral theory shows that morality is still the framework on top of which we form ethical views, but it at the same time shows that a successful theory of justice in an ethically pluralistic society must be limited to only the moral, and the degree of its success crucially depends on how much the theory excludes the ethical.

1.3 The Great Separation

Like Forst, Habermas draws a distinction between the moral and the ethical. While the moral refers to the abstract and the universal, the ethical refers to the contextual and the particular. Nevertheless, unlike Hegel who proposes that the ethical order will dissolve into morality through his philosophy of history, Habermas argues that the embodiment of the moral principle "is dependent upon the perpetual regeneration of 'norms' and values in concrete contexts of communicative action through the actions and 'collective efforts' of 'sociopolitical movements.'"[29] In other words, the achievement of this incarnation of the moral and universal principle involves two aspects: on the one hand, the moral must be separated from the ethical; on the other hand, the moral principle needs to be transformed into practical principles to address corresponding issues.

As for the first aspect, Rousseau's approach is especially significant to Habermas, because in a way it influenced Kant, Hegel, and most of Habermas' predecessors. Although Rousseau comes closer to a mode of democracy whose legitimacy is produced through its procedure, he nevertheless "gives the idea of self-legislation more of an ethical than a moral interpretation," which not only makes his own approach too contextual to be effective in the modern pluralistic society but also particularly influenced Hegel's grand moral project to culminate in the constitutional monarchy that bears the risk of justifying totalitarianism. Born into a world shaped by National Socialism, this Hegelian dilemma is especially pertinent to Habermas: "an ethic based on the forms of life existing within a culture, would, and in fact did, legitimate acts which we know to be the very contradiction of ethical behavior."[30] Here the difference between Habermas and previous thinkers becomes clear. While his predecessors still work to *solve* this contexualist dilemma within a teleological and metaphysical framework, Habermas seeks to *transcend* it by precisely breaking from the traditional philosophical orientations. The idea is that if the failures of the

[29] Jürgen Habermas, *Moral Consciousenss and Communicative Action*, trans. C. Lenhardt and S. Weber Nicholson (Cambridge: Polity Press, 1990), 203, 208.

[30] David Rasmussen, *Reading Habermas* (Cambridge, Mass.: Basil Blackwell, 1990), 57.

predecessors are caused by their ambition to maintain both the moral and ethical aspects in an equally absolute sense, then it is only reasonable to lower the burden to deal with them individually. Furthermore, Habermas not only makes a distinction between morality and ethics, he also radically breaks from the ethical. In order to do so, Habermas introduces his discourse or communicative ethics.

Discourse ethics is a "normative theory that is implicit in the rules of communication that are presupposed by the competent members of society."[31] Following the linguistic turn of philosophy as well as Lawrence Kohlberg's theory of moral development, Habermas is able to argue that the center of discourse ethics is the discourse principle, which states that "only those norms can claim validity that could meet with the acceptance of all concerned in practical discourse."[32] In other words, discourse principle takes the form of a universalizing principle that distances itself from the ethical and particular contexts.

It is not difficult to recognize the Kantian implication of Habermas' discourse ethics. It is obvious that discourse ethics "is indebted to Kant's *Foundation to the Metaphysics of Morals* and involves a procedural reformulation of the Categorical Imperative."[33] However, as Gulshan Khan points out, Hegel is not at all dismissed in Habermas' discourse ethics. In contrast, "Habermas' use of the term morality shares important similarities with Hegel's notion of a *sittlich* relation or ethical life, that is, as a binding social force rather than a Kantian abstract and formulaic notion of a self-legislative 'rational' principle."[34] Khan goes on to argue that "Habermas' conception of political 'morality' refers not to an abstract rational principle of individual conduct but rather to a *civic* bond, that is, a republican concord on a mode of conduct to be adhered to by all members of the political community."[35] Although I submit that the Hegelian intersubjective emphasis, or the element of social recognition, is absolutely present in Habermas' discourse ethics, it does not follow that it is strong enough to offer what Khan calls a "*civic* bond" that essentially puts deliberative democracy on the same shelf with the Rousseauian democracy. For that matter, one might even go so far as to argue that the intersubjective element was already present in the state of nature, yet it does not follow that the state of nature offers a civic bond as such. Rather, the intersubjective aspect of discourse ethics is generic to the discourse principle and present at the factual level, because Habermas builds his system on the basis of Charles Sanders Peirce's idea of the ideal community of speech, which claims that "the possibility of scientific truth presupposed a scientific community which could make judgments on the validity or invalidity of

---

[31] Andrew Edger, *Habermas: The Key Concepts* (Routledge, 2006), 44.

[32] Jürgen Habermas, *The Inclusion of the Other: Studies in Political Theory* (Cambridge, MA: MIT Press, 1998), 41.

[33] Thomas McCarthy, "Kantian Constructivism and Reconstructivism: Rawls and Habermas in Dialogue," *Ethics*, 1990, 105 (1): 44.

[34] Gulshan Khan, "Politics and Morality in Habermas' Discourse Ethics," *Philosophy & Social Criticism* (forthcoming), 2.

[35] Ibid.

scientific achievements."[36] Since language and the search for consensual truth presuppose a communicative community, the intersubjective aspect of discourse ethics is not something Habermas deliberately import from Hegel. Quite the contrary, it is a universal principle always present in communication.

Nevertheless, the motivation behind Khan's argument is well taken. Habermas' radical separation between the moral and the ethical *does* raise serious questions, especially when such issues as pluralism and social disintegration are taken into consideration. One of the key purposes of this chapter is to examine whether Habermas' notion of morality in the sense of universalizability is adequate enough to create at least a theoretical foundation for the common bond necessary in a pluralist society. Although the separation of morality from ethics prevents Habermas from following the failures of his predecessors, it runs the risk of presenting an oversimplified and incomplete view of reality, which will eventually render the approach inadequate in dealing with the tension between the universal and the particular. In the next section, I will focus on Habermas' reconstructive approach to law as the medium of social integration in *Between Facts and Norms* as an example of discourse ethics in practice.

1.4 Tensions and Separations

Before offering a reconstruction of law based on the system of rights in the famous third chapter of *Between Facts and Norms*, Habermas declares that thus far "no one has succeeded in satisfactorily reconciling private and public autonomy at a fundamental conceptual level."[37] According to Habermas, Kant introduces the element of autonomy by opposing Hobbes with a structural difference between the social contract, which serves as a model for legitimation, and the private contract, which basically regulates exchange relationships.[38] The merit of the social contract is precisely its lack of specific content, because it provides the "performative conditions under which rights acquire legitimate validity."[39] For Kant, "right is the limitation of each person's freedom so that it is compatible with the freedom of everyone, insofar as this is possible in accord with a universal law."[40] On the one hand, Kant links the concept of private autonomy with human rights. Insofar as a person is an autonomous human being, the system of natural rights belongs inalienably to him or her. On the other hand, with the "performative conditions" created essentially by private and autonomous people via the formal social contract, the sovereign lawgiver

[36] David Rasmussen, *Reading Habermas* (Cambridge, Mass.: Basil Blackwell, 1990), 58.

[37] Jürgen Habermas, *Between Facts and Norms: Contributions to A Discourse Theory of Law and Democracy*, trans. William Rehg (Cambridge, Mass.: The MIT Press, 1996), 84.

[38] Ibid., 92.

[39] Ibid., 93.

[40] Immanuel Kant, "On the Proverb: That May Be True in Theory. But Is of No Practical Use," *Perpetual Peace and Other Essays*, trans. T. Humphrey (Indianapolis, 1983), 72.

follows from the "natural rights" of private autonomy.[41] Therefore, political autonomy is explained by Kant *on the basis* of the internal connection between popular sovereignty and human rights.

Rousseau's approach of the general will is the opposite process. Instead of beginning with private autonomy and human rights, Rousseau "starts with the constitution of civic autonomy and produces a fortiori an internal relation between popular sovereignty and human rights."[42] In Rousseau, then, "the exercise of political autonomy no longer stands under the proviso of innate rights. Rather, the normative content of human rights enters into the very mode of carrying out popular sovereignty."[43] In other words, contrary to the Kantian approach, the connection between popular sovereignty and human rights is *the consequence of* the constitution of civic autonomy.

Nevertheless, there is "an unacknowledged competition between morally grounded human rights and the principle of popular sovereignty" in both Kant and Rousseau.[44] In Kant's case, "if the rational will can take shape only in the individual subject, then the individual's moral autonomy must reach through the political autonomy of the united will of all in order to secure the private autonomy of each in advance via natural law."[45] In Rousseau's case, "if the rational will can take shape only in the macrosubject of a people or nation, then political autonomy must be understood as the self-conscious realization of the ethical substance of a concrete community; and private autonomy is protected from the overpowering force of political autonomy only by the nondiscriminatory form of general laws."[46] Both views thus miss the alternative "legitimating force of a discursive process of opinion- and will-formation, in which the illocutionary biding forces of a use of language oriented to mutual understanding serve to bring reason and will together—and lead to convincing positions to which all individuals can agree without coercion"—this is Habermas' discourse principle in a political context.[47] Getting rid of the disadvantages of both approaches, Habermas' discourse principle absorbs the best parts from both Kant and Rousseau. From Kant, it absorbs the formal relationship between individual autonomy and the universal law. From Rousseau, it absorbs the mode of legitimation through democratic procedure. Adding a third and communicative dimension, the discourse principle is able to assume co-originality of private and public autonomy. On the one hand, publicly autonomous sovereignty is legitimated through the procedure of rational deliberation among privately autonomous citizens. On the other hand, participating citizens are privately autonomous because their individual freedom is the

[41] Jürgen Habermas, *Between Facts and Norms: Contributions to A Discourse Theory of Law and Democracy*, trans. William Rehg (Cambridge, Mass.: The MIT Press, 1996), 101.

[42] Ibid.

[43] Ibid.

[44] Ibid., 94.

[45] Ibid., 103.

[46] Ibid.

[47] Ibid.

precondition of the rational procedure. Accordingly, the discourse principle creates the condition to produce legitimacy without succumbing to either the overly subjective Kantian tradition or the overly contextual Rousseauian tradition.

Based on the primary separation between the moral and the universal, and the ethical and the particular, Habermas' discourse principle is essentially a principle of universalization, because "a norm is valid when the foreseeable consequence and side effects of its general observance for the interests and value-orientations of *each individual* could be *jointly* accepted by *all* concerned without coercion."[48] In *Between Facts and Norms*, the discourse principle transforms itself into the democratic principle in the legal and political contexts to deal with the modern disintegration of society and value pluralism. In a nutshell, Habermas argues that law functions as the modern medium of social integration, through which the democratic principle obtains its actual force.

Similar to the self-transformation of the discourse principle into the democratic principle, the primary tension between the universal and the particular also takes a different form from a legal perspective between validity and facticity. On the one hand, there is the political tension between compliance and coercion, which solidifies itself in the need of norms that bring about the "willingness to comply *simultaneously* by means of de facto constraint and legitimate validity."[49] On the other hand, there is also the legal tension between form and substance, which is illustrated by Ronald Dworkin's search for a liberal ethic that is both "sufficiently formal to go along with the disagreements one can reasonably anticipate in regard to preferred life orientations" and at the same time "substantial enough to constitute a motivational base for implementing abstract liberal principles."[50] Both tensions, according to Habermas, are reducible to the separation of validity from facticity as a result of social evolution.

In order to demonstrate this point, Habermas offers an imaginary account of two mechanisms of social integration in the pre-pluralistic world, where validity and facticity were perfectly fused. The first one involves the concept of the "lifeworld," which he draws from Edmund Husserl, and refers to "the horizon of shared, unproblematic beliefs [that]...are nourished by these resources of the *always already familiar*."[51] In other words, the universal and the particular are fully fused together within this "'forgotten' foundation of meaning inhabiting everyday practice and experience," thus creating an identity between facticity and validity—what *is* is what *ought* to be.[52] The other one reveals itself in archaic institutions where "cognitive and normative expectations merge and harden into an unbroken complex of convictions linked with motives and value orientations."[53] Unlike the previous case,

---

[48] Gulshan Khan, "Politics and Morality in Habermas' Discourse Ethics," *Philosophy & Social Criticism* (forthcoming), 5.

[49] Jürgen Habermas, *Between Facts and Norms: Contributions to A Discourse Theory of Law and Democracy*, trans. William Rehg (Cambridge, Mass.: The MIT Press, 1996), 27.

[50] Ibid., 63.

[51] Ibid., 22.

[52] Ibid.

[53] Ibid., 23.

the second mechanism functions through "an authority that imperiously confronts us and arouses ambivalent feelings."[54] Any imposed human sanctions are therefore only secondary because they obtain their actual force from the higher fusion between the factual and the valid in the authority. Therefore, these two "primitive" conditions of social integration fused together facticity and validity in an indissoluble manner, and the tensions mentioned earlier did not exist.

However, social evolution and the advent of pluralism gradually eliminate such "metasocial guarantees" as the lifeworld certainties and the sacred authorities.[55] Consequently, facticity and validity no longer enjoy the indissoluble fusion and tensions arise. Modern law, according to Habermas, now functions as the third mechanism of social integration. Yet the presupposition is that the cohesion of law is its power of enforcement, and law is a coercive instrument only when it is valid. Social integration thus requires "the facticity of the *enforcement* of law [to be] intertwined with the *legitimacy* of a genesis of law that claims to be rational because it guarantees liberty" (emphasis added).[56] In other words, the tension between private and public autonomy, as well as that between popular sovereignty and human rights must be reconciled before the facticity and validity of the law can be juxtaposed.

As shown in the previous section, Habermas' co-originality thesis precisely answers this demand. Using rights as the starting point of his reconstructive approach to law and on the basis of the democratic principle, which states that "only those statutes may claim legitimacy that can meet with the assent (*Zustimmung*) of all citizens in a *discursive process of legislation* that in turn has been legally constituted," Habermas argues that rights "should not only institutionalize a rational political will-formation, but should also guarantee the very *medium* in which this will-formation can express itself as a common will of freely associated consociates under law" (emphasis added).[57] In the meantime, the actualization of the system of rights requires a constitutional state as the rational instrument of the production of legitimate law. Under the framework created by the democratic principle, the system of rights and the constitutional state are able to create a deliberative democracy where citizens' subjective rights are guaranteed through legal enforcement whose validity is justified through the process of democratic legislation in the constitutional state. Hence, the tension between facticity and validity is reconciled, and the discourse principle in the form of the democratic principle creates a framework capable of dealing with not only social disintegration but also value pluralism.

Because of the intrinsically universal and context-transcending characters of the discourse principle, the reconstructed modern law is now the new mechanism of social integration, and both the political and the legal dilemmas are diminished. Nevertheless, the seeming advantage of the discourse ethics produces some further problems.

---

[54] Ibid., 24.

[55] Ibid., 26.

[56] Ibid., 28.

[57] Ibid., 110, 143.

1.5 The Motivation Problem

The superiority of Habermas' approach is twofold. On the one hand, stretched across the entire spectrum of validity claims, discourse ethics offers only "a *guide* for reconstructing the network of discourses that … provides the matrix from which democratic authority emerges."[58] On the other hand, it also pertains to insights so as to offer (a weak) necessity.[59] In other words, discourse ethics is able to avoid the teleological "ought" by decentering itself and get rid of the metaphysical "must" by "innerworldly" transcending itself.[60] However, this advantage raises another perennial question. How to motivate people to become a member of a certain community and participate in its political function is sometimes referred to as the "motivation problem" in political philosophy, which is also one of the central criteria of testing the success of a political theory. Facing modern pluralism and social disintegration, Habermas must be able to solve the motivation problem before claiming any final superiority over his predecessors. Nevertheless, his approach precisely faces some rather serious challenges here.

Among Habermas' predecessors, the motivation problem is dealt with in a variety of ways. In Hobbes' Leviathan, the motivation is simply fear—whoever does not comply with the Sovereign cannot be a citizen and hence loses his or her privilege of being protected against the brutal state of nature. In Locke's state, people's motivation to join the social compact coincides with the desire to protect their private property. Finally in Rousseau's community, the motivation becomes the transformative experience citizens have in order to become organic parts of the general will. Unlike those who try to directly reconcile the universal and the particular, Habermas deliberately separates the two and tries to show that the two can be unified through the universal because the particular is co-original with the universal.

However, this strategic move to avoid direct confrontation with the universal-particular problem is not cost-free. In fact, the strength it gains it loses in justification. Unlike Hobbes, Locke, and Rousseau, Habermas faces a twofold motivation problem. Based on the separation between morality and ethics, Habermas' discourse and democratic principles must be able to motivate not only people within the moral and political system to engage in discourses and communicative actions, but also people within the ethical and civil society to transcend their particular and contextual views in order to contribute to the moral procedure. As for the people already in the community of discourse ethics, the co-originality thesis works, because people's motivation lies in the anticipation to reach consensus. Nevertheless, even here the bargaining process does not necessarily lead to consensus. In fact, according to Alastair MacIntyre, some of the major moral claims in modern societies are in fact

[58] Ibid., 5.

[59] Ibid.

[60] Ibid.

incommensurable with one another.[61] Furthermore, Habermas' discourse ethics has been attacked most frequently because "its requirement of consensus in the face of the multiplicity of value-perspectives that characterize modern democracies would make moral judgments impossible to achieve."[62] The difficulty—or perhaps the impossibility—of achieving consensus is "reinforced by the fact that participants in discourses are not required to deny their actual, empirical needs and desires but only to distance themselves from them temporarily; the consensus reached in practical discourse is *a union of empirical wills*" (emphasis added).[63] Similar to the macro-case of the current European Union where different nationalisms keep competing with one another even under the same union, it is very doubtful if this "union of empirical wills" will reach true consensus in the organic sense of the term. If not, even with democratic procedures and proper legislation, it remains to be seen how modern laws based on democratic consensus do not in fact coerce citizens, since after all the participants reach the foundational consensus only by distancing from, not transforming, their needs and desires.

One way out of this problem is of course to insist further on Habermas' moral principle by arguing that consensual norms and principles are able to become even more abstract, and that the set of questions which can be answered rationally from the moral point of view can be restricted to even smaller circles.[64] However, this intensified strategy to separate morality from ethics puts Habermas in an awkward position. In order to maintain his discourse principle in the moral and political sphere, he has to abstract norms and principles and restrict himself in dealing only with the question of the just. However, as it shall become clearer in the next section, the theoretical separation between the two realms does not mean that the two are not interrelated. The more abstract and simple discourse ethics makes the moral sphere, the more substantial and complex the ethical sphere becomes, which is deeply problematic.

As for the people in the ethical sphere, although "every person, by definition, has the capacity to respond to validity claims and, hence, to engage in communicative action, not every person is able or willing to engage in that reflective form of communicative action that Habermas calls discourse."[65] This is especially the case for citizens with religious beliefs who have to at least to some extent translate their private and religious languages to the public and political language before engaging in any moral discourses. Since people in the ethical sphere have to form public opinion through the public sphere in order to influence the moral sphere and the political system, it is essential that people in the civil and ethical realm be nurtured with "the background culture in which the practice of critical evaluation of validity

[61] Alasdair MacIntyre, *After Virtue: A Study in Moral Theory*, 3rd Ed (Indiana: University of Notre Dame Press, 2007).

[62] Maeve Cooke, "Habermas, Autonomy and the Identity of the Self," *Philosophy & Social Criticism*, 1992, vol. 18 (3–4), 276.

[63] Ibid.

[64] Ibid., 277.

[65] Ibid., 279.

claims is established" and equipped with the motivation "to enter into the kind of critical and open discussion of validity claims that Habermas describes as discourses."[66] But with the abstraction and simplification of the moral sphere, the discourse ethics becomes more and more of a "formal ethic, in the sense that it offers no substantive ethical orientation."[67] People are then free not to choose to engage in the Habermasian discourse precisely because of the Habermasian reason. In order for the Habermasian project to work, citizens must in the first step be motivated to choose to become a member of the community of critical discourse and then be motivated once again to reach a consensus that might or might not be in conformity with their own needs and desires. Both steps appear precarious to say the least. The inadequacy of dealing with the motivation problem points to the essential problem in Habermas' approach, which is better illustrated in the context of pluralism.

1.6 Two Pluralisms

As a formal ethic, discourse ethics "does not provide a basis for adjudication between alternative value systems," which means that "a differentiation has been made between questions of justice, which are derived from universalistic procedures, and questions of the good life, which are posed within a particular life-context."[68] Another way of understanding this distinction is to draw a distinction between moral pluralism and ethical pluralism; the former of which refers to the different systems of political values, and the latter of which refers to the different orientations and ways of life. Habermas makes it clear that philosophy is no longer capable of intervening in the latter, and his strategy to separate morality from ethics and constructing discourse ethics on the principle of universalizability are precisely modern applications of the Delphic motto of "know thyself."[69]

However, as shown in the previous section, Habermas' discourse ethics has a difficult time satisfying the criterion of motivation, which is essential in dealing with modern pluralism. The reason is that Habermas must motivate people twice in order for them to engage in discourses and democratic procedures, first in the ethical and contextual sphere, and then in the moral and political sphere. However, because of the formalistic nature of discourse ethics, it does not produce any substantial ethical orientation to deal with ethical pluralism and motivate people to create the condition for moral and political discourses. Furthermore, even if a

---

[66] Ibid.

[67] David Rasmussen, *Reading Habermas* (Cambridge, Mass.: Basil Blackwell, 1990), 62.

[68] Ibid.

[69] Jürgen Habermas, "Are There Postmetaphysical Answers to the Question: What is the "Good Life," *The Future of Human Nature* (MA: Polity Press, 2003).

consensus is achieved, it remains to be seen if the "union of empirical wills" is able to motivate people to act accordingly and adequately deal with value pluralism.

With *Between Facts and Norms*, Habermas deals with the second part of the problem by utilizing modern law as the new mechanism of social cohesion. Granted that laws generated through the democratic procedure and proper legislation on the basis of a consensus reached under the guidance of the discourse principle are both formal enough to deal with pluralism and substantial enough to motivate people to act, Habermas still has to deal with the fact that although everybody is born into the ethical sphere, not everybody is born a proper member of the discourse and democratic community, especially when the interplay between the two spheres is limited to say the least.[70] Within the ethical sphere, an equally pressing pluralism is present. Unlike value or moral pluralism in the political realm, the ethical pluralism includes competing and incommensurate ways of life that disintegrate civil society. Accordingly, there should be two interrelated mechanisms of social integration dealing with two corresponding pluralisms. While Habermas' reconstructed modern laws are able to function as a medium of cohesion in the moral sphere, there is nothing of the kind in the ethical sphere. The immediate result is that the more universal, impartial, and simple the moral sphere is reconstructed, the more particular, contextual, and complex the ethical realm becomes. The ethical consequence of this process is therefore the privatization of life, which produces "extreme forms of individualism…[that] threaten the very social fabric."[71] Facing a wide variety of forms of collective identification, the civic bond that is able to unite a democratic political association as Khan demands is available only accidental. This is because "the free and unconstrained public deliberation of all on matters of common concern is a conceptual impossibility, since the particular forms of life which are presented as its 'impediments' are its very condition of possibility."[72] Through this

---

[70] People in the ethical sphere do not necessarily have to leave their contextual background to engage in moral and political procedures. According to Habermas, in complex societies, "the public sphere consists of an intermediary structure between the political system, on the one hand, and the private sectors of the lifeworld and functional systems, on the other hand." However, in Chap. 8 of *Between Facts and Norms*, Habermas qualifies his argument by saying that only "*under certain circumstances* civil society can acquire influence in the public sphere…and compel the political system to switch over to the official circulation of power." Then what are the "certain circumstances" under which civil society is able to do so? Usually the public sphere is at rest, and the "certain circumstances" are "periods of mobilization" or crisis of the public sphere. In other words, while actors in civil society essentially do not influence the political system when the public sphere is at rest, they can, "in a perceived crisis situation,…assume a surprisingly active and momentous role." During the usual rest of public sphere, the public sphere and hence the political system are influenced mostly by such "insiders" as officeholders or political leaders and "mobilizers" who actively initiate the mobilization of the public sphere, such as the mass-media. Therefore, actual actors in civil societies are only "outsiders" who are only able to passively influence the political system, provided that they are "fortunate" enough to experience crises in public sphere in the first place. Jürgen Habermas, *Between Facts and Norms: Contributions to A Discourse Theory of Law and Democracy*, trans. William Rehg (Cambridge, Mass.: The MIT Press, 1996), 373, 380.

[71] Ibid., 96.

[72] Ibid., 98.

"vicious" circle, the critical preparation for deliberative democracy—the separation between the moral and the ethical—undermines its effects. This is the central problem with Habermas' approach.

To demonstrate this point, it is useful to go back to the biographical note in the beginning of this chapter that supposedly motivated Habermas. Focusing on the Hegelian ethical dilemma materialized in the Nazi movement, Habermas seems to have neglected the opposite danger of an overly formal system of democracy. For instance, the American ethicist Peter Haas tries to answer the question of "how an entire society, not just Nazi party members, willingly participated for over a decade in a state-sponsored program of mass torture that culminated in genocide without serious oppositions from political, legal, medical or regions leaders."[73] Unlike Hannah Arendt's idea of "the banality of evil," Haas' argument focuses on the human ability to redefine good and evil accordingly through an ethic that legitimates behaviors.[74] Although in a different context, Haas' argument brings in the element of legitimation that is central in Habermas' discourse ethics. "The power of an ethic," argues Haas, "ultimately resides in the fact that it provides a system for judging every action in a coherent, non-self-contradictory and intuitively correct way."[75] Moreover, crucial to Haas' theory is his definition of an ethic as "any *formal* system that permits human beings to characterize some actions as good and others as evil, *irrespective of the system's contents*," which, according to Haas, was shared not only by the Nazis but also by most European and American political and religious leaders.[76] Back to Habermas, Haas' argument points to the opposite consequence of the Hegelian and contextual dilemma: an overly formal system bears the risk of being manipulated by the substantial contents within. In the context of pluralism, if the opportunity cost of dealing with the moral pluralism in the political system with discourse ethics is the addition to the complexity of the ethical pluralism in civil society, Habermas' solution, though sufficient to avoid contextualism in the first place, is nevertheless burdened with the dilemma and danger of formalism.

This worry motivates Khan to take odds with the popular reading of Habermas and show that Habermas' "notion of 'morality' is able to provide a theoretical basis for the common bond necessary in a pluralist society."[77] I take Khan's "common bond" to be twofold. On the one hand and ethically speaking, this common bond is

---

[73] Richard Rubenstein, "The Vatican Statement on the *Shoah* and Pius XII," *Remembering for the Future: The Holocaust in an Age of Genocide,* Vol. 2: Ethics and Religion, ed. Margo Levy (Palgrave, 2001), 459.

[74] Ibid.

[75] Peter J. Haas, *Morality After Auschwitz: The Radical Challenge of the Nazi Ethic* (Philadelphia Fortress Press, 1988), 4.

[76] Richard Rubenstein, "The Vatican Statement on the *Shoah* and Pius XII," *Remembering for the Future: The Holocaust in an Age of Genocide,* Vol. 2: Ethics and Religion, ed. Margo Levy (Palgrave, 2001), 459.

[77] Gulshan Khan, "Politics and Morality in Habermas' Discourse Ethics," *Philosophy & Social Criticism* (forthcoming), 2.

the condition for people to be motivated to engage in critical discourses on a communicative level. On the other hand and morally speaking, it is "a democratic procedure that legitimates norms of conduct (moral norms)" in actual discourses on a political level.[78] However, the reason Khan gives—"Habermas' notion of morality incorporates aspects of Hegel's notion of ethical life understood as a 'general mode of behavior'"—is not convincing.[79] To begin with, as pointed out in the beginning of this chapter, Khan misinterprets the *generic* presupposition of communication as the *imported* Hegelian *Sittlichkeit*. Furthermore, Khan goes so far as to argue that "Habermas goes beyond the limitations of Hegelian ethical life by turning to a Rousseauian notion of democracy to determine the content of the *sittlich* relation."[80] But the Rousseauian ethical and contextual aspect is precisely what Habermas is determined to get rid of. Contrary to Khan's argument, there is no clear "common bond" substantial enough to function in the moral sphere and there is no such thing at all in the ethical sphere, because Habermas' strategy is predicated on the choice not to prescribe it.

Nevertheless, one might challenge this analysis by arguing that there is indeed such a common bond in the moral and political sphere as the "modern Western democracy in its various manifestations."[81] In particular, the democratic atmosphere of the American culture is precisely its *Sittlichkeit* that binds people together even in the ethical sphere. But even Habermas himself would be suspicious of this response, since the possibility of having the democratic culture as one's civic bond is inconceivable to those "who do not have the good fortune to be heirs of the Founding Fathers."[82] Turning to their own traditions for a source of democracy, the problem of coordinating between the moral and the ethical sphere becomes a serious challenge. To advocate this essentially contextual point is therefore to defeat the principle universalizability, the very essence of discourse ethics. Furthermore, this suggestion also undermines Habermas' point because it shows just how much Habermas fails to transcend the modern context to begin with—if this were the case, as "Marx once questions German thought: why does Habermas have to achieve in theory what some countries have achieved in actuality?"[83]

Consequently, how to motivate citizens to become proper participants of deliberative democracy becomes *the* problem. Unfortunately, this problem is not only a matter of the just but also a matter of the good. Moreover, as Plato's *Republic* already shows thousands of years ago that the just does not necessarily lead to the good. As long as Habermas insists on the separation between morality and ethics, and that between the questions of the just and the good, this problem is by no means

[78] Ibid., 16.

[79] Ibid., 15.

[80] Ibid., 16.

[81] David Rasmussen, *Reading Habermas* (Cambridge, Mass.: Basil Blackwell, 1990), 71.

[82] Jürgen Habermas, *Between Facts and Norms: Contributions to A Discourse Theory of Law and Democracy*, trans. William Rehg (Cambridge, Mass.: The MIT Press, 1996), 2.

[83] David Rasmussen, *Reading Habermas* (Cambridge, Mass.: Basil Blackwell, 1990), 73.

easy to solve. In the final section, I wish to show that the moral question of the just cannot be sufficiently answered without at least creating the condition for answering the ethical question of the good.

1.7 The Just and the Good

In "On the Question: What is the 'Good Life'," Habermas declares that "theories of justice and morality take their own separate path today."[84] This statement is both the end of and motivation for Habermas' separation of morality from ethics. Yet Habermas is not alone in advocating this distinctively modern approach, John Rawls represents the other side of the deliberative democracy story. Similar to Habermas, Rawls also develops a clear-cut separation "between the realm of the *private*—where a plurality of different and irreconcilable comprehensive views coexist—and the realm of the *public*, where an overlapping consensus can be established over a shared conception of justice."[85] However, in *Between Facts and Norms*, Habermas criticizes Rawls' approach by dividing it into two stages. The first stage is concerned with the normative justification of his model of Rawls' well-ordered society, which states that the "self-stabilization of a well-ordered society is…based not on the coercive force of law but on the socializing force of a life under just institutions, for such a life simultaneously develops and reinforces the citizens' dispositions to justice."[86] However, according to Habermas, "all this holds only on the assumption that just institution already exists. It is another question how these can be *established* or at least promoted in present circumstances."[87] Besides, since the sociological disenchantment shows the collapses of the traditional institutions of social integration, Habermas argues that despite Rawls' "overlapping consensus" in the second stage, his version of democracy eventually falls victim of the inadequate philosophical traditions.

Instead of grounding valid law on the precarious claim of the just institution, Habermas advocates the procedural mechanism of discourse ethics that allows him to "leave more questions open because it entrusts more to the *process* of rational opinion and will formation."[88] However, in the famous debate between Rawls and Habermas, Rawls retorts by arguing that Habermas' approach cannot be as strictly procedural as he thinks, and it must include a substantive dimension, "given that

---

[84] Jürgen Habermas, "Are There Postmetaphysical Answers to the Question: What is the "Good Life," *The Future of Human Nature* (MA: Polity Press, 2003), 3.

[85] Chantal Mouffe, "For an Agonistic Model of Democracy," *The Democratic Paradox* (London: Verso, 2000), 90.

[86] Jürgen Habermas, *Between Facts and Norms: Contributions to A Discourse Theory of Law and Democracy*, trans. William Rehg (Cambridge, Mass.: The MIT Press, 1996), 58.

[87] Ibid.

[88] Jurgen Habermas, "Reconciliation Through the Public Use of Reason: Remarks on John Rawls' Political Liberalism," *The Journal of Philosophy* XXCII, 3, 1995, p. 131.

issues concerning the result of the procedures cannot be excluded from their design."[89] The debate between the two deliberative democracy theorists precisely shows that "both are unable to separate the public from the private or the procedural from the substantial as clearly as they declare."[90] In other words, the question of the just cannot be as absolutely separated from the question of the good as Habermas proposes.

According to Chantal Mouffe, "the domain of politics—even when fundamental issues like justice or basic principles are concerned—is not a neutral terrain that could be insulated from the pluralism of values and where rational, universal solutions could be formulated."[91] Furthermore, drawing inspiration from Wittgenstein's view that "to agree on the definition of a term is not enough and we need agreement in the way we use it," Mouffe argues that "in order to have agreement in opinions, there must first be agreement in forms of life."[92] These suggestions indicate that the Habermasian separation between the procedural morality and the substantial ethics cannot be maintained, because the internal connection between the moral and the ethical is not eliminated after a mere conceptual separation. Instead, discourse ethics must presuppose ethical elements to begin with because participants first emerge from the ethical sphere and they are concerned first and foremost with the question of the good.

A different way of putting the problem is that Habermas does not give a theory of the democratic self to support his theory of the democratic state. For such classical philosophers as Hobbes, Locke, and Rousseau, an adequate social and political theory devoted to the universal-particular or facticity-validity problem is contingent upon an equally sufficient understanding of the individual self. Accordingly, Hobbes analyzes the Leviathan as if it were a human body; Locke first develops his psychology in *An Essay Concerning Human Understanding*; and Rousseau educates the fictional Emile as an ideal civic candidate.

Despite Habermas' criticism, Rawls argues in *Political Liberalism* that the stability of what he calls "justice as fairness" cannot be maintained without a preceding stage that is "worked out as a freestanding political (but of course moral) conception for the basic structure of society."[93] Specifically, the issue of stability involves two questions. Before addressing the second question concerning the "overlapping consensus" that directly deals with "reasonable pluralism," Rawls claims that the first question has to do with "whether people who grow up under just institutions (as the political conception defines them) acquire a normally sufficient sense of justice so that they generally comply with those institutions."[94] According to Rawls, the first

[89] Chantal Mouffe, "For an Agonistic Model of Democracy," *The Democratic Paradox* (London: Verso, 2000), 91.

[90] Ibid.

[91] Ibid., 92.

[92] Ibid., 97.

[93] John Rawls, *Political Liberalism*, 2nd Ed. (New York: Columbia University Press, 2005), 140.

[94] Ibid., 141.

question, which is key in dealing with the motivation problem, is answered "by setting out the moral psychology in accordance with which citizens in a well-ordered society acquire a normally sufficient sense of justice so that they comply with its just arrangements."[95] In other words, the reason why the democratic citizens will be willing to participate in and contribute to the shaping of the just political system is because they are already in a sense just as a result of a well-ordered society. The condition of a just society and the condition of a just people are thus interconnected in an almost Durkheimian manner.

Following the linguistic turn and the footsteps of Peirce, Habermas lays the foundation of his theory on communication. Although communicative reason works very well to deal with the complexity of the pluralistic and post-metaphysical world, it lacks a substantial account about the individual self that previous theorists deem essential in adequately understanding the social and political realm. In other words, Habermas' discourse ethics is so dependent on idealization and abstraction for the purpose of impartiality and open process that individual actors engaging in critical discourses and democratic procedures are accordingly and unfortunately idealized and abstracted "from social and power relations, language, culture and the whole set of practices that make agency possible."[96] The opportunity cost of achieving the impartial and open procedure of deliberative democracy in the moral and political sphere is thus the neglecting of the "crucial role played by passions and affects in securing allegiance to democratic values" in the civil and ethical sphere.[97] The solution to this problem, as pointed out earlier, belongs to the question of the good. A condition among the participating citizens—one that "abstracts from the knowledge of citizens' determinate conceptions of the good"—must be established first in order to answer the question of the just.[98] But what is required for such establishment to properly reconcile the moral and the universal on the one hand, and the ethical and the particular on the other? Will a justificatory framework suggested by Forst work? To this topic we now turn.

[95] Ibid.

[96] Chantal Mouffe, "For an Agonistic Model of Democracy," *The Democratic Paradox* (London: Verso, 2000), 95.

[97] Ibid.

[98] Ibid.

Chapter 2
The Problem of Justification and the *Proviso*

Abstract This chapter elevates Rawls's *proviso* from procedural footnote to a structuring framework of pluralistic justification, allowing comprehensive doctrines to inform public reason if translated into reciprocal terms. It contrasts Rawls's political domain with Habermas's comprehensive discourse ethics, arguing the *proviso* better excludes ethical intrusion while preserving motivational resources from citizens' traditions. This reinterpretation positions the *proviso* as the book's core mechanism for sustaining legitimacy amid ethical pluralism, extensible to non-liberal contexts like Confucianism and AI.

Keywords Rawls proviso • Public reason • Overlapping consensus • Political liberalism • Reciprocity • Moral motivation

2.1 Introduction

We now know that pluralism is nothing new. One of the implications of this modern situation is precisely the Hobbesian disillusionment that "there is no such *Finis ultimus* nor *Summum Bonum* as is spoken of in the books of the old moral philosophers."[1] Instead of asking how one *should* live one's life, the best we can strive for without infringing upon another's freedom and equality is to inquire which way of life one *must* choose. Nevertheless, without a sense of "should," it would appear that all would be lost. Given reasonable pluralism and the lack of moral criterion, how can a state maintain its authority, how can a person address another person in moral terms, and how can we keep society united and stable? As we saw

[1] Thomas Hobbes, *Leviathan*, ed. and intro. Edwin Curley (Indianapolis: Hackett, 1994), 57.

Z. Li, *Pluralism, Confucianism, and Artificial Intelligence*, Philosophy and Politics - Critical Explorations 35, https://doi.org/10.1007/978-3-032-25605-8_2

in Chap. 1, a successful solution must be able to properly reconcile the tension between the moral and the universal on the one hand, and the ethical and the particular on the other. Otherwise, some failed solutions are regarded as authoritarian and even tyrannical, because the fact of pluralism dictates that a successful solution cannot be singular in nature.

With *Political Liberalism*, John Rawls proposes yet another approach to address pluralism by reconciling the universal and the particular in the context of politics. According to Rawls, "the diversity of reasonable comprehensive religious, philosophical, and moral doctrines found in modern democratic societies is not a mere historical condition that may soon pass away; it is a permanent feature of the public culture of democracy."[2] With this observation as the starting point, Rawls goes on to outline his version of liberalism with a family of innovative concepts that justifies the existence of a domain of the political which maintains the sense of "should" in public despite the fact of reasonable pluralism. However, a question immediately arises: what about the rest of society—the domains of the nonpolitical, where moral people also need a private sense of "should" to address one another, especially when moral claims are regarded as illocutionary? Rawls' answer is simple enough: it is not the business of political liberalism to deal with the nonpolitical, and any attempt to maintain this private sense of "should" with state power is tyranny; instead, we should leave the rest of the world as it is. Even if Rawls is right, there is still a further question: By applying the principle of toleration to philosophy, does Rawls change the role of (moral) philosophy in modernity? In other words, how should we think about ethics in a Rawlsian society if full justification can only be political? This problem is anticipated by Bernard Williams' controversial work *Ethics and The Limits of Philosophy*, in which Williams argues that the task of moral philosophy needs to be reconsidered. Gerald Gaus also disagrees with Rawls in his ambitious book *The Order of Public Reason*, where he tries to grant public reason a much broader justificatory scope than the mere political.

In this chapter, I will argue that the justificatory strength we gain in the domain of the political is contingent upon the loss of justificatory strength in the domain of the ethical. A truly successful solution to the problem of modernity must address both the fact of reasonable pluralism and the loss of justification in society *as a whole*. Specifically, I will first outline the contribution Rawls makes to the urgent problem of modernity, and I will argue that Rawls' solution is by far the most effective. Then, I will point out the "opportunity cost" of the Rawlsian solution and argue that there is a trade-off between the domain of the political and the domain of the ethical when it comes to the problem of justification. With Williams' insight, I will then argue that the demand of ethics in modernity differs from that of its traditional counterpart, and it requires an even more substantive understanding of pluralism that I refer to as "deep reasonable pluralism." Finally, I will conclude by appealing to Rawls' *proviso* as a potential starting point for a more competent political theory to address the issue of pluralism. In the remaining two parts of the book, I will lay out the main components of a pluralistic political theory in the context of an increasingly pluralistic East Asia and then in the age of artificial intelligence.

---

[2] John Rawls, *Political Liberalism* (New York: Columbia University Press, 2005), 36.

2.2 Confronting Reasonable Pluralism

The best place to start outlining the position of the later Rawls is his reply to Jürgen Habermas during the famous Rawls-Habermas debate. The biggest difference between their positions, according to Rawls, is that Habermas' "is comprehensive while [Rawls'] is an account of the political and is limited to that."[3] This statement shows the first among many distinctions the later Rawls draws. To Rawls, reasonable pluralism manifests itself in modern democratic societies through a variety of comprehensive doctrines that include conceptions of what are of value in human life, ideals of personal virtue and character, and the like, that inform life as a whole.[4] Religious and philosophical concepts, like Augustine's theological position and Kant's "Kingdom of Ends," tend to be general and comprehensive. Traditionally, the criterion of justification for comprehensive doctrine is epistemological. In other words, advocates of different comprehensive doctrines endorse and impose their beliefs not because these are their beliefs but because they think their beliefs are true.[5] Nevertheless, accepting the Hobbesian observation that an event may seem like a miracle to one man and the opposite to another, Rawls argues that epistemological claims supported by private reason can be made equally among citizens, and the imposition of one of the claims cannot be reasonably justified among all citizens.[6] Habermas' philosophical doctrine, though brilliant in its own way, nevertheless falls into the category of comprehensive doctrine that tries to establish its legitimacy by justifying its truth, which cannot be fully justified and equally applied to modern pluralistic societies. Furthermore, this uniquely modern problem of justification on the basis of reasonable pluralism would never occur to a comprehensive thinker like Habermas because the only justificatory tool for the latter is epistemological. Nevertheless, confronting reasonable pluralism requires a different manner of justification, and Rawls' solution is going to change the role philosophy plays in modernity.

In contrast to Habermas' position, Rawls' political liberalism is founded upon a freestanding conception of right and justice limited to the domain of the political. The central idea, in Rawls' own words, is that "political liberalism moves within the category of the political and leaves philosophy as it is. It leaves untouched all kinds of doctrines—religious, metaphysical, and moral—with their long traditions of development and interpretation."[7] This statement highlights the three basic features of a political conception of justice: first, it is concerned only with the basic structure of society; second, it can be formulated independently of any particular comprehensive doctrine; and finally, its fundamental ideas belong

---

[3] Ibid, 373.

[4] John Rawls, "The Domain of the Political and Overlapping Consensus," *Collected Papers* (Harvard University, 1999), 480.

[5] John Rawls, *Political Liberalism* (New York: Columbia University Press, 2005), 61.

[6] Ibid.

[7] Ibid., 375.

to the category of the political alone.[8] Inspired by the evolution of the social and historical conditions of modern democratic regimes as well as the history of the Wars of Religion following the Reformation, Rawls realizes that a workable conception of justice "must allow for a diversity of general and comprehensive doctrines, and for the plurality of conflicting, and indeed incommensurable, conceptions of the meaning, value, and purpose of human life [i.e. conceptions of the good] affirmed by the citizens of democratic societies."[9] The only sensible thing to do is to "apply the principle of toleration to philosophy itself: the public conception of justice is to be political, not metaphysical."[10] The reason why the domain of the political needs to be freestanding and stays deliberately on the surface of all the religious and philosophical debates is not because "these questions are unimportant or regarded with indifference, but because we think them too important and recognize that there is no way to resolve them politically."[11] In other words, modernity and pluralism demand political theories to subordinate the rational to the reasonable and apply what Rawls call the "method of avoidance" to avoid disputed religious, philosophical, and moral questions.[12] What political theorists and philosophers are able to propose is at best "a framework within which permissible conceptions can be advanced" and mutually acceptable way of resolving disagreements can be publicly established.[13] Consequently, justification for such a political framework should not be epistemological and "regarded simply as valid argument from listed premises"; instead, the justification must be practical and more importantly it must be "addressed to others who disagree with us, and therefore it must always proceed from some consensus, that is, from premises that we and others publicly recognize as…acceptable."[14] Like Kant's innovation in the first critique to limit the scope of pure reason, *Political Liberalism* is a similar critique of the limit of political philosophy by shifting the paradigm from the rational and the comprehensive to the reasonable and political.

Realizing what cannot be the proper justification in a reasonably pluralistic world, the question remains whether Rawls' political liberalism is up to the modern task of justification. In other words, how does the freestanding political conception of justice exert the sense of "should" and motivate assured and stable cooperation among citizens? Here Rawls distinguish three kinds of justification. The first two stages are the stages of *pro tanto* and full justifications, which occur only when citizens both construct a political conception of justice from shared judgments (the *pro tanto* stage) and accept the political conception from within

[8] Ibid., 376.

[9] John Rawls, "The Idea of an Overlapping Consensus," *Collected Papers* (Harvard University Press, 1999), 424.

[10] John Rawls, "Justice as Fairness: Political not Metaphysical," *Collected Papers* (Harvard University Press, 1999), 388.

[11] Ibid., 394.

[12] Ibid., 395.

[13] Ibid., 413.

[14] Ibid., 394.

their comprehensive doctrines (the full justification stage).[15] Nevertheless, citizens' comprehensive doctrines can easily override these justifications, and this possibility poses serious threat to the stability of the state. The third stage is public justification by political society: "reasonable citizens take one another into account as having reasonable comprehensive doctrines that endorse that political conception, and this mutual accounting shapes the moral quality of the public culture of political society."[16] Two related concepts are at work here: the concept of the reasonable and the concept of the overlapping consensus. Giving W. M. Sibley's original term a more restricted sense, Rawls associates the reasonable with "the willingness to propose and honor fair terms of cooperation...and the willingness to recognize the burdens of judgment and to accept their consequences."[17] In other words, a reasonable citizen, in contrast to a merely rational citizen who thinks only about herself, takes others and their comprehensive doctrines into consideration. Furthermore, there are both a political and non-political components in each comprehensive doctrine. Although citizens holding different comprehensive doctrines might seriously disagree in terms of the non-political (religious, philosophical, moral, etc.) components, a consensus can be established in terms of the political component. In other words, public justification depends on an overlapping consensus in the domain of the political alone. The contents of this overlapping consensus have "no normative role in public justification; citizens do not look into the content of others' doctrines, and so remain within the bounds of the political."[18]

This overlapping consensus in the domain of the political consequently solves the stability problem because this political conception of justice is not only the most reasonable but also the deepest. It is the most reasonable because it is "endorsed, or in some way supported by, all reasonable (or the reasonable) comprehensive doctrine in society.[19] It is the deepest simply because "the fundamental ideas of the political conception are endorsed by the reasonable comprehensive doctrines, and these doctrines represent what citizens regard as their deepest convictions—religious, philosophical, and moral."[20] With these innovative concepts, Rawls shows that stability for the right reasons and democratic legitimacy are at least possible in a society marked by reasonable pluralism on the basis of public justification.

[15] John Rawls, *Political Liberalism* (New York: Columbia University Press, 2005), 386.

[16] Ibid., 387.

[17] Ibid., 49.

[18] John Rawls, *Political Liberalism* (New York: Columbia University Press, 2005), 387.

[19] Ibid., 391.

[20] Ibid., 392.

2.3 The Limits of Public Reason and the Problem of Justification

Rawls' attempt to publicly justify the domain of the political is closely related to his idea of public reason. The concept of public reason is nothing new, and one can easily find origins in many early thinkers such as Emile Durkheim, who argues that society has its own consciousness consisting of but not reducible to the individual and private consciousness. Rawls, on the other hand, gives public reason a political twist. According to Rawls, a political society, like an individual or a family, "has a way of formulating its plans, of putting its ends in an order of priority and of making its decisions accordingly. The way a political society does this is its reason."[21] Specifically, public reason is public in three ways: "as the reason of citizens as such, it is the reason of the public; its subject is the good of the public and matters of fundamental justice; and its nature and content is public, being given by the ideals and principles expressed by society's conception of political justice, and conducted open to view on that basis."[22] Thus, similar to a variety of other concepts Rawls uses, public reason is distinguished from nonpublic reason, such as that of churches and universities. Furthermore, public reason is also limited to the domain of the political, which necessarily limits its scope of influence. For instance, although religious, philosophical, and moral considerations *do* influence people's contribution to the public domain, Rawls explicitly argues that they do not play a role in the domain of the political and thereby do not influence public reason. What is at work is the overlapping consensus among these reasonable comprehensive doctrines. Asking for more is to reach beyond the limits of public reason.

Gerald Gaus has a different view of public reason in his *The Order of Public Reason*, in which the authority of social morality is the central concern, and the political falls within the bigger domain of social morality. For Gaus, reasonable pluralism poses a far greater problem than Rawls realizes: how can we maintain the authority of social morality and also hold on to the free and equal status of moral persons in a "diverse and bounded world"? The answer lies in what Gaus calls "real public reason" endorsed by the reasons of all the public. From the very beginning Gaus shows his very different concern from that of Rawls. Instead of the domain of the political, Gaus argues that social morality constitutes "the basic framework for a cooperative and mutually beneficial social life."[23] Moreover, Gaus stresses the individual and the nonpublic dimension by arguing that social morality also "provides rules that we are required to act upon and…the basis for authoritative demands of one person addressed to another."[24] Taking moral demands for granted, Gaus asks: "How can free and equal moral persons claim authority to prescribe to other

[21] Ibid., 212.

[22] Ibid., 213.

[23] Gerald Gaus, *The Order of Public Reason: A Theory of Freedom and Morality in a Diverse and Bounded World* (Cambridge University Press, 2011), 1.

[24] Ibid.

free and equal moral persons?"[25] This question is absent in the later Rawls because it is not the business of a political conception of justice to care about the dealings among individual moral persons. In fact, social morality is a public concern only insofar as it is part of the domain of the political. In contrast, Gaus has a much more ambitious project in mind and he intends to solve the problem of justification as a whole in the domains of not only the political but also the moral.

Despite their difference in scope, both Rawls and Gaus acknowledge the nature of modernity. For instance, both recognize the difference between ancient and modern ethics. Like Rawls who argues for the priority of the right over the good, Gaus also argues that modern ethics concerns what we *must* do rather than what we *should* do, the former of which implies the binding or obligatory "right" and the latter of which implies the teleological or imperative "good."[26] Moreover, both recognize that the rational alone can no longer function as the sole justificatory standard. Nevertheless, rather than starting with the political, Gaus begins by talking about moral authority among free and equal citizens. The problem here is the justification for moral demand. With reasonable pluralism on the one hand, and the lack of justificatory standard on the other, Gaus wonders how we can ever morally *demand* another person that is as free and equal as we are. It would appear that one can only advise and not demand any more, because the other person would simply respond to our claim with two quintessentially modern questions: "So what? Who are you to tell me what to do?"[27] To these responses another free and equal person would be at a loss: "what do I have that is so different from the other person that also justifies my demand?" One might argue that it is only to morality, not the moral person who utters the claim, that the demand appeals to. Nevertheless, reasonable pluralism dictates that morality be interpreted among people with different background knowledge and their unique comprehensive doctrines so that no private disagreement will ever contribute to the problem of justification.[28] This is also why citizens need to be "forced to be free" in a Rousseauian regime and why citizens need to be held in awe and fear in a Hobbesian state. But these solutions are obviously unacceptable in modern democratic societies.

So, both Rawls and Gaus recognize the twofold task of modern political philosophy—acknowledging reasonable pluralism and solving the problem of justification, but they differ in terms of strategy and scope. Although Gaus also resorts to public reason, his version is quite different from Rawls', mainly because the former does not restrict itself to the domain of the political alone. After a lengthy discussion of social morality and the emotion and reason involved in social morality, Gaus introduces his "Basic Principle of Public Justification":

[25] Ibid.

[26] Ibid., 7.

[27] Ibid., 12.

[28] Jean-Jacques Rousseau, "On the Social Contract," in *The Basic Political Writings*, trans. and ed. Donald A. Cress (Indianapolis: Hackett, 1987), 150.

> A moral imperative "ϕ!" in context C, based on rule L, is an authoritative requirement of social morality only if each normal moral agent has sufficient reasons to (a) internalize rule L, (b) hold that L requires ϕ-type acts in circumstances C and (c) moral agents generally conform to L.[29]

On the basis of this principle, Gaus formulates his model of public justification and thereby his version of public reason. Unlike Rawls, Gaus does not treat the domain of the political as freestanding, and his version of public reason has a much broader scope that also covers the nonpolitical. Which version of public reason is more reasonable is another question, but the difference between the two views raise an interesting issue. Even if Rawls' view works perfectly in the domain of the political and even if in his defense political liberalism should not care about the domain of the nonpolitical, the problem of justification remains in the latter domain, where the nonpolitical components of a variety of comprehensive doctrines keep clashing. Traditionally the burden of justification is shouldered by moral philosophy or ethics, and Rawls explicitly argues that he leaves philosophy as it is with the method of avoidance. However, not taking religious, philosophical, and moral issues into consideration does not mean that those issues are not in turn influenced by the freestanding domain of the political. Gaus recognizes this point, which is why his version of public reason wishes to cover both the political and the moral. In contrast, the Rawlsian public reason has its limits and these limits have deep implications in the domain of the nonpolitical, which brings us to the problem of influence.

Although one of the major themes of liberal thought is that the state must try to be neutral, Rawls nevertheless abandons the neutrality of effect or influence, because "it is surely impossible for the basic structure of a just constitutional regime not to have important effects and influences on which comprehensive doctrines endure and gain adherents over time, and it is futile to try to counteract these effects and influences."[30] This statement confirms Rawls' subscription to a basic political sociology that links the universal and the particular aspects. Specifically, Rawls argues that justice as fairness is a good in two ways. The first way is as a good for persons individually in terms of both experiencing moral powers in the domain of the political as good and securing for citizens the social bases of mutual self-respect.[31] The second way is that establishing just democratic institutions over a long period of time is a great social good and appreciated as such.[32] Furthermore, Rawls argues that political liberalism further affirms the superiority of certain forms of moral character and encourages certain political virtues—"the virtues of fair social cooperation such as civility and tolerance, reasonableness and the sense of fairness."[33] This point becomes much clearer in *Political Liberalism*, where Rawls says: "Think,

[29] Gerald Gaus, *The Order of Public Reason: A Theory of Freedom and Morality in a Diverse and Bounded World* (Cambridge University Press, 2011), 263.

[30] John Rawls, "The Priority of Right and Ideas of the Good," *Collected Papers* (Harvard University Press, 1999), 460.

[31] John Rawls, *Political Liberalism* (New York: Columbia University Press, 2005), 203.

[32] Ibid., 204.

[33] Ibid.

then, of the principles of justice as designed to form the social world in which our character and our conception of ourselves as persons, as well as our comprehensive views and their conceptions of the good, are first acquired, and in which our moral powers must be realized, if they are to be realized at all."[34] In other words, although Rawls intentionally designs the domain of the political as freestanding so as to exclude the nonpolitical components of the comprehensive doctrines, the problem of influence shows that there are interactions between the domains of the political and the nonpolitical especially in that the former has certain influence over the latter. Connected to the problem of justification in general and Gaus' broader concern for moral justification, it is imperative that we not only look at the freestanding Rawlsian domain of the political, however successful it might be, but also pay attention to the possible changes in the domain of the nonpolitical under the influence of the political, and this will reveal some inadequacies of Rawls' political approach.

2.4 The Domain of the Nonpolitical and the Challenge to Traditional Ethics

According to Rawls, the domain of the nonpolitical consists of a variety of comprehensive doctrines that contribute to the fact of reasonable pluralism. The reason why the domain of the political needs to be freestanding and stays deliberately on the surface of all the religious, philosophical, and moral debates is not because "these questions are unimportant or regarded with indifference, but because we think them too important and recognize that there is no way to resolve them politically."[35] Accordingly, a successful political theory "must allow for a diversity of general and comprehensive doctrines, and for the plurality of conflicting, and indeed incommensurable, conceptions of the meaning, value, and purpose of human life [i.e. conceptions of the good] affirmed by the citizens of democratic societies."[36] The reason that the later Rawls is able to see things so clearly and propose a political theory that directly answers the demand of modernity is that he dares to "reshuffle the cards" and begin anew the task given to us by Hobbes. The Rawlsian strategy, unlike the Hobbesian one, is to first acknowledge reasonable pluralism absolutely by treating different reasonable comprehensive doctrines with equal validity and avoiding favoring any one of them. Then, through overlapping consensus among different reasonable comprehensive doctrines, Rawls give back the justificatory power to the domain of the political and restore the sense of "should" in public. By claiming that he tries to leave the world as it is, Rawls is not aiming for actual consensus; instead, he tries to maintain the differences in a unified and stable way with

[34] Ibid., 41.

[35] John Rawls, "Justice as Fairness: Political not Metaphysical," *Collected Papers* (Harvard University Press, 1999), 394.

[36] Ibid.

the help of a political conception of justice. However, what he takes away from the domain of the nonpolitical Rawls never quite gives back. On the one hand, treating traditional justificatory standards equally is to preclude the possibility that any one of these standards can be used by itself to offer justification. On the other hand, granting justificatory power only to the domain of the political is to give back to the domain of the nonpolitical nothing of the kind. Consequently, the problem of justification remains in the domain of the nonpolitical where comprehensive doctrines clash, and this seems to be the price of Rawls' political strategy to accommodate reasonable pluralism and deal with the problem of justification at the same time. In other words, the justificatory strength we gain in the domain of the political is contingent upon the loss of such strength in the domain of the ethical. Furthermore, since Rawls takes away justification for comprehensive doctrines in the domain of the nonpolitical, what happens to ethical theories whose basis is precisely moral justification? In a Rawlsian society, while the political component might be well and stable, the Socratic question that founded the discipline of (moral) philosophy—"how should one live"—needs to be reconsidered both in breadth and depth to redefine the task of moral philosophy in a world characterized by reasonable pluralism.[37]

Socrates brings up the question of how one should live during his debate with the Sophist Thrasymachus in Plato's *Republic*. Arguing that justice is by no means the power of the stronger, Socrates convinces Thrasymachus that it is at least something general, in the sense that every kind of *techne* requires a degree of justice. Eventually, the discussion of justice transitions into the discussion of the just way of life near the end of the first book, which sets the tone for the rest of the dialogue. Bernard Williams' *Ethics and the Limits of Philosophy* rightly begins with this Socratic question to carry out an evaluation of the task of modern ethics. Nevertheless, instead of treating the question of how one should live as *the* question of ethics, Williams argues that it does not presuppose much about ethics. Instead, its primary implication is that the issue of how to live can be properly addressed at a high level of generality that "embraces or shapes the individual ambitions each person may bring to the question."[38] This is only part of the story, the other part hinges upon the term "should." From our discussions above, it is apparent that "should" goes hand in hand with the problem of justification, since even the question of "what should I do now" presupposes certain justification for the motivation behind my following action. But Williams' argument about the generality of the founding question of moral philosophy is equally crucial, because it offers the standard for the content of traditional moral philosophy. From Plato to the utilitarianists, moral philosophy sets the goal to address everyone on a general level.

Rawls is clearly aware of this characteristic of traditional ethics. In *A Theory of Justice*, he argues that the structure of an ethical theory depends on how it defines and connects two basic notions: the right and the good. A teleological theory, for

[37] Plato, *Republic*, trans. and intro. Allan Bloom (Basic Books, 1968), 352d.

[38] Bernard Williams, *Ethics and the Limits of Philosophy* (Routledge Classics, 2011), 5.

instance, generally defines the good independently and prior to the right, in that the right is defined as that which maximizes the good.[39] This is the approach of most traditional ethical theories. For instance, Aristotelian ethics requires the same highest *telos* for every virtuous person sharing a community; whoever fails to share the good/end is not following the right ethical principle. Certainly not all the traditional moral theories are teleological, a deontological theory like Kant's moral philosophy, on the other hand, tries to stay abstract and prioritizes duty so as to apply to as many situations as possible. Regardless of how the right and the good are defined and connected, these traditional ethical theories stay loyal to the Socratic question and try to address morality and ethics on a comprehensive level. In the appendix to his book, Gaus recognizes the same thing and argues that traditionally moral theories presuppose a unity of morality and assume that "all moral judgments must be of a single type, reducible to single type, or the various type must be capable of being organized into a coherent system."[40] This phenomenon, according to Williams, shows that the ambition of traditional ethical theories is to find an Archimedean point to objectively justify morality from the ground up. However, this ambition sounds too good to be true, because on the one hand there are non-ethical considerations equally capable of justifying and answering the Socratic question, and on the other hand traditional ethics neglect those who simply will not find their theories appealing to begin with. Therefore, any successful answer to the Socratic question must first address the complexity of reality itself, especially when reasonable pluralism becomes the primary characteristic of modern society.

According to Williams, answering the Socratic question requires some prior justification. First of all, *to whom* is it addressed? Second, *from where* is it addressed? Third, *against what* is it addressed?[41] By asking to whom the question is addressed, Williams asks us to consider the possibility that there might be people incapable of being convinced by ethical considerations alone. By asking from where the question is addressed, Williams shows that one needs to be aware that there is no Archimedean point where one's ethical position can be objectively justified, and that one is always inside the domain of the ethical. Perhaps most importantly by asking against what the question is addressed, Williams warns us to also take into consideration of alternatives by which the person might be convinced. The history of philosophy is on Williams' side. Historically, ethical theory has undergone several phases of transformation. From the earliest teleological stage where different ethical theories were coherent with a variety of moral and metaphysical *telos* to the Enlightenment Project when rationality became the sole criterion of justification and post-metaphysical thinking began to dominate, and finally to the Rawlsian paradigm shift from the rational to the reasonable, moral philosophy has gone a long way from the Socratic question that first founded it. The hope to objectively justifying

---

[39] John Rawls, *A Theory of Justice: Original Edition* (Belknap Press of Harvard University Press, 2005), 23.

[40] Gerald Gaus, *The Order of Public Reason: A Theory of Freedom and Morality in a Diverse and Bounded World* (Cambridge University Press, 2011), 552.

[41] Bernard Williams, *Ethics and the Limits of Philosophy* (Routledge Classics, 2011), 27.

morality from the ground up grows dimmer, whereas the Berlinian realization that there are ethical choices "between ends equally ultimate, and claims equally absolute, the realization of some of which must inevitably involve the sacrifice of others" grows stronger.[42] All of these culminate in Rawls' comments that there are "a diversity of general and comprehensive doctrines, and for the plurality of conflicting, and indeed incommensurable, conceptions of the meaning, value, and purpose of human life [i.e. conceptions of the good] affirmed by the citizens of democratic societies."[43]

However, the Socratic question that founded moral philosophy is still with us, so is moral philosophy in general. One thing that none of the previous thinkers fully addresses is the fundamental reason behind the generality of traditional ethical theory. First, why general theories at all? And second, why do we wait so long to realize that public endorsement of a comprehensive doctrine is equivalent to tyranny? Certainly, a singular and general theory that comprehensively covers most areas of human moral reality is aesthetically appealing, but the reasons must be more than that. To answer these questions is to go beyond the scope of this chapter, but they are helpful to bring out the influence of reasonable pluralism and Rawls' political liberalism over moral philosophy. If remaining faithful to the generality of the Socratic mission is no longer an option, what does that leave moral philosophy? It would appear that we have two options: First, we simply cannot do moral philosophy in its traditional sense any more, because moral philosophy is by definition comprehensive. Second, we need to redefine the task of moral philosophy.

If we take both Rawls and Williams seriously, the first choice *does* make sense. On the one hand, the Rawlsian solution to reasonable pluralism is to take the easy way out and leave all the problems to the domain of the nonpolitical. On the other hand, however, there is no adequate way of justification for morality in the domain of the nonpolitical, as Williams points out, and there is little philosophy can do about that. Soren Kierkegaard's *Either/Or* brilliantly captures this impasse by presenting two points of view, one of them ethical and the other aesthetic, without at the same time offering any overarching standard of justification. The implication is clear: without a criterion or a sense of "should," an ethical theory cannot necessarily convince another person holding a different point of view. Williams draws the same conclusion by asking to whom the Socratic question should be addressed. Furthermore, if there are alternative points of view, a hyper-reflective person, like "A" in *Either/Or*, will find it even harder to have the *confidence* to adopt one of the options, according to Williams.[44] Thus, to accept the first hypothesis is to declare death of moral philosophy, and this is unacceptable.

Then we are left with the second choice, or rather task, to redefine moral philosophy in modern society. The fulfilling of this task would appear to complete the Rawlsian solution to reasonable pluralism by giving back justification not only to

---

[42] Ibid.

[43] John Rawls, "Justice as Fairness: Political not Metaphysical," *Collected Papers* (Harvard University Press, 1999), 394.

[44] "Confidence" is a term Williams uses.

the domain of the political but also the domain of the nonpolitical. But one should be cautious not to violate the overall Rawlsian principle that the rational subordinates to the reasonable absolutely.[45] For instance, although Habermas' discourse ethics based on his theory of communicative action is a brilliant justificatory theory in itself, it will not fit into the overall Rawlsian scheme because it is a comprehensive doctrine. One might wonder if *any* theory would be sufficient to give justification back to the domain of the nonpolitical without violating the principle of reasonability. This is absolutely correct, which is why a moral philosophy or an ethical theory up to the modern task must be fundamentally different from its traditional counterparts. This observation also means that what Rawls calls reasonable pluralism might not be the perfect term to capture what is really going on in modern societies. Even in mature liberal democracies, strong disagreements among citizens might not be limited to only ethical issues. As Alessandro Ferrara points out, citizens might disagree strongly with one another even over the nature of the constitutional essentials, which are the defining examples of the universal. Ferrara refers to this as "hyperpluralism," which represents a less idealized understanding of modern pluralism.[46] Among emerging liberal democracies, such as some East Asian societies, pluralism is also not idealized in the way Rawls imagines. In these societies, pluralism runs much deeper because liberal and democratic way of life is not necessarily the only game in town. Competing legacy doctrines, such as Confucianism and Daoism, continue to exert substantial moral and ethical influence over citizens. This "deep reasonable pluralism," to which I will refer in Chap. 3, poses challenges to Rawls' political liberal solution to the issue of pluralism.

2.5 Habermas and Rawls: A Comparison

It will be recalled that Habermas shares Rawls' ambition to reconcile the universal and the particular in the context of politics. We are now in a good position to also clarify their subtle differences. According to Habermas, Rawls' political liberalism "should make a sharper separation between questions of justification and questions of acceptance," and the (ethical) neutrality Rawls achieves is "at the cost of forsaking its cognitive validity claim."[47] Rawls thus "fails to achieve his goal of bringing the liberties of the moderns into harmony with the liberties of the ancients."[48] Habermas' criticism of Rawls relies, I think wrongly, on a dichotomy between a functionalist view and an epistemic view of a theory of justice. After agreeing with

---

[45] John Rawls, "Kantian Constructivism in Moral Theory," *Collected Papers* (Harvard University Press, 1999), 319.

[46] Alessandro Ferrara, *The Democratic Horizon: Hyperpluralism and the Renewal of Political Liberalism* (New York: Cambridge University Press, 2014).

[47] Jürgen Habermas, "Reconciliation Through the Public Use of Reason: Remarks on John Rawls' Political Liberalism," *The Journal of Philosophy* (Vol. 92), 110.

[48] Ibid.

Rawls that the domain of the political and the reasonable overlapping consensus should not merely lead to a *modus vivendi*, Habermas goes on to say that "if Rawls rules out a functionalist interpretation of justice as fairness, he must allow some epistemic relation between the validity of his theory and the prospect of its neutrality toward competing worldviews being confirmed in public discourses."[49] Accordingly, Habermas thinks that "we have reason to ask why Rawls does not think his theory admits of truth and in what sense he here uses the predicate 'reasonable' in place of the predicate 'true'."[50] These remarks are important primarily because they get to the center of any approach that tries to accomplish a successful separation of the moral from the ethical, and they demand an answer from Rawls to clarify his central concept of "the political." Furthermore, they also raise an interesting question regarding Rawls' theory. In an earlier section, I argued that the moral and the ethical share an intimate relationship: on the one hand, the moral shapes the ethical in a foundational sense; on the other hand, the ethical reshapes the moral in a justificatory sense. It remains to be seen how Rawls' reasonable and political overlapping consensus can be entirely free from the ethical influences, because as long as it needs justification, the moral and the ethical seem to be both present.

Rawls' response is very illuminating, and especially so in terms of explaining the difference between Habermas' and his own theories as well as clarifying some main concepts in greater details. Rawls argues that the difference with Habermas' theory is twofold: the first is that while Habermas' is comprehensive, political liberalism is not; the second concerns the difference between their devices of representation. The first difference is more important because that is where Rawls' theory shows its superiority. Instead of a simple distinction between the moral and the ethical, Rawls draws the distinction between the political, within which a reasonable overlapping consensus can be established as the basis of public justification, and comprehensive doctrines, among which ethical conflicts occur, leading to the permanent fact of reasonable (ethical) pluralism. Political liberalism as a doctrine falls under the domain of the political and it "works entirely within that domain and does not rely on anything outside it."[51] Like Habermas, one might wonder how that is even possible. To this Rawls answers that political liberalism attributes only two reasonable (not rational) characteristics to persons: "first, a willingness to propose fair terms of social cooperation that others as free and equal also might endorse, and to act on these terms, provided others do, even contrary to one's interest; and second, a recognition of the burdens of judgment and accepting their consequences for one's attitude (including toleration) toward other comprehensive doctrines."[52] In other words, reasonable persons do not depend on any of their comprehensive doctrines to create an overlapping consensus in the domain of the political. Consequently,

---

[49] Ibid., 122.

[50] Ibid., 122.

[51] John Rawls, "Political Liberalism: Reply to Habermas," *The Journal of Philosophy* (Vol. 92), 133.

[52] Ibid., 134.

regardless of how their comprehensive doctrines might differ in terms of truth and validity, a shared interest can be found in each comprehensive doctrine that overlaps in the domain of the political. Immediately one is able to see that Rawls' concept of the political is a much purer counterpart to Habermas' concept of the moral, because "the aim of [the latter's] theory of communicative action is to give a general account of meaning, reference, and truth or validity both for theoretical reason and for the several forms of practical reason."[53] To further illustrate this difference, Rawls characterizes Habermas' theory as broadly Hegelian: "a philosophical analysis of the presuppositions of rational discourse (of theoretical and practical reason) which includes within itself all the allegedly substantial elements of religious and metaphysical doctrines."[54] I think this characterization is fair, mainly because like Hegel, Habermas' theory of communicative action and his discourse ethics manifested in *Between Facts and Norms* both show a gradual transformation from the ethical to the moral not through an artificial separation but through a process of dialectical overcoming that very much resembles what Hegel argues in the *Phenomenology of Spirit*. Hence, the ethical is not in fact separated but rather overcome and maintained in the final moral perspective, because the inputs made to the discourse scenario come from concrete ethical participants. The reason why a religious doctrine does not make it to the Habermasian moral and universalizing perspective is not because it is excluded from the start but rather because it is *judged* as inappropriate to be included, and this cognitive aspect concerning "meaning, reference, and truth or validity" is precisely what Rawls, and indeed any successful theory of justice should exclude.[55] Incidentally, Forst's defense of Habermas that Habermas' theory does not qualify as comprehensive in Rawls' sense since it does not try to answer the question of the good life that are at the center of comprehensive doctrines does not stand, since the comprehensive doctrine includes not only the question of the good life but also everything associated with it, such as meaning, reference, and truth or validity.[56] In a nutshell, the difference between the two theories is one of locations—"one in a comprehensive doctrine, the other limited to the political."[57] Habermas' approach to separate the moral from the ethical is a priori and becomes substantial only a posteriori, whereas Rawls begins from an a posteriori standpoint, enabling it to separate the ethical much more successfully.

Nevertheless, the concept of the political remains obscure for two reasons. First, since Rawls' political liberalism fundamentally relies on the distinction between the moral and the ethical, and since we saw that the exclusion of comprehensive doctrines does a better job at excluding the ethical from the moral, does this mean that the political is a purely moral domain? Second, it is not clear how the exclusion of

[53] Ibid., 135.

[54] Ibid., 137.

[55] Ibid., 135.

[56] Rainer Forst, *The Right to Justification: Elements of a Constructivist Theory of Justice*, trans. Jeffery Flynn (New York: Columbia University Press, 2011), 92.

[57] John Rawls, "Political Liberalism: Reply to Habermas," *The Journal of Philosophy* (Vol. 92), 138.

comprehensive doctrines is carried out, since at the outset I argued that our moral justification seems to be inevitably influenced by our ethical views, which is also the reason why Habermas asks if the concept of "the reasonable" truly replaces the predicate of "true."[58] As for the first question, Forst offers a useful account through his reductive approach to ground not only the moral but also the political on the right to reasonable justification. After claiming that human beings are first and foremost justificatory beings, Forst goes on to argue that "we can call a social context 'political' when human beings find themselves in an 'order of justification', which consists of norms and institutions that are to govern their lives together—in cooperation as well as in conflict—in a justified or justifiable way"; and the "most important normative concept that applies to this order is that of justice."[59] Furthermore, since Forst also argues that morality is self-justifying and serves as the basis of any meaningful justification, it follows that this "order of justification" is precisely what Rawls means by "the domain of the political," where nothing ethical in included and only the moral exits as the foundation of justification. In other words, a sense of "ought" is fully justified in this order because it relies on nothing but the moral, and to question this sense of "ought" is to be less human. In the chapter on Rawls, Forst offers a more concrete account by arguing that the domain of the political has "a political as well as moral character: a 'political' character insofar as they do not originate in a 'comprehensive doctrine'…; and a moral character insofar as both 'moral' powers are still characteristic of the 'political' conception of the person."[60] In other words, an investigation from the aspect of the political also confirms that Rawls' theory excludes more fully the ethical from the moral, because the political is a purely moral domain, where only the justificatory basis exists.

It should now be clear that, judging from both the comprehensive doctrines and the domain of the political, Rawls' political liberalism does a better job in excluding the ethical and thereby is the superior theory in comparison with that of Habermas. However, how do *actual* ethical persons and communities exclude the ethical and reach a reasonable overlapping consensus in the domain of the political? This issue not only motivates Habermas' criticism but also thinkers like Gerald Gaus to argue: "there is nothing wrong with philosophers painting their personal pictures of ideal moralities and social orders…[but] we must not forget that…they remain personal ideals: they are personal ideals of philosophers about what a social morality should look like. If they are in the eligible set, they may be selected, but they have no authority until they are."[61] This remark becomes relevant when we take into consideration the relationship between the moral and ethical, especially when we closely examine some of Rawls' own comments. For instance, Rawls argues that "in pre-

[58] Jürgen Habermas, "Reconciliation Through the Public Use of Reason: Remarks on John Rawls' Political Liberalism," *The Journal of Philosophy* (Vol. 92), 122.

[59] Rainer Forst, *The Right to Justification: Elements of a Constructivist Theory of Justice*, trans. Jeffery Flynn (New York: Columbia University Press, 2011), 1.

[60] Ibid., 84.

[61] Gerald Gaus, *The Order of Public Reason: A Theory of Freedom and Morality in a Diverse and Bounded World* (Cambridge University Press, 2011), 549.

senting a freestanding political conception and not going beyond that, it is left entirely open to citizens and associations in civil society to formulate their own ways of going beyond, or of going deeper, so as to make that political conception congruent with their comprehensive doctrines."[62] This claim is problematic because it offers two interpretations of the actual mechanism of separating the moral and the ethical. On the one hand, it is possible that the political as well as the possible overlapping consensus already exist within each comprehensive doctrine, and what each ethical person needs to do is to separate this natively political component with other native parts of their comprehensive doctrines. In turn, political liberalism focuses on only these native political components and the mechanism needed is to separate, natively, the moral and the ethical. On the other hand, it is also possible that the political is freestanding in the same sense that the moral is behind every ethical view. In other words, the political is the order of morality working as a framework so fundamental that it is part and parcel of who we are. The mechanism needed is one that helps to lift the veil of the ethical and see the moral. Since we share the same self-justifying moral framework, so long as the political is constructed purely on the basis of the moral, it is able to fulfill the Rawlsian requirements of being both freestanding and capable of exerting moral/political demands.

Rawls' own remarks seem to point to the first interpretation, and some of the examples demonstrate this point. For instance, Quakers, despite being pacifists, are able to support a constitutional regime and accept the legitimacy of majority or other plurality rule.[63] However, this example, as well as Rawls' general remarks regarding the actual mechanism suggests that his own understanding of the domain of the political and its moral content is perhaps narrower than the one Forst has in mind. Rather than identifying the political with self-justifying moral framework, Rawls has in the center of the moral the political values of American democratic society. As a result, the domain of the political works in tandem not only with a reasonable overlapping consensus, but also "stability for the right reasons and legitimacy."[64] Imagine finding a domain of the political in a state where the Quaker religion exists but the American democratic culture is missing, can anyone still be able to see a reasonable overlapping consensus as Rawls puts it? In other words, the domain of morality in Rawls' theory, though stripped of much, perhaps even most of ethical views, is still laden with the value of the American democratic culture, which not only is an ethical view in itself but also requires further moral justification. This is exactly what Habermas was worried about, and despite its superiority to Habermas' theory, Rawls' political liberalism does not go as far as it should have gone in terms of excluding the ethical from the moral.

If the first interpretation of the mechanism that separates the moral from the ethical does not work, what about the second, which says that it is also possible for the

---

[62] John Rawls, "Political Liberalism: Reply to Habermas," *The Journal of Philosophy* (Vol. 92), 136.

[63] Ibid., 148.

[64] Ibid., 143.

political to be freestanding in the same sense that the moral is behind every ethical views. This approach is taken by Gaus in his work on public reason, which begins with social morality and ends with a moral equilibrium within what he calls a "maximal eligible set" that includes different optimal moral proposals.[65] Although Gaus' initial project seems to follow the broad Rawlsian line in that he tries to reconstruct social morality as a basis for moral and political justification, the introduction of the "maximal eligible set" and the mechanism to pick the public justifiable moral principles makes Gaus' project in the end a rational theory of choice, like the one we witness in *A Theory of Justice*. Nevertheless, Gaus' ambitious project *does* suggest that without embedding a democratic culture into morality, Rawls' method to separate the moral from the ethical by making the political a freestanding domain is insufficient, despite its superiority to Habermas' approach.

2.6 Enters the *Proviso*

It is indeed very difficult to envision a moral philosophy that relies on none of its traditional justificatory criteria. To accommodate reasonable pluralism, a working moral philosophy within the broader Rawlsian scheme must rely on neither teleology nor metaphysical rationalism, and above all it must not be comprehensive; instead, it must be a reasonable moral philosophy—a form of justification grounded in reciprocity rather than truth. Gaus tries to sketch such a model through his "real public reason," yet perhaps Rawls himself leaves a subtler clue in what appears, at first glance, to be a procedural footnote: the *proviso*. The significance of the *proviso* has often been underestimated, but it reveals how Rawls implicitly recognizes that even a freestanding political conception of justice cannot hermetically seal itself off from the ethical sources that sustain citizens' moral motivation. It is, as Paul Weithman has argued, a *porous boundary principle* rather than an exclusionary one, allowing the circulation of reasons between the political and nonpolitical domains under disciplined conditions of translation.[66]

According to Rawls, "reasonable comprehensive doctrines, religious or nonreligious, may be introduced in public political discussion at any time, provided that in due course proper political reasons—and not reasons given solely by comprehensive doctrines—are presented that are sufficient to support whatever the comprehensive doctrines introduced are said to support."[67] The *proviso* therefore institutes a hermeneutic economy between the reasonable and the rational: citizens may begin from their particular moral vocabularies, but they are obliged to seek convergence at

---

[65] Gerald Gaus, *The Order of Public Reason: A Theory of Freedom and Morality in a Diverse and Bounded World* (Cambridge University Press, 2011), 321.

[66] Paul Weithman, *Religion and the Obligations of Citizenship* (Cambridge, MA: Harvard University Press, 2002), 77–84.

[67] John Rawls, *Political Liberalism*, expanded ed. (New York: Columbia University Press, 2005), 453.

the level of public justification.[68] In this sense, the *proviso* functions as an ethical discipline of justificatory citizenship. It embodies the duty of civility, not as a suppression of conviction but as a moral disposition to reconstruct one's private reasons into publicly acceptable forms. What is prohibited is not the expression of comprehensive doctrines in political debate, but their *closure*—their refusal to submit to the test of reciprocity. The *proviso* thereby reaffirms the Rawlsian understanding of the reasonable: citizens are free to affirm any conception of the good, yet when coercive power is at stake, they must justify their political proposals by reasons that others, as free and equal, can reasonably accept.

The deeper logic of the *proviso* also illuminates Rawls's understanding of the relation between justification and legitimacy. In *Political Liberalism*, legitimacy depends on what citizens can reasonably accept, not on what is metaphysically true. Yet if public reason were strictly delimited to secular or noncomprehensive premises, the justificatory resources of actual citizens—who invariably reason from within ethical traditions—would be impoverished. The *proviso* prevents such impoverishment by allowing citizens to draw motivational strength from their comprehensive views while maintaining justificatory fairness. In doing so, it also secures a subtle continuity between political liberalism and moral anthropology: citizens remain embedded moral agents rather than abstract bearers of public reason.

This feature becomes evident in Rawls's "Idea of Public Reason Revisited," where he emphasizes that the *proviso* "specifies a way in which the limits imposed by public reason may be extended."[69] Here Rawls concedes that comprehensive doctrines can contribute to the political culture by offering moral insight, provided that they accept the priority of the political conception when justifying coercive laws. The *proviso* thus works as a *filter*, not a wall: it admits ethical materials that can be reconstructed in terms of public values such as fairness, equality, or reciprocity, while excluding those that cannot undergo this translation without loss of reasonableness. In practice, this means that religious or perfectionist moral claims can inform public discourse if they are ultimately re-expressed through the grammar of political justification. In effect, the *proviso* transforms the act of justification itself into a civic virtue. To speak publicly under the *proviso* is to practice what Rawls calls "reasonableness as a moral power"—the disposition to see one's own reasons as revisable in light of others.[70] If we push this insight further, the *proviso* may also serve as the embryonic principle of a *pluralistic ethics* that extends beyond the political domain. By establishing a procedural bridge between comprehensive and public reason, the *proviso* implicitly models a form of moral reasoning capable of addressing disagreement without denying moral depth. It suggests that moral justification in modernity is neither purely epistemological nor purely procedural, but

[68] Micah Schwartzman, "The Ethics of Reasoning from Conjecture," *Philosophy & Public Affairs* 41, no. 1 (2013): 3–29.

[69] John Rawls, "The Idea of Public Reason Revisited," *University of Chicago Law Review* 64, no. 3 (1997): 765.

[70] John Rawls, *Political Liberalism*, expanded ed. (New York: Columbia University Press, 2005), 19, 54.

dialectical: it arises through the iterative translation of reasons across moral vocabularies under the regulative ideal of reciprocity. This dialectic of translation—so central to Rawls's later thought—could, in turn, inspire the reconstruction of moral philosophy itself. Instead of seeking a single Archimedean standpoint, moral philosophy in a Rawlsian age would study the norms governing this circulation of reasons between distinct moral languages. It would analyze the conditions under which ethical claims may be rendered reasonable without being neutralized—a task that becomes indispensable in societies marked by deep pluralism.

The *proviso*'s promise, however, extends beyond abstract moral theory. It has profound implications for cross-cultural legitimacy. In contexts such as contemporary East Asia, where Confucian, Buddhist, and liberal values coexist within the same political framework, the *proviso* offers a procedural grammar through which culturally specific reasons may enter public justification without collapsing into relativism or domination.[13] A Confucian citizen, for instance, may defend filial piety or social harmony as public values, provided these are recast in the language of civic equality and mutual respect rather than inherited hierarchy. The *proviso* thereby allows tradition to remain a moral interlocutor rather than a political authority. Understood this way, the *proviso* becomes the moral infrastructure of public reason itself—the condition of its vitality in pluralistic societies. It transforms the procedural ideal of legitimacy into an ongoing practice of mutual justification that simultaneously respects difference and constructs commonality. This will be the topic of Part II.

What begins as a modest qualification in *Political Liberalism* culminates in a general model of pluralistic justification. The *proviso* allows Rawlsian liberalism to absorb moral particularity without surrendering to relativism, to maintain civic unity without imposing metaphysical uniformity. It represents the reconciliation of the universal and the particular—the very task of modern moral and political philosophy. In this sense, the *proviso* is not merely an "injunction to present proper political reasons," but a philosophical insight into the nature of moral reasoning under conditions of freedom and equality: that justification is always both situated and shared, both ethical in its origin and political in its form. In Part III of this book, I will suggest that this same logic—the translation of comprehensive moral insight into shareable political reason—can guide our collective confrontation with the social, moral, and political challenges posed by artificial intelligence. For if the *proviso* teaches anything, it is that even in an age of algorithmic reason, the legitimacy of power depends not on intelligence but on justification.

Part II
Confucianism

Chapter 3
Deep Reasonable Pluralism, Moderate Political Confucianism, and Pluralistic Neutrality

Abstract Moderate Confucian perfectionism aims to take advantage of both the capacity of liberalism to accommodate reasonable pluralism and the richness of Confucianism to endorse shared values without much controversy. Drawing from John Rawls's *proviso*, Franz Mang offers an internal critique of moderate Confucian perfectionism by constructing a "wide view of moderate perfectionism" according to which active promotion of Confucianism or Confucian values violates the liberal condition to accommodate reasonable pluralism. In this chapter, I will argue that Mang's internal critique not only reveals the weakness of moderate Confucian perfectionism but also pushes moderate perfectionism closer to neutrality, which can be demonstrated by adopting a pluralistic understanding of liberal neutrality. Furthermore, the pluralistic understanding of liberal neutrality leads to a convergent view of the relationship between political liberalism and moderate perfectionism, on the basis of which a modified *proviso* can be constructed to take advantage of both freestanding political reasons and freestanding perfectionist reasons. This modified *proviso* not only meets the liberal condition to accommodate reasonable pluralism but also strengthens the case for political liberalism.

Keywords Political liberalism • Moderate perfectionism • Liberal neutrality • Confucianism reasonable pluralism • Public justification • Liberal democracy

3.1 Introduction

Despite the historical legacies and contemporary prevalence of many non-Confucian traditions, Confucian values and ideals are often regarded by comparative political theorists as both culturally dominant and politically relevant in many East Asian societies. Filial piety, for instance, remains one of the key "habits of the heart" for

Z. Li, *Pluralism, Confucianism, and Artificial Intelligence*, Philosophy and Politics - Critical Explorations 35, https://doi.org/10.1007/978-3-032-25605-8_3

many East Asians and continues to exert its cultural and political influence. In 2013, China implemented a revised version of its Law for the Protection of the Rights and Interests of the Elderly, which led a local court to rule that a Chinese woman and her husband must visit the woman's elderly mother "at least once every two months, and during at least two public holidays every year."[1] This new law requires that "adult children provide mental support, in addition to financial support and life care, to their partners once they reach the age of 60."[2] A 2018 case in Taiwan also made the news when the Supreme Court of Taiwan ruled that a dentist must pay his mother nearly $1 million of "upbringing fee."[3] Beneath people's divisive opinions regarding these controversial cases is a shared understanding of the value of filial piety. Is it then reasonable for filial piety to serve as a basis of relevant legislative and judicial processes? More generally, is it reasonable to draw from Confucianism to justify laws that directly or indirectly coerce citizens to live up to certain Confucian ideals and doctrines? Should Confucianism play a dominant role in shaping and reshaping the relationship between the state and civil society? Liberal-minded Confucian political theorists offer largely positive answers to these questions. Instead of striving toward neutrality, they claim that the state ought to adopt a perfectionist position and publicly advocate at least some Confucian ideals and doctrines, which should be used to structure its constitutionalism and to justify state actions, policies, and legislation for the betterment of its citizens who also commit to basic liberal values and ideals.

But liberal democracies tend to be pluralistic. The idea of reasonable pluralism, which was popularized by John Rawls to describe the co-existence of a plurality of reasonable religious, philosophical, and moral comprehensive doctrines, has become an integral part of contemporary liberal political theory. Both liberal perfectionists and political liberals incorporate different strategies to accommodate reasonable pluralism so as not to cross the boundary of liberalism. Taking reasonable pluralism seriously, the co-existence of liberalism and Confucianism often leads to conflicts between the liberal necessity to accommodate reasonable pluralism and the perfectionist necessity to maintain at least moderately Confucian public characteristics in East Asian societies. This chapter will first introduce the idea of deep reasonable pluralism and then argue that the tension between liberalism and perfectionism (Confucianism in this case) is substantial enough to undermine even moderate attempts to bridge the two. Furthermore, pushing theories to be even more moderate for the sake of alleviating this tension will effectively approach a form of liberal neutrality, which perfectionists reject. Specifically, I will first outline the idea of deep reasonable pluralism and its role in contemporary Confucian political theory. Then, I will focus on Franz Mang's critique of and attempt to revise Joseph

[1] Xuyang Pi, "China Filial Piety Law Draws First Blood," *The Wall Street Journal*, July 4, 2013, https://www.wsj.com/articles/BL-CJB-18029.

[2] Ibid.

[3] Chris Horton, "Taiwan Dentist Must Pay His Mother Nearly $1 Million for 'Upbringing,'" *The New York Times*, January 2, 2018, https://www.nytimes.com/2018/01/02/world/asia/taiwan-dentist-court-mother-filial-son.html.

Chan's Confucian political perfectionism. I will argue that Mang correctly diagnoses that the key problem with Confucian political perfectionism is the tension between the liberal and the Confucian components of the theory. However, drawing from John Rawls's *proviso*, Mang's solution to make a clean break between the two components and to appeal to Confucianism only when freestanding justification is obtained pushes his position dangerously close to liberal neutrality. Finally, I will argue that a pluralistic understanding of liberal neutrality can help illustrate a converging relationship between moderate perfectionism and political liberalism. Despite their different positions on perfectionism, moderate liberal perfectionists and political liberals' shared goal of approaching liberalism in a non-comprehensive way leads to some common ground, on the basis of which I will propose a modified version of the *proviso* that strengthens the case of political liberalism. Finally, I will conclude by responding to some potential objections and highlighting the role that Confucianism can still play under the demand of liberal neutrality.

3.2 Deep Reasonable Pluralism in East Asia

It will be remembered that reasonable pluralism, as Rawls understands it, refers to "the co-existence of highly diverse religious, philosophical, and moral doctrines that is the necessary outcome of human reason under burdens of judgment and enduring free instructions," defines modern liberal democracies.[4] Hence, one of the most urgent questions any political theorist can ask is: "How is it possible that there may exist over time a stable and just society of free and equal citizens profoundly divided by reasonable though incompatible religious, philosophical, and moral doctrines?"[5] Among liberal-minded Confucian political theorists, Rawls's question can be revised to better reflect the condition of East Asian societies that are becoming increasingly pluralistic and still highly saturated with Confucian values and mores. One might wonder: How is it possible that there may exist over time a stable and just society of free and equal citizens profoundly divided by reasonable though incompatible religious, philosophical, and moral doctrines *that also exhibits publicly recognizable Confucian characteristics*?[6] A variety of moderately perfectionist Confucian political theories have tried to maintain both the liberal and democratic

[4] John Rawls, *Political Liberalism*, Expanded ed. (New York: Columbia University Press, 2005), 61.

[5] Ibid., xviii.

[6] For instance, despite his preference for liberal democracy, Sungmoon Kim argues that "the Confucianism in public reason Confucianism holds substantively Confucian perfectionist values that give the East Asian people a Confucian public character. And this publicly intelligible Confucianism binds citizens horizontally as equal members of one political community, notwithstanding their internal differences and moral disagreements." Sungmoon Kim, "Public Reason Confucianism: A Construction," *American Political Science Review* 109, no. 1 (2015): 193.

ideals and institutions and the Confucian values and mores in East Asian societies.[7] However admirable the question is, it is a fundamentally misguided one for both theoretical and empirical reasons. From a theoretical perspective, the political liberal nature of Rawls's original question fundamentally conflicts with the moderately perfectionist addition of Confucianism. What Rawls wants to ask is how a society can maintain its justice and stability without resorting to any specific comprehensive doctrine, regardless of how reasonable it might be. Asking how a society can do so while maintaining a decidedly Confucian outlook is simply courting contradiction. Moreover, insisting on having publicly recognizable Confucian characteristics is going against the permanent fact of reasonable pluralism. If human reason under burdens of judgment and enduring free instructions could not figure out which reasonable comprehensive doctrine ought to rule over others, which is the premise of the question, why must Confucianism be publicly and recognizably endorsed? Thus, recent liberal theories of political Confucianism seem to have been caught in a dilemma from the outset: Either the theory favors the liberal and democratic ideals and institutions for the sake of reasonable pluralism but loses its ground for also favoring Confucianism, or the theory must disown its strong commitment to liberal and democratic ideals and institutions in favor of Confucian values and mores. As I argue elsewhere, the former approach leads to a series of problems that ultimately lead to the collapse of the approach itself.[8] As for the latter approach, scholars have proposed much more perfectionist theories of political Confucianism that are beyond the scope of this chapter.[9]

From an empirical perspective, one might also recognize how the question posed earlier is out of sync with the history and condition of modern and contemporary East Asian societies. The New Culture Movement in China in the 1910s and 1920s, for instance, tried to promote progressive and modern ideals of politics to replace traditional Chinese culture defined by Confucianism. The competition between Confucianism and alternative doctrines already existed at the outset of waves of liberalization and democratization that would follow the movement. Even today, the co-existence and even competition between Confucianism and alternative doctrines, such as liberalism, is evident in many East Asian societies. In South Korea, Article

[7] See Joseph Chan, *Confucian Perfectionism: A Political Philosophy for Modern Times* (Princeton, NJ: Princeton University Press, 2014). Sungmoon Kim, *Public Reason Confucianism: Democratic Perfectionism and Constitutionalism in East Asia* (Cambridge: Cambridge University Press, 2016). Shaun O'Dwyer, *Confucianism's Prospects: A Reassessment* (Albany, NY: State University of New York Press, 2019).

[8] See Zhuoyao Li, *Political Liberalism, Confucianism, and the Future of Democracy in East Asia* (Cham, Switzerland: Springer International Publishing, 2020). Zhuoyao Li, "The Discontents of Moderate Political Confucianism and the Future of Democracy in East Asia," *Philosophy East & West* 68, no. 4 (2018): 1193–1218.

[9] See Tongdong Bai, *Against Political Equality: The Confucian Case* (Princeton, NJ: Princeton University Press, 2019). Daniel A. Bell, *Beyond Liberal Democracy: Political Thinking for an East Asian Context* (Princeton, NJ: Princeton University Press, 2006). Qiang Jiang, *A Confucian Constitutional Order: How China's Ancient Past Can Shape Its Political Future*, ed. Daniel A. Bell and Ruiping Fan (Princeton, NJ: Princeton University Press, 2013).

9 of the Korean Constitution explicitly stipulates that "The State shall strive to sustain and develop the cultural heritage and to enhance national culture."[10] In Sungmoon Kim's view, Article 9 shows that the Constitution is committed to "non-liberal, characteristically Confucian, goods and values…and encourages the Korean state to promote them publicly."[11] But this article, which is embedded in an otherwise substantively liberal constitutional framework, also demonstrates that liberalism and Confucianism co-exist in a well-ordered society and are competitively, if not equally, significant to the lives of its citizens.

The key problem with the misguided question is not so much its ambition to accommodate reasonable pluralism and promote Confucianism at the same time as its failure to take pluralism in East Asia truly seriously. What Rawls has in mind when it comes to reasonable pluralism is quite different from its manifestation in East Asia. In the Western context, reasonable pluralism developed after "the Wars of Religion following the Reformation and the subsequent development of the principle of toleration…the growth of constitutional government and of large industrial market economies."[12] In a way, the history of reasonable pluralism in the West *is* the history of liberalism. In East Asia, without the history of liberalism to historically define reasonable pluralism, liberalism, like Confucianism, Daoism, and many other domestic counterparts, is only one of many reasonable comprehensive doctrines that are either imported or homegrown. In other words, the kind of reasonable pluralism in East Asia is not a by-product of liberalism and democracy, as Rawls suggests in the Western context, but rather a form of deep reasonable pluralism that includes liberalism as a competing way of life.

The fact that liberalism can co-exist with Confucianism in East Asian societies should prompt theorists to move beyond Rawlsian reasonable pluralism and take deep reasonable pluralism seriously. The question one ought to ask is not how Confucianism can stand out in a society where reasonable pluralism is accommodated with liberal and democratic ideals and institutions, but how deep reasonable pluralism, which encompasses liberalism rather than being defined by it, ought to be accommodated. Framing the question in terms of deep reasonable pluralism has two distinct advantages. First and foremost, the question bypasses the key problem mentioned above confronting both moderate and extreme Confucian perfectionists. There is no need to pick a side between liberalism and Confucianism since both are parts of the deep reasonable pluralism prevalent in East Asia. Second, it opens up a range of possibilities to reconceive the domain of the political without the need to be fully liberal or Confucian, which in actuality matches the socio-political condition of many East Asian societies.

---

[10] Constitution of the Republic of Korea, accessed 2022, https://elaw.klri.re.kr/eng_service/lawView.do?hseq=1&lang=ENG.

[11] Sungmoon Kim, *Public Reason Confucianism: Democratic Perfectionism and Constitutionalism in East Asia* (Cambridge: Cambridge University Press, 2016), 121.

[12] John Rawls, *Political Liberalism*, Expanded ed. (New York: Columbia University Press, 2005), 61.

3.3 Moderate Confucian Perfectionism and the Wide View of Moderate Perfectionism

How could one maintain some substantively liberal and democratic ideals on the one hand and still remain faithful to the Confucian tradition on the other? Joseph Chan's Confucian political perfectionism offers an ingenious answer to the question by choosing a road less traveled. Instead of succumbing to comprehensive Confucian perfectionism that encourages Confucian values and ideals to be publicly endorsed by the state, and instead of adopting a thoroughly political liberal and neutralist approach that risks banishing Confucianism to the private sphere, Chan develops an intermediate position that justifies Confucian values and ideals in a "piecemeal and moderate" way.[13] On the one hand, piecemeal judgments about the good life need not be controversial. Instead of appealing to specific comprehensive doctrines, judgments about what Chan calls agency goods and prudential goods are widely shared by reasonable persons, and they can serve as a non-controversial foundation for a moderately perfectionist political structure.[14] On the other hand, moderate perfectionism dictates that Confucian values and ideals should not be justified and endorsed by the state by appealing to Confucianism in a comprehensive way. Instead, they should be justified with reasons that do not require prior acceptance of Confucianism as a comprehensive doctrine. Thus, Chan's strategy is to start with Confucian values that can ground the basic institutions of liberal democracy and are justifiable by appealing to reasons not tied to Confucianism in a comprehensive sense. A key assumption behind Chan's Confucian political perfectionism is that a political philosophy for modern times must be able to accommodate reasonable pluralism. If Confucianism were the only meaningful doctrine practiced by citizens in an East Asian society, then there would be little need to be moderate about promoting certain Confucian values and ideals. The motivation behind Chan's moderate turn is precisely to avoid the problematic implication of the extreme form of Confucian perfectionism that disrespects non-Confucian doctrines.

However, Chan's position is inherently unstable because it oscillates between its liberal commitment to accommodate reasonable pluralism and its Confucian commitment to promote Confucian values and ideals.[15] Franz Mang proposes a similar critique where he argues that many liberal-minded Confucian perfectionists, Chan included, try to satisfy two conditions at once:

(1) The liberal accommodation condition: Any liberal society is characterized by a wide plurality of conceptions of the good, moral outlooks, and religious doc-

[13] Joseph Chan, *Confucian Perfectionism: A Political Philosophy for Modern Times* (Princeton, NJ: Princeton University Press, 2014), 199–200.

[14] Joseph Chan, "Legitimacy, Unanimity, and Perfectionism," *Philosophy & Public Affairs* 29, no. 1 (2000): 11.

[15] See Zhuoyao Li, "The Discontents of Moderate Political Confucianism and the Future of Democracy in East Asia," *Philosophy East & West* 68, no. 4 (2018): 1193–1218.

trines. A political theory for liberal societies seeks to accommodate as many reasonable conceptions of the good and religious doctrines as possible.
(2) The intelligibility condition: A Confucian political theory must have a recognizable Confucian character.[16]

In Chan's case, the two conditions come into conflict. In order to fulfill the liberal accommodation condition, Chan's theory must be intentionally moderate so as to make room for non-Confucian doctrines, which necessarily dilutes the Confucian characteristics of his position. In order to fulfill the intelligibility condition, Chan's theory must appeal to Confucian values, albeit in a piecemeal and moderate way, which raises the question of "why Confucianism" and risks turning his moderate position into a more extreme one. By advocating Confucian political perfectionism, Chan faces a dilemma: "either he maintains his version of moderate perfectionism where Confucianism cannot have a central place in moderate perfectionism and therefore, his political philosophy lacks a recognizable Confucian character or he should present Confucianism as a comprehensive doctrine and as a result, he can no longer uphold moderate perfectionism."[17] Moderate perfectionism in the form of Confucian political perfectionism thus does not live up to its ambition.

Sympathetic to Chan's overall project, Mang proposes some modifications that push moderate perfectionism even further. Inspired by Rawls's wide view of public political culture, Mang draws a distinction between the narrow view and the wide view of moderate perfectionism.[18] In contrast to the narrow view that prohibits citizens from appealing to any particular comprehensive doctrines for political justification, Mang defines the wide view of moderate perfectionism as follows:

> In political justification, citizens may appeal to perfectionist reasons whose validity does not rely on the truth of any particular comprehensive doctrine. In addition, citizens may appeal to any reasonable and fully comprehensive doctrine to support their positions in political justification, given that their positions are already supported by sufficient reasons whose validity does not rely on the truth of any particular comprehensive doctrine.[19]

Following the general spirit of Rawls's *proviso*, Mang reintroduces a reasonable comprehensive doctrine to Chan's political and moderate take on perfectionism. Instead of narrowly barring citizens to appeal to their reasonable comprehended doctrines altogether, which Chan's approach does, the wide view of moderate perfectionism allows citizens to appeal to their reasonable comprehended doctrines to

---

[16] Franz Mang, "Confucianism, Perfectionism, and Liberal Society," *Dao: A Journal of Comparative Philosophy* 17 (2018): 30.

[17] Ibid., 38.

[18] Rawls refers to this exception as the *proviso*: "[R]easonable comprehensive doctrines, religious or nonreligious, may be introduced in public political discussion at any time, provided that in due course proper political reasons—and not reasons given solely by comprehensive doctrines—are presented that are sufficient to support whatever the comprehensive doctrines introduced are said to support. This injunction to present proper political reasons I refer to as the *proviso*." See John Rawls, *Political Liberalism*, Expanded ed. (New York: Columbia University Press, 2005), 462.

[19] Franz Mang, "Confucianism, Perfectionism, and Liberal Society," *Dao: A Journal of Comparative Philosophy* 17 (2018): 45.

justify their positions on the condition that there are already sufficient freestanding reasons that support their positions. There are two types of perfectionist reasons at work. On the one hand and primarily, there are piecemeal and moderate perfectionist reasons not tied to any particular reasonable comprehensive doctrine. On the other hand and secondarily, there are perfectionist reasons strongly associated with citizens' reasonable comprehensive doctrines. The latter kind of reason can but need not be utilized, depending on how well citizens' positions at stake are supported by the former kind of reason. With this strategy to designate different perfectionist reasons with distinct roles without associating either reason with Confucianism, Mang tries to meet the liberal accommodation condition without being weighed down by the intelligibility condition.

In my view, Chan's emphasis on civility for the purpose of accommodating reasonable pluralism might push his theory toward neutrality. Mang's modified version of moderate perfectionism is susceptible to a similar criticism, namely that by prioritizing the liberal accommodation condition over the intelligibility condition and drawing from Rawls's wide view of public political culture, which is associated with liberal neutrality, the wide view of moderate perfectionism might be so moderate that the perfectionist connotation wears thin. Mang might object by arguing that the wide view of moderate perfectionism is not associated with liberal neutrality because it "allows citizens to justify their views *at any time* in terms of perfectionist reasons that are freestanding from any particular doctrine."[20] Moreover, "when and only when citizens have justified their views in terms of reasons that are freestanding from any particular doctrine can they further explain their views and their perfectionist reasons by appealing to their doctrines."[21] But one might wonder why citizens feel the need to take the extra step of appealing to their comprehensive doctrine when they are required and already can justify their positions in terms of reasons that are freestanding from any particular reasonable comprehensive doctrine. Since Mang rejects the intelligibility condition, the reason why citizens might be motivated to appeal to their reasonable comprehensive doctrines cannot be because they wish to maintain public characteristics that are intelligibly associated with their own reasonable comprehensive doctrines. Another possible reason is that so doing might make justifications for citizens' positions stronger. This might be the case. After all, even Rawls admits that sometimes introducing reasonable comprehensive doctrines to the domain of the political can eventually strengthen public reason, which serves as the justificatory basis for public political discussions. If some citizens decide to promote certain positions supported by freestanding reasons but also cite reasons associated with specific reasonable comprehensive doctrines as further support, then it is unclear what the intention of these citizens truly is. Similarly, if a Supreme Court Justice tries to first justify the Court's decision in neutral language by appealing to freestanding political reasons, and then add that parts of her reasonable comprehensive doctrine, which others need not fully

[20] Ibid., 45.

[21] Ibid.

embrace, can also lend a justificatory hand, what would citizens feel about this two-step explanation? I think many would suspect that the Justice is probably not sincere in her freestanding justification in the first step. Moreover, one might also argue that by allowing the second step to be incorporated into the general justificatory process, citizens and state officials might be motivated to either disguise their private reasons with neutral language or abandon the first step of freestanding justification altogether. After all, if citizens and state officials can appeal to their reasonable comprehensive doctrines in the domain of the political, why bother with freestanding political reasons at all? All these are likely to undermine the degree of civility established by appealing to freestanding justification in the first place, which is foundational for a well-ordered liberal democracy.

It is therefore quite surprising for Mang to argue that even if a Confucian value cannot be justified by freestanding reasons, "allowing citizens to appeal to Confucianism in political justification in some cases would give them the opportunity to appreciate the merits of Confucianism."[22] Is not the point of the liberal accommodation condition to promote only values that are justifiable by freestanding reasons, and should not appealing to Confucianism in political justification come only after freestanding justification is achieved? This confusing statement leads to the realization that the wide view of moderate perfectionism is subject to the same criticism Mang levies against Chan's version of moderate perfectionism, only to a lesser degree. Allowing citizens (and the state) to appeal to their reasonable comprehensive doctrines to support positions that are already justified with freestanding reasons inevitably casts a shadow over the motivations of citizens and the state to advocate their positions. In the examples Mang gives, state promotions of humanity-based moral education and filial piety, so long as Confucian reasons are introduced to the process of justification, there will always be a lingering concern that the state in fact prioritizes the intelligibility condition over the liberal accommodation condition, which the wide view of moderate perfectionism criticizes.

Finally, Mang might still insist that "Confucianism as a fully comprehensive doctrine to shed light on a wide range of social and political issues in a liberal society," and that it can "enrich public deliberation."[23] In other words, public reason can be strengthened by including Confucian reasons in the second step of the two-step justificatory process. However, one ought to be careful with what else is strengthened with the reintroduction of non-freestanding perfectionist reasons. It will be recalled that a key reason why Rawls introduces the *proviso* is because so doing might strengthen the ideal of public reason, which is strongly associated with liberal neutrality. With the wide view of moderate perfectionism, a similar move cannot be said to strengthen public reason, which makes references only to public values of a political conception of justice and public standards that all citizens could reasonably endorse. Instead, it strengthens only a platform of freestanding reasons not contin-

---

[22] Ibid., 46.

[23] Ibid., 46, 48.

gent upon the truth of any particular reasonable comprehensive doctrines. Despite the difference, both strategies effectively approach some form of neutrality. In the case of Rawls, a sense of neutrality is established with the help of public reason in the domain of the political, where the conception of justice is not subordinated to any particular comprehensive doctrine. In the case of Mang, a sense of neutrality is established with the help of the platform of freestanding reasons, where the truth of any particular comprehensive doctrines becomes irrelevant. Since the intelligibility condition needs to be severed from the liberal accommodation condition, the wide view of moderate perfectionism seems to be so modest that it takes on a neutral perspective, which is why it needs perfectionist compensation by reintroducing non-freestanding reasons. Therefore, a political approach to perfectionism inevitably inches closer to neutrality the more moderate the theory becomes. Mang's attempt to focus only on the liberal accommodation condition makes the tendency even clearer. This revelation leads to a more profound question regarding the nature of liberal neutrality. In the final section of this chapter, I will first explore a pluralistic view of liberal neutrality as the point of convergence between moderate perfectionism and political liberalism. Then I will conclude by addressing the relationship between Confucianism and liberal neutrality.

3.4 A Pluralistic View of Liberal Neutrality

Liberal neutrality has always been a contested idea and a point of divergence between political liberals and liberal perfectionists. However, in the case of moderate perfectionism, the tendency toward liberal neutrality is often regarded as a strong criticism against its largely political approach to perfectionism. In the cases of Chan and Mang, the increasing degree of moderation effectively pushes their perfectionist positions closer to liberal neutrality. In this section, I will go beyond the point of divergence and argue that my critique that Mang's wide view of moderate perfectionism shares affinity toward liberal neutrality should serve more as a point of convergence than a piece of criticism against moderate perfectionism.

It will be recalled that one of my lines of critique against the wide view of moderate perfectionism is that it is unclear why citizens would want to appeal to their private reasons to justify positions that can be and are required to be justified in terms of reasons that are freestanding from any reasonable comprehensive doctrine. The same issue applies to the state, which may offer two types of perfectionist reasons for endorsing a certain position, one being freestanding and the other not. In these cases, the intention of the citizens and the state becomes questionable and can conflict with the liberal accommodation condition. Thus, in addition to the justificatory dimension, whether or not a position or a state can be labeled "neutral" also hinges upon the intentional dimension. Collis Tahzib argues against the justificatory focus of contemporary liberal theory in favor of a pluralist view that understands neutrality as "a complex, multifaceted, gradable concept with consequential, justificatory, and intentional dimensions."[24] After a survey of arguments that try to give answers to the question of what is meant by "state neutrality" from consequential, justificatory, and intentional perspectives alone, Tahzib comes to the conclusion that "each account captures something of the concept of neutrality" but at the same time also produces implausible implications.[25] Instead, Tahzib proposes two unidimensional ways to think about neutrality. First, there is the "all-or-nothing pluralism with thresholds," which is "a natural first attempt to formulate a pluralist account of neutrality":

> A state is neutral if and only if: (1) the reasons and justifications given in support of its laws, policies, and institutions do not appeal to any particular controversial conception of the good life, but rather are based on publicly accessible or intelligible considerations; *and* (2) the state does not act with the aim or intention of promoting one or another conception of the good life; *and* (3) the effects of state action are not such as to make it exceedingly difficult for some individuals to live out their reasonable conception of the good life.[26]

The main problem with this formulation is that the "exceeding difficulty" threshold in clause (3) might still be too strong. Trying to adjust this threshold leads to a dilemma: either the threshold we set is too strong for neutrality to achieve, or the threshold we set is too weak to produce sufficient sensitivity to non-neutral consequences that significantly advantage some conception of the good over others. In Tahzib's view, the problem is that the "all-or-nothing" perspective regarding neutrality is implausibly dichotomous between the maximally neutral state that appeals to no perfectionist values at all, and the maximally perfectionist state that appeals only to comprehensively perfectionist values.[27]

To avoid this problem, Tahzib proposes a second unidimensional approach to a pluralist account of neutrality, which he calls "matter-of-degree pluralism without thresholds." On this view:

> A state is neutral *to the extent that*: (1) the reasons and justifications for its laws, policies, and institutions do not appeal to any particular controversial conception of the good life, but rather are based in publicly accessible or intelligible considerations; *and* (2) the state does not act with the aim or intention of promoting one or another conception of the good life; *and* (3) state action does not have the effect of advantaging some reasonable conceptions of the good life and of disadvantaging others.[28]

Although there are many questions to be answered (for instance, how the three dimensions of neutrality interact with one another and how they should be weighed and ordered), this pluralist account of neutrality seems to me to be on the right path. On the one hand, it collects in a package what the three dimensions each captures about the idea of liberal neutrality. On the other hand, it breaks ground for an

---

[24] Collis Tahzib, "Survey Article: Pluralist Neutrality," *The Journal of Political Philosophy* 26, no. 4 (2018): 508.

[25] Ibid., 519.

[26] Ibid.

[27] Ibid., 520.

[28] Ibid., 521.

alternative understanding of neutrality without the unnecessary constraint of the all-or-nothing dichotomy. It has become somewhat a consensus among contemporary liberal political theorists that perfectionism, comprehensive or moderate, is necessarily against neutrality. As our discussion in the previous section has demonstrated, moderate perfectionism can inch toward neutrality under certain circumstances. As a matter of fact, I will argue that the wide view of moderate perfectionism fits the pluralist account of neutrality almost perfectly, which further demonstrates that pushing moderate perfectionism too much is equivalent of meeting political liberalism halfway at the point of neutrality.

Tahzib's pluralist account of neutrality aims to connect the consequential, justificatory, and intentional perspectives of neutrality in such a way as to avoid an all-or-nothing dichotomy. Mang's wide view of moderate perfectionism touches upon all three perspectives. By avoiding comprehensively Confucian reasons and appealing to reasons that are independent of the truth of any comprehensive doctrine, the wide view of moderate perfectionism precisely tries to achieve clause (1). By severing the liberal accommodation condition from the intelligibility condition, the wide view of moderate perfectionism tries to avoid the possibility that the state intentionally favors Confucianism through moderately perfectionist policies, which stays in line with clause (2).[29] As for the consequential perspective in clause (3), Mang makes it clear that it is an advantage of moderate perfectionism to advocate policies that do not necessarily disadvantage some reasonable conceptions of the good life. For instance, the state's decision to promote sociality through supporting the business of flea markets and other gathering activities hardly seems contentious, nor does it obviously make it exceedingly difficult for hermits to practice their way of life, which values solitude more than solidarity.[30] In this case, the wide view of moderate perfectionism achieves clause (3) in both the all-or-nothing and matter-of-degree versions of the pluralist account of neutrality. If Tahzib's view is reasonable, which I think it is, then it is clear that Mang's position actually supports state neutrality, despite its moderate perfectionist structure.

3.5 Between Political Liberalism and Moderate Perfectionism: A Convergent View

The wide view of moderate perfectionism is thus perfectionism pushed to its moderate limit. It will be recalled that instead of public reason, the wide view of moderate perfectionism draws from publicly justifiable reasons that are independent of the

[29] As I discuss in this section, the widening of moderate perfectionism by appealing to private reason might introduce some uncertainty over intentionality, which poses enough problems to question the validity of the wide view of moderate perfectionism. I will propose a modified *proviso* in the next section that avoids this issue.

[30] Franz Mang, "State Perfectionism and the Importance of Confucianism for East Asia," *The Philosophical Forum* 52 (2021): 5–16.

truth of any particular comprehensive doctrines. Unlike public reason, which draws only from political values that are freestanding, publicly justifiable reasons that Mang alludes to are moderately perfectionist beyond the domain of the political. For instance, humanity-based moral education can be justified by appealing to the value of human excellence, which includes "practical wisdom, courage, compassion, and a sense of responsibility."[31] In my view, Rawls's political conception of justice can be interpreted as occupying a narrower space within a broader domain of a public conception of morality, which includes values that are:

(1) reasonably justified;
(2) publicly endorsed;
(3) devoid of the traditionally ontological character of morality, meaning that the objective prescriptivity of morality no longer hinges upon the independent truth regarding the foundation of morality but on its possibility of being reasonably justified; and
(4) justificatory only in structure, meaning that the principle of reasonable justification cannot itself play a foundationalist role.[32]

If this view is reasonable, then there seems to be a point of convergence between the wide view of moderate perfectionism and political liberalism. On the one hand, prioritizing the liberal accommodation condition over the intelligibility condition, as the wide view of moderate perfectionism does, pushes moderate perfectionism toward state neutrality. On the other hand, political liberalism must be able to justify its inclusion of some perfectionist elements without giving up its position on state neutrality. The point of convergence hinges upon state neutrality created by publicly justifiable reasons independent of the truth of any particular reasonable comprehensive doctrines. Although appealing to these reasons pushes the wide view to its perfectionist limit, doing so can strengthen the case of political liberalism. As Kim points out, political liberalism has "a back door allowing comprehensive doctrines to sneak into the domains of public reason."[33] In Kim's view, the fact that Rawls allows citizens to arrive at different conceptions of justice in *Political Liberalism* suggests the possibility for citizens' reasonable comprehensive doctrines to influence their interpretation of public reason.[34] Rawls's *proviso*, which inspires the wide view of moderate perfectionism, also suggests that political liberalism reserves at least some room for perfectionism. However, since the wide view of moderate perfectionism eventually leads to a form of state neutrality, which provides a point of convergence between moderate perfectionism and political liberalism, political liberalism can take advantage of this convergence and justifies its inclusion of some

[31] Franz Mang, "Confucianism, Perfectionism, and Liberal Society," *Dao: A Journal of Comparative Philosophy* 17 (2018): 46.

[32] Zhuoyao Li, "The Public Conception of Morality in John Rawls' Political Liberalism," *Ethics & Global Politics* 9 (2016): 1–23.

[33] Sungmoon Kim, *Public Reason Confucianism: Democratic Perfectionism and Constitutionalism in East Asia* (Cambridge: Cambridge University Press, 2016), 80.

[34] Kim builds his public reason Confucianism on this assumption.

perfectionist elements without losing its neutral appeal. For instance, the original *proviso* can be modified in the following way: Instead of reasonable comprehensive doctrines, *publicly justifiable reasons that are independent of the truth of any particular reasonable comprehensive doctrines can be introduced in public political discussion, provided that in due course proper political reasons are presented that are sufficient to support whatever the publicly justifiable reasons introduced are said to support.* This modified *proviso* offers three advantages. First, it closes the back door through which specific reasonable comprehensive doctrines may influence political justification as suggested by the original *proviso*. What the wide view of moderate perfectionism intends as a way to suppress the intelligibility condition is now used as a means to strengthen political liberalism. Second, the freestanding and moderately perfectionist values introduced into public political discussion can meet the liberal accommodation condition, which is key to both the wide view of moderate perfectionism and political liberalism, without the problem of intentionality caused by reintroducing comprehensive perfectionist reasons. Finally, both political liberalism and moderate perfectionism can further converge on liberal neutrality as a matter of degree because adopting the modified *proviso* satisfies all three clauses of Tahzib's pluralist account of neutrality.

One might certainly object to the structure of the modified *proviso* by questioning the priority of public reason over publicly justifiable reasons. In other words, why can't moderate perfectionists turn things around and focus solely on publicly justifiable reasons, which are moderately perfectionist? One might also object that the modified *proviso* seems to presuppose the superiority of political liberalism over moderate perfectionism. Regarding the first objection, our previous discussion has shown that adopting and prioritizing publicly justifiable reasons over reasons associated with specific reasonably comprehensive doctrines pushes moderate perfectionism toward state neutrality, which is undesirable even for moderate perfectionists like Chan and Mang, who still see value in promoting Confucian doctrines and ideals. Thus, although Mang's wide view of moderate perfectionism takes advantage of publicly justifiable reasons to hopefully move moderate perfectionism away from the risk of becoming too comprehensive, it cannot break from perfectionist reasons that are not publicly justified. Consequently, the second objection ceases to be an objection and in fact captures what logically follows from Mang's experiment with the wide view of moderate perfectionism and my attempt to modify the *proviso*. Because political liberalism does not aim to fulfill the intelligibility condition, it is not burdened with the task of justifying perfectionist reasons independent of specific reasonable comprehensive doctrines.[35] Moderate perfectionism, on the other hand, only pushes itself further away from perfectionism by focusing on publicly justifiable reasons and avoiding the intelligibility condition. This contrast precisely highlights the superiority of political liberalism over moderate perfectionism.

---

[35] One might argue that political liberalism also needs to fulfill the intelligibility condition so that it is recognizably liberal. This is true, and part of the condition is fulfilled by the liberal accommodation condition. Since the discussion is within the realm of liberal political theory, the liberal intelligibility is taken as given.

From a Confucian perspective, one might object that it would appear that Confucianism is further banished from the public sphere since the moderately perfectionist values allowed into public political discussion need to be freestanding as well. This is a reasonable concern. Following the non-comprehensive spirit shared by political liberalism and moderate perfectionism, the modified *proviso* is designed to keep comprehensively perfectionist, and in this case Confucian, values out of public political discussion. A key reason why the wide view of moderate perfectionism ultimately gets too close to neutrality has to do with Mang's strategy to abandon the intelligibility condition that makes Confucian political theories recognizably Confucian. If meeting the liberal accommodation condition makes it impossible for a political theory to maintain its Confucian characteristics, then the question becomes: How should liberal neutrality be understood in the context of Confucian political theory? As Mang admits, since the state has strong reason to remain impartial in light of civility and mutual respect, "we should not expect too much from Confucianism for the improvement of liberal societies."[36] Take filial piety as an example. Instead of serving as the justification and the end for laws that coerce citizens to take care of their aging parents, the little that we *can* expect from Confucianism lies in the possibility for Confucianism to "offer insight into how we can better understand familial relationship and at the same time, citizens can consider the potential contributions of Confucianism to public policy making, such as public policies that concern family matters."[37] So, the above objection is misconstrued. In the case of the wide view of moderately perfectionism, appealing to Confucian values is allowed only if citizens' positions are already justified with freestanding reasons. In other words, the contribution that Confucianism can directly make to public political discussion is supplemental at best. Furthermore, it is difficult for Confucianism to take credit for any meaningful contributions that it may make anyway, because freestanding reasons almost always take the credit for the contributions because they publicly justify citizens' positions. The modified *proviso* does not add substantially more barriers to Confucianism in increasingly pluralistic societies, and it does not mean that Confucianism cannot make any meaningful contribution in the public sphere. As Mang points out, Confucianism may offer insight into how we can better understand important social, cultural, and political issues. It is up to the citizens to justify their inspirations with public reason and/or freestanding perfectionist reasons. It is true that Confucianism cannot play as significant a role as it could in a comprehensively perfectionist state, but the same loss is shared by all reasonable comprehensive doctrines in the face of reasonable pluralism, through which we maintain the liberal spirit. In the next three chapters, I will apply this pluralistic point of view to three key areas of concern: legitimacy, constitutionalism, and global justice.

---

[36] Franz Mang, "Confucianism, Perfectionism, and Liberal Society," *Dao: A Journal of Comparative Philosophy* 17 (2018): 47.

[37] Ibid.

Chapter 4
Confucian Meritocracy, Political Legitimacy, and Constitutional Democracy

Abstract The chapter will argue that neither what may be called 'multiple legitimacies' nor what Leigh Jenco refers to as the hybrid view of legitimacy provides substantial guidance in reconceiving legitimacy in the increasingly pluralistic region of East Asia. Instead, a more helpful view of political legitimacy can be drawn from John Rawls's liberal principle of legitimacy. I will demonstrate that Rawls's classic formulation can be deprived of its liberal connotation by taking constitutional essentials as the source of legitimation for political authority. On the basis of this principle of pluralistic legitimacy, it will become clear that a pluralistic understanding of political legitimacy does not rule out Confucian meritocracy, but it does make a strong case for an antiperfectionist state, even if it might be nondemocratic.

Keywords Meritocracy • Legitimacy • Constitutionalism • Confucian hierarchy • Public reason • Pluralism

4.1 Introduction

The increasing diversity in East Asian societies has led to a new wave of political theories that attempt to situate Confucianism in a liberal and democratic background so that both the historical and cultural influence of Confucianism and the accommodating capacity of liberal democracy can be maintained.[1] Despite their

[1] Sungmoon Kim, "Public Reason Confucianism: A Construction," *American Political Science Review* 109, No. 1 (Feb., 2015): 187–200. On the basis of public reason Confucianism, Kim recently advances a pragmatic interpretation of the relationship between Confucianism and democracy that aims to strike the right balance between the two. See Sungmoon Kim, "Pragmatic

Z. Li, *Pluralism, Confucianism, and Artificial Intelligence*, Philosophy and Politics - Critical Explorations 35, https://doi.org/10.1007/978-3-032-25605-8_4

differences, these theories share a similar aversion toward Confucian political meritocracy, by which I mean a political system that publicly endorses Confucianism and selects political leaders based on their merits in accordance with Confucianism. Interestingly and somewhat counterintuitively, some theories of Confucian political meritocracy *do* include democratic elements. For instance, both Daniel Bell and Jiang Qing include a democratic house in their respective systems of legislature that are supposed to contribute to the legitimacy of a meritocratic Confucian state.[2] However, it would be missing the big picture if Bell's and Jiang's approaches are understood as attempts to democratize Confucian political meritocracy. Quite the opposite. Both Bell and Jiang have very negative views on liberal and especially democratic ideals and institutions.[3] Their disappointment and even disdain toward democracy pave the road for their proposals for Confucian political meritocracy in replacement of liberal democracy.

This seeming contradiction between the willingness to adopt democratic elements and the harsh criticisms against democracy prompts Sungmoon Kim to ask, "why should we bother with democracy if its disvalue is so obvious and practically unbearable?"[4] In my view, two other questions need to be answered before Kim's question can be fully addressed, which requires an exploration of the relationship between legitimacy, meritocracy, and democracy. First, in the backdrop of pluralism in East Asian societies, how should the concept of legitimacy be understood? Second, can a nondemocratic meritocracy be nonetheless legitimate? These are the guiding questions of this chapter. In the next section, I will go through what may be called "multiple legitimacies" and what Leigh Jenco refers to as the hybrid view of legitimacy. I will argue that both fail to provide substantial guidance in reconceiving legitimacy in pluralistic societies. Instead, I will propose a more helpful view of legitimacy by drawing from John Rawls's liberal principle of legitimacy. I will demonstrate that Rawls's classic formulation can be deprived of its liberal connotation by taking constitutional essentials as the source of legitimation for political authority, to which citizens can relate in a plurality of manners from within their comprehensive doctrine, or for partially or even fully prudential reasons. I will refer

Confucian Democracy: Rethinking the Value of Democracy in East Asia," *The Journal of Politics* 79, No. 1 (Jan., 2017): 237–249. See also Joseph Chan, *Confucian Perfectionism: A Political Philosophy for Modern Times* (Princeton: Princeton University Press, 2014). Franz Mang, "Confucianism, Perfectionism, and Liberal Society," *Dao* 17 (2018): 29–49.

[2] Qing Jiang, *A Confucian Constitutional Order: How China's Ancient Past Can Shape Its Political Future*, eds. Daniel Bell and Ruiping Fan, trans. Edmund Ryden (New Jersey: Princeton University Press, 2013). Daniel Bell, *The China Model: Political Meritocracy and the Limits of Democracy* (New Jersey: Princeton University Press, 2015).

[3] Take Jiang as an example. He argues that the major flaw of democracy is that the popular will is the only source of legitimacy. In addition, democracy also lacks morality and ideals. See Qing Jiang, *A Confucian Constitutional Order: How China's Ancient Past Can Shape Its Political Future*, eds. Daniel Bell and Ruiping Fan, trans. Edmund Ryden (New Jersey: Princeton University Press, 2013), 33–34.

[4] Sungmoon Kim, *Public Reason Confucianism: Democratic Perfectionism and Constitutionalism in East Asia* (Cambridge: Cambridge University Press, 2016), 9.

to this as the principle of pluralistic legitimacy. In the following section, I will address the second question by applying the principle of pluralistic legitimacy to nondemocratic meritocracy. I will argue that nondemocratic meritocracy, of which Confucian political meritocracy is an example, need not be illegitimate under all circumstances. However, the lack of practicality and conflict with contemporary pluralism make it a less likely candidate for East Asian societies. Finally, it will become clear that a pluralistic understanding of legitimacy does not rule out meritocracy, but it *does* make a strong case for an antiperfectionist state, even if it might be nondemocratic. Thus, Kim's concern in the original question quoted in the beginning might be misplaced. The problem with Bell's and Jiang's theories of Confucian political meritocracy is not so much that the inclusion of democratic elements leads to theoretical inconsistency, or that Confucian political meritocracy is necessarily illegitimate, but that the comprehensively perfectionist nature of their proposals make them unfit for contemporary East Asian societies.

4.2 From Multiple Legitimacies to Hybridity: Political Legitimacy in East Asia[5]

There is no denying that East Asia has always been an exceptionally diverse region with a plurality of cultural traditions and religions. However, because of the dominant and enduring influence of Confucianism, the region is sometimes (and wrongly) considered homogeneously Confucian. What is even more misleading is the belief that a Confucian cultural background necessarily leads to a Confucian state. As a matter of fact, few scholars believe that a comprehensively Confucian state is practical in East Asia. Instead, the most vibrant discussions in Confucian political theory in the past decade has been about the relationship between Confucianism and democracy, as well as the most reasonable arrangement to accommodate both Confucian ideals and democratic institutions. From the democratic side, a Confucian state has a legitimacy problem on two levels. First, a Confucian state needs to legitimatize its superiority over competing cultural traditions and religions to become publicly endorsed by the state and to influence legislation and policy making. Second, granting the superiority of Confucianism still leaves the legitimacy problem unsolved. Meritorious rule is central to Confucian political thought, but the essence of "merit" or "worth" is less clear in contemporary societies.[6] Selecting rulers based on such a vague and easily manipulated criterion risks misrepresenting

[5] I draw arguments from Zhuoyao Li, *Political Liberalism, Confucianism, and the Future of Democracy in East Asia* (Cham, Switzerland: Springer, 2020).

[6] Wide disagreement on what counts as "worth" or "merit" also existed throughout the Warring State period. Yuri Pines, "Between Merit and Pedigree: Evolution of the Concept of 'Elevating the Worthy' in Pre-imperial China," The East Asian Challenge for Democracy: Political Meritocracy in Comparative Perspective, eds. Daniel A. Bell and Chenyang Li (New York: Cambridge University Press, 2013), 161–202.

and even suppressing the will of the people. From the Confucian side, democracy represents at best one of the many criteria of legitimacy and at worst a highly problematic political system for East Asian societies.[7] Connecting both sides is the mutual criticism that the other side lacks sufficient or complete legitimacy. However, it is not clear if the two sides hold a similar concept of legitimacy, which is somewhat understandable given the complexity of the concept itself. Most would agree that the concept of legitimacy has both a descriptive and a normative perspective.[8] Contemporary theories of Confucian political meritocracy, Jiang's Confucian constitutionalism for instance, adopts a mixture of both perspectives in constructing the idea of legitimacy. The descriptive or empirical perspective is necessary given the long history and influence of Confucianism in East Asia and China in particular. The normative perspective, on the other hand, is present for two reasons. First, even a Confucian state needs to justify its use of coercive power, which calls for a normative understanding of political legitimacy. Second, the inclusion of democratic elements also strengthens the normative perspective of political legitimacy, that is, political authority at least partially relies on the endorsement of the popular will. As mentioned in the introduction, the inclusion of democratic elements in an otherwise Confucian and meritocratic theory of politics raises some serious questions. It is not unreasonable to assume more comprehensive Confucian political theories that do away with any reference to democratic ideals and institutions altogether. In this case, a purely descriptive understanding of legitimacy might be adopted. For example, a comprehensively Confucian meritocracy can be viewed as fully legitimate simply because the majority of citizens genuinely subscribe to Confucianism. In other words, citizens have faith in the leadership deemed worthy according to Confucian doctrines. Alternatively, citizens might also endorse such a political arrangement simply because the state has been an excellent provider and caretaker of their economic well-being.

The complexity and diversity within the concept of legitimacy leads to exploration of new ways to conceive legitimate political arrangement, especially in East Asia where a plurality of cultural traditions and religions coexist. In this section, I will first outline two such attempts in the discussion of Confucian political theory and then argue that both Jiang Qing's multiple legitimacies and Leigh Jenco's hybrid legitimacy fail to capture what is at stake with political legitimacy in East

[7] For criticisms of (liberal) democracy, see Qing Jiang, *A Confucian Constitutional Order: How China's Ancient Past Can Shape Its Political Future*, eds. Daniel Bell and Ruiping Fan, trans. Edmund Ryden (New Jersey: Princeton University Press, 2013), 32–37. Also see Tongdong Bai, "A Confucian Improvement to Democracy," *New Perspectives Quarterly* 29, No. 1 (Winter 2012): 12–14.

[8] According to Max Weber, "the basis of every system of authority, and correspondingly of every kind of willingness to obey, is a belief, a belief by virtue of which person exercising authority are lent prestige." Weber is thus considered one of the advocates of purely descriptive account of legitimacy. Max Weber, T*he Theory of Social and Economic Organization*, ed. Talcott Parsons (New York: Free Press, 1964), 382. As we will see soon, John Rawls proposes an influential normative account of legitimacy that he calls the liberal principle of legitimacy. John Rawls, *Political Liberalism*, Expanded Edition (New York: Columbia University Press, 2005), 137.

Asia. While Jiang's approach fails because its focus is too narrow to be practical, Jenco's approach fails because its scope is too broad to be meaningful.

Jiang Qing is arguably one of the most controversial contemporary Confucian political theorists. The controversy surrounding him and his theory is manifold, but the most obvious theoretical controversy has to do with his proposal of a tricameral parliamentary political system for China on the basis of his Confucian constitutionalism. To preface his proposal, Jiang says that the way ahead for China's political development is "the Way of the Humane Authority and not democracy," and that this is "the *only* way in which Chinese culture can respond to the challenge of Western culture."[9] Jiang draws two crucial distinctions in this statement. There is the distinction between "the Way" and democracy, and there is the distinction between Chinese and Western cultures. Because of the "inherent pattern of Chinese history," Jiang claims, democracy cannot be the answer to the future of China.[10] Instead, drawing from the *Gongyang Commentary* to the *Spring and Autumn Annals*, Jiang proposes a threefold view of political legitimacy that points to what he refers to as "the Way of the Humane Authority" that involves the heaven, the earth, and the human:

> The legitimacy of 'heaven' refers to transcendent, sacred legitimacy. In Chinese culture 'heaven' has both the character of a ruling will, personal yet hidden, and a transcendent, sacred sense of natural morality. The legitimacy of 'earth' refers to the legitimacy that comes from history and culture because cultures are formed through history in particular places. The legitimacy of the 'human' refers to the legitimacy of the will of the people because conformity to the will of the people directly determines whether or not people will obey political authorities.[11]

This threefold view of legitimacy serves to address the problems with democracy by ending the exclusivity of the popular view, putting morality back into politics, and setting up high ideals to inspire political perfection.[12] To implement the Way of the

---

[9] Qing Jiang, "The Way of the Humane Authority: The Theoretical Basis for Confucian Constitutionalism and A Tricameral Parliament," *A Confucian Constitutional Order: How China's Ancient Past Can Shape Its Political Future*, eds. Daniel Bell and Ruiping Fan, trans. Edmund Ryden (New Jersey: Princeton University Press, 2013), 27. Emphasis mine. Jiang's dismissive attitude toward democracy is based on not only the uniqueness of the Chinese culture but also the inherent deficiencies of democracy as a political system. As for the latter, he lists three most obvious problems. First, the sole reliance of political legitimacy on the popular will leads to "extreme secularization, contractualism, utilitarianism, selfishness, commercialism, capitalization, vulgarization, hedonism, mediocritization, this worldliness, lack of ecology, lack of history, and lack of morality." Second, democracy lacks morality, according to Jiang, because the authority and legitimacy of the government are determined by a formal will "with no respect for the quality of the opinions," which in Jiang's view is "a matter of head counting" that gives rise to "imperialism, fascism, and hegemonism." Finally, there are no ideals in the running of a democracy because of the stress on the will of the people as the sole source of legitimacy. Thus, it is clear that the central flaw of democracy in Jiang's view has to do with its exclusive reliance on the popular will as the justification of political legitimacy. Ibid., 33–34.

[10] Ibid., 27.

[11] Ibid., 28.

[12] Although the three forms of legitimacy are supposed to be mutually restraining, the sacred legitimacy of heaven has a higher status, because the cultural and popular forms of legitimacy are also

Humane Authority, Jiang proposes a parliamentary system consisting of three houses that each represents one of the three forms of legitimacy:

> The three are the House of Ru (*Tongruyuan*), which represents sacred legitimacy, the House of the People (*Shuminyuan*), which represents popular legitimacy, and the House of the Nation (*Guotiyuan*), which represents cultural legitimacy. The Scholars (*Ru*) are chosen by recommendation and nomination. The People are chosen by universal suffrage and by election from functional constituencies. The members of the Nation are selected by hereditary criteria and by assignment.[13]

The House of *Ru* consists of Confucian scholars, and the House of the People are chosen according to the norms and processes of Western democratic parliaments. Perhaps the most controversial component is the House of the Nation, whose leader is to be "a direct descendant of Confucius."[14] The three Houses are supposed to be mutually restraining when it comes to legislation and policy making. For instance, if a bill passes the House of *Ru* and the House of the Nation, which means that it is good for the Way of heaven and culture, but fails to pass the House of the People, it will become a weak bill. But if a bill is opposed by both the House of the People and the House of the Nation, then it will not be passed into law. However, Jiang insists that the House of *Ru* "enjoys a permanent power of veto."[15] The implication is that even if a bill can pass the other two Houses, a veto from the House of *Ru* will put an end to the process. Jiang explicitly gives the example of a bill that permits homosexual marriages: "A bill, such as one permitting homosexuals to found a family, that passes the House of the People but is against the Way of heaven will be vetoed by the House of *Ru*."[16] In Jiang's view, this tricameral system "enables each form of legitimacy to cooperate with the others and to restrain them when necessary. Each also wins the recognition of the others and does not interfere in their legitimate proceedings," which offers definite advantage over Western democracies.[17] Once the legitimacy problem is addressed, Jiang is ready to propose his Confucian constitutional structure, which consists of the tricameral parliament, the Academy to supervise the state, and symbolic monarch republicanism, which is controversial on its own.[18]

---

heaven's embodiment in politics. Qing Jiang, "The Supervisory System of Confucian Constitutionalism: Reflections on the Supervision of the State by the Academy," *A Confucian Constitutional Order: How China's Ancient Past Can Shape Its Political Future*, eds. Daniel Bell and Ruiping Fan, trans. Edmund Ryden (New Jersey: Princeton University Press, 2013), 50.

[13] Qing Jiang, "The Way of the Humane Authority: The Theoretical Basis for Confucian Constitutionalism and A Tricameral Parliament," *A Confucian Constitutional Order: How China's Ancient Past Can Shape Its Political Future*, eds. Daniel Bell and Ruiping Fan, trans. Edmund Ryden (New Jersey: Princeton University Press, 2013), 41.

[14] Ibid.

[15] Ibid.

[16] Ibid.

[17] Ibid., 42.

[18] Qing Jiang, "The Supervisory System of Confucian Constitutionalism: Reflections on the Supervision of the State by the Academy," *A Confucian Constitutional Order: How China's*

Jiang's theory of multiple legitimacies is as innovative as it is problematic.[19] The main innovation is the attempt to combine Confucian meritocracy with democratic values. According to Daniel A. Bell, it is "tempting to conceive of the possibility of reconciling the Confucian emphasis on rule by wise and virtuous elites with the democratic values of popular participation, accountability, and transparency."[20] The reason for this temptation has to do with the Confucian doctrine of ruling by merits, which can be demonstrated from both the perspective of the ruler and that of the ruled. From the ruler's perspective, cultivating virtues will have a ripple-like effect that leads to moral transformation of the entire community. The ruler is in a unique position to set the example of virtue. Confucius offers a comparison between the virtuous ruler and the North Star when he says, "One who rules through the power of Virtue is analogous to the Pole Star: it simply remains in its place and receives the homage of the myriad lesser stars."[21]

> From the perspective of the people who follow the example of the ruler, the legitimacy of the state and the ruler also relies on his virtue and merits. Consider, for instance, the following exchange between Zigong and Confucius on the issue of government:The Master said, "Simply make sure there is sufficient food, sufficient armaments, and that you have the confidence of the common people."
> Zigong said, "If sacrificing one of these three things became unavoidable, which would you sacrifice first?"
> The Master replied, "I would sacrifice the armaments."
> Zigong said, "If sacrificing one of the two remaining things became unavoidable, which would you sacrifice next?"
> The Master replied, "I would sacrifice the food. Death has always been with us, but a state cannot stand once it has lost the confidence of the people."[22]

Ancient Past Can Shape Its Political Future, eds. Daniel Bell and Ruiping Fan, trans. Edmund Ryden (New Jersey: Princeton University Press, 2013), 55.

[19] Jiang's approach also inspired many contemporary Confucian political theorists to follow his lead. For instance, Bai Tongdong proposes a bicameral legislature with a democratically elected house and a meritocratic house composed of deputies selected through exams and performance at lower levels of government. Joseph Chan also advocates, in addition to a democratic house, a meritocratic house composed of retired civil servants with a proven record of public experience. Fan Ruiping, on the other hand, endorses a reconstructionist Confucian meritocracy by drawing from a substantive Confucian view of human well-being that ought to be written into the Chinese constitution in order to direct legislation and governance. See Tongdong Bai, "A Confucian Version of Hybrid Regime: How Does It Work, and Why Is It Superior?" *The East Asian Challenge for Democracy: Political Meritocracy in Comparative Perspective*, eds. Daniel A. Bell and Chenyang Li (New York: Cambridge University Press, 2013). Joseph Chan, "Political Meritocracy and Meritocratic Rule: A Confucian Perspective," *The East Asian Challenge for Democracy: Political Meritocracy in Comparative Perspective*, eds. Daniel A. Bell and Chenyang Li (New York: Cambridge University Press, 2013). Ruiping Fan, "Confucian Meritocracy for Contemporary China," *The East Asian Challenge for Democracy: Political Meritocracy in Comparative Perspective*, eds. Daniel A. Bell and Chenyang Li (New York: Cambridge University Press, 2013).

[20] Daniel Bell, *Beyond Liberal Democracy: Political Thinking for an East Asian Context* (Princeton: Princeton University Press, 2006), 152.

[21] Confucius, *Analects with Selections from Traditional Commentaries*, trans. Edward Slingerland (Indianapolis: Hackett Publishing, 2003), 8 (2.1).

[22] Ibid., 128 (12.7).

It is clear from the conversation that virtue is prioritized above all else in the evaluation of the ruler. If the ruler is virtuous, then other problems will be solved in due course, and the people ought to sincerely trust and endorse the ruler. In Bell's opinion, this meritocratic sentiment, juxtaposed with the respect for scholar-official in Confucian history, provides substantial ground for rethinking the exclusivity of democracy, especially in East Asia. A modern person in East Asia influenced by both Confucianism and democracy will likely to be confronted with the dilemma that "while Western-style democratic institutions do not fully accommodate concerns for the 'rule of the wise,' the 'Parliament of Scholar-Officials' idea goes too far in the elitist direction by failing to incorporate any form of political decision making by the people."[23] The solution, according to Bell, is a bicameral legislature "with a democratically elected lower house and a 'Confucian' upper house composed of representatives selected on the basis of competitive examinations."[24] Specifically, Bell refers to the upper house as the House of Virtue and Talent (*Xianshiyuan*) so as to reflect the meritocratic nature of the ruling elites.[25] Bell's proposal obviously resonates with Jiang's extreme Confucian reform in that both approaches adopt multiple legitimacies to make a stronger case for Confucian political meritocracy.

Recently, however, Bell revises his earlier stance. Criticizing Jiang's proposal as unrealistic, especially in the likely scenario that the popular support for political leaders chosen on the basis of one person, one vote clashes with the meritocratic endorsement of leaders chosen by Confucian standards, Bell says:

> If we want something better than one person, one vote—such as a political institution that secures the interests of future generations, with the power to complement, and sometimes override, the decisions of politicians elected by one person, one vote—it cannot be done in the form of proposals for bicameral or tricameral legislatures, no matter what the context.[26]

Ironically, the problem with Jiang's Confucian constitutionalism from Bell's perspective is that it is too democratic, because there is a slippery slope "toward a powerful House of the People could not be stopped, and the House of Exemplary Persons (as well as the House of the Nation) would almost certainly be marginalized, if not made completely irrelevant."[27] Bell's critique of Jiang's Confucian constitutionalism points to the deeper problem with multiple legitimacies: multiple legitimacies will clash and lose balance if the overarching project clearly favors some forms of legitimacies over others.[28] Classical Confucianism offers some sup-

[23] Daniel Bell, *Beyond Liberal Democracy: Political Thinking for an East Asian Context* (Princeton: Princeton University Press, 2006), 165.

[24] Ibid., 165–166.

[25] Ibid., 167.

[26] Daniel Bell, *The China Model: Political Meritocracy and the Limits of Democracy* (Princeton: Princeton University Press, 2016), 167.

[27] Ibid.

[28] Bell's most recent proposal is "a vertical model with political meritocracy at the level of the central government and democracy at the local level." Bell's new position is partly inspired by the Chinese context, where direct village elections were introduced by the central government in 1988

port. While the House of People still requires one person, one vote, which is an active practice of the democratic will, the Heaven in classical Confucianism plays only a passive and mediating role between the ruler and the ruled. What eventually determines whether or not the Mandate will be maintained or removed has little to do with the people. Instead, it is fundamentally determined by the virtue of the ruler. As Mencius puts it, "If a ruler is benevolent, no one will fail to be benevolent. If a ruler is righteous, no one will fail to be righteous."[29] What classical Confucianism reveals is a disregard for the democratic will and a strong emphasis on the meritocratic nature of political rule. Multiple legitimacies for the narrow focus of promoting Confucian meritocracy lead to internal clash and problematic consequences.

Unlike Jiang, Leigh Jenco recently proposes the concept of hybridity as "a new lens to interpret legitimacy in East Asia."[30] According to Jenco,

> Hybridity is not simply a mixture or juxtaposition of different elements. Rather, the concept portrays social realities as always constituted (as opposed to, say, merely episodically enhanced) by multiple elements—regime types, allegiances, values, cultures, interests, motives—whose relative content and relationship change dynamically over time, both producing and being produced by the conditions in which they are found.[31]

This hybrid view of legitimacy is superior to multiple legitimacies in two significant ways. First, it is not necessarily bound by a narrow focus to promote Confucianism, which avoids the drawback of multiple legitimacies. Second, it adopts a dynamic view of elements influencing our understanding of legitimacy. Moreover, hybridity has its unique advantage in that it emphasizes three overlapping characteristics of human practice: dynamism, novelty, and instability.[32] In Jenco's view, hybridity, understood as a dynamic process rather than an end result, "offers a way of grasping the complex phenomena [of multiple and even competing legitimacies], one that is more nuanced than simple binaries such as East/West, democratic/nondemocratic, or traditional/modern may suggest."[33] This dynamic process of hybridization emphasizes "the way in which social constructs—whether cultures or states, institutions, or individuals—often cannot always be easily classified as one thing rather than another."[34] Acknowledging hybridity also means that unpredictable and novel

---

to maintain social order and combat corruption of leaders, and became mandatory in 1998, giving more than nine hundred million Chinese farmers the right to vote by 2008. Theoretically, by limiting one person, one vote to village and other local governments, Bell wishes to eradicate popular vote from the selection mechanism for central government officials so that meritocratic rule will not clash with democratic chambers.

[29] Mencius, *Mengzi with Selections from Traditional Commentaries*, trans. Bryan W. Van Norden (Indianapolis: Hackett Publishing, 2008), 105 (4B.5).

[30] Leigh Jenco, "Legitimacy as a Hybrid Phenomenon," East Asian Perspectives on Political Legitimacy, eds. Joseph Chan, Doh Chull Shin, and Melissa Williams (New York: Cambridge University Press, 2016), 247.

[31] Ibid., 238–239.

[32] Ibid., 240.

[33] Ibid., 239.

[34] Ibid.

theories will come out of unorthodox and adaptive theorizing. Finally, hybridity "resists prefigured expectations of Asian or Western political behavior by refusing the stability of such distinctions in the first place."[35] The hybrid view of legitimacy is appealing for a variety of reasons, mainly because it depicts the socio-political condition of East Asian societies more accurately as changing, distinct, and pluralistic. However, unlike Jiang's multiple legitimacies, it has the opposite problem. The hybrid view of legitimacy does not offer anything more substantial than a broad picture. In contrast to the narrow focus of multiple legitimacies that ultimately leads to incoherence, the broad stroke of Jenco's hybridity does not generate enough substantive guidance for reconceiving the concept of legitimacy. To be fair, the concept of hybridity is deliberately loose and works as a "lens" in order to make room for the hybridized character of political phenomena in general. When it comes to the issue of legitimacy, it also makes room for nondemocratic and other forms of legitimacy, which are often overlooked by Confucian political theorists. But meaningful discourse on legitimacy requires a tighter but equally flexible focus on the concept itself in addition to capturing the socio-political construct on which the concept is based. In the next section, I will propose such an approach.

4.3 From the Liberal Principle of Legitimacy to the Principle of Pluralistic Legitimacy

Although the concept of hybridity is too abstract to provide substantive guidance regarding the issue of political legitimacy, it *does* highlight the fact that East Asian societies have become increasingly pluralistic. How to understand political legitimacy when a plurality of comprehensive doctrines are competing for socio-political attention becomes an urgent matter. It will be recalled that Jiang's multiple legitimacies represent a backward-looking approach to address pluralism and legitimacy at the same time. On the liberal and democratic side, John Rawls's political liberalism is also inspired by the need to accommodate pluralism in well-ordered liberal societies, which prompts Rawls to ask the fundamental question of political liberalism: "how is it possible for there to exist over time a *just and stable* society of free and equal citizens, who remain profoundly divided by reasonable religious, philosophical, and moral doctrines?"[36] What is of special interest to us is Rawls's attempt to define the legitimacy of political authority in a liberal democracy. According to Rawls,

> our exercise of political power is fully proper only when it is exercised in accordance with a constitution the essentials of which all citizens as free and equal may reasonably be

---

[35] Ibid., 243.

[36] John Rawls, *Political Liberalism*, Expanded Edition, (New York: Columbia University Press, 2005), 4.

> expected to endorse in the light of principles and ideals acceptable to their common human reason.[37]

This is known as the liberal principle of legitimacy. In this section, I will argue that Rawls's classic formulation can be stripped of its liberal connotation to provide meaningful guidance in reconceiving political legitimacy in East Asia.

Rawls's liberal principle of legitimacy touches upon two important aspects of political legitimacy that give it the potential to go beyond its liberal boundary. First of all, the source of legitimation lies with the constitutional essentials. Rawls has in mind the constitutional essentials as concerning "questions about what political rights and liberties, say, may reasonably be included in a written constitution, when assuming the constitution may be interpreted by a supreme court, or some similar body."[38] Frank Michelman further develops this point with what he calls "legitimation-worthy constitution," by which he means "one whose terms are such as to allow you or me to say, with clear conscience, that any law whose process of enactment, and whose content, pass muster under that constitution's requirements can ipso facto be deemed a law that all within range have good enough reason to accept, even if they disagree with it."[39] In other words, the kind of constitutions that can serve as the source of political legitimacy must be such that citizens can count on to serve as the ultimate law-giving entity. But Rawls does not specify the content of constitutional essentials, nor does he suggest that only liberal democracies can have meaningful constitutions.[40] In fact, as Alessandro Ferrara points out, the term "constitution" need not be interpreted in the modern sense of a written authoritative document "but could be understood in the more general sense of what Plato and Aristotle used to call 'politeia,' namely a structured complex of interrelated institutions and principles (whether positively codified or customary) regulating their functioning."[41] Understood in this way, constitutional essentials do not necessarily have to take on a liberal or a democratic connotation. Imagine an East Asian society where the vast majority of citizens genuinely subscribe to and actively practice Confucianism following a long history of Confucian influence, the kind of inherited socio-political structure complex is rich enough to provide a justifiable foundation for legislation, which is usually assumed in Confucian political theories that aim to actively endorse or at least accommodate political Confucianism.[42]

The second aspect of the liberal principle of legitimacy that also gives it the potential to go beyond its liberal context is Rawls's emphasis that the justification of

---

[37] Ibid., 137.

[38] Ibid., 442, Footnote 7.

[39] Frank I. Michelman, "Legitimation by Constitution (and the News from South Africa)," *Valparaiso University Law Review* 44, No. 4 (2010): 1017.

[40] As a matter of fact, neither the EU nor the UK have constitutions as Rawls understand the term.

[41] Alessandro Ferrara, "Authority, Legitimacy and Democracy: Narrowing the Gap Between Normativism and Realism," *Philosophy & Social Criticism* 41, No. 2 (2015): 121–131.

[42] For a recent discussion on how liberalism and political Confucianism can interactively support a hybrid constitution, see Part II of Sungmoon Kim, *Public Reason Confucianism: Democratic Perfectionism and Constitutionalism in East Asia* (Cambridge: Cambridge University Press, 2016).

constitutional essentials, which further justifies the legitimacy of political authority, is contingent upon reasonable citizens' endorsement based on their practice of common human reason.[43] It is unrealistic to expect that all citizens in a liberal democracy are reasonable in the Rawlsian sense.[44] It is equally unrealistic to expect reasonable citizens to be able to stay absolutely neutral regarding their comprehensive doctrines when participating in public reason.[45] In the world we actually reside, societies consist of people who endorse a wide variety of comprehensive doctrines, such as Catholicism, Islam, and Confucianism. Some elements of the constitutional essentials, even if the latter are legitimation-worthy, could become problematic at least for some of citizens.[46] But this does not mean that there is simply no way that citizens can still endorse the constitutional essentials. Sungmoon Kim recently proposes what he calls a pragmatic theory of Confucian democracy by combining the Schumpeterian and instrumental conception of democracy with the Deweyan and intrinsic conception of democracy. According to Kim, being pragmatic about Confucian democracy means that the instrumental value of democracy should be emphasized in the initial and transition stage of democratization. The Schumpeterian model looms large "because the instrumental value is the key motivating force of regime transition on which this model of democracy is undergirded."[47] This pragmatic turn is necessary because people are more likely to be motivated by the instrumental than the intrinsic value of democracy. According to Kim, the purpose of pragmatic Confucian democracy when it comes to realize the instrumental value of

[43] According to Rawls, persons are reasonable when (1) among equals, they are "ready to propose principles and standards as fair terms of cooperation and to abide by them willingly, given the assurance that others will likewise do so," and that (2) they are willing to "recognize the burdens of judgment and to accept their consequences for the use of public reason in directing the legitimate exercise of political power in a constitutional regime." John Rawls, *Political Liberalism*, Expanded Edition (New York: Columbia University Press, 2005), 49, 54.

[44] The meaning and implication of reasonableness is the subject of considerable debate in contemporary literature. I do not intend to go into details here. For a more recent exchange see Steven Wall, "Perfectionism, Reasonableness, and Respect," *Political Theory* 42, No. 4 (2014): 468–489. Martha Nussbaum, "Perfectionist Liberalism and Political Liberalism," *Philosophy & Public Affairs* 39, No. 1 (Winter, 2011): 3–45. See also Margaret Moore, "On Reasonableness," *Journal of Applied Philosophy* 13, No. 2 (1996): 167–178. Simon Caney, "Liberal Legitimacy, Reasonable Disagreement and Justice," *Critical Review of International Social and Political Philosophy* 1, No. 3 (1998): 19–36. David Estlund, "The Insularity of the Reasonable: Why Political Liberalism Must Admit the Truth," *Ethics* 108, No. 2 (January, 1998): 252–275.

[45] Although Rawls's ideal theory is well taken.

[46] Alessandro Ferrara, *The Democratic Horizon: Hyperpluralism and the Renewal of Political Liberalism* (Cambridge: Cambridge University Press, 2014), 90. I think another way to put this challenge is in terms of Rawls's idealization of a majority of reasonable people in liberal democratic society. As it shall become evident soon, Ferrara's proposal is a direct response to the more realistic scenario that a sizable population of a pluralistic, liberal, and democratic society may not be able to meet the requirement of being reasonable proposed by Rawls. Bai Tongdong makes a similar point when constructing what he calls "Confu-China". See Sect. 3.5 of Chap. 3 in Tongdong Bai, *The New Mission of an Old State: The Contemporary and Comparative Relevance of Classical Confucian Political Philosophy* (Beijing: Peking University Press, 2009).

[47] Kim, 241.

democracy is "not so much to faithfully serve what classical Confucianism requires ethically by means of state perfectionism as to theorize a principled way in which democracy both as a political system and as a way of life can acquire its instrumental and intrinsic values in a way intelligible to citizens of East Asia."[48] Although Kim's theory is divided into two stages to reflect the difference between the instrumental and intrinsic values of democracy, it is difficult, if not impossible, to realistically tell when the first stage ends and the second stage begins. So, it is reasonable to assume that there are different types of citizens endorsing democracy and the constitutional essentials for different reasons. For instance, there are citizens who embrace all the constitutional essentials in the light of principles rooted in Confucianism.[49] There are citizens who embrace some of the constitutional essentials in the light of principles rooted in Confucianism and other constitutional essentials out of instrumental reasons. There are also citizens who embrace all of the constitutional essentials out of purely instrumental reasons. The important thing to note is that the endorsement of the constitutional essentials, which in turn justifies the legitimacy of political authority, can be based upon both comprehensive and prudential reasons without requiring citizens to also subscribe to liberalism. Because of the pluralistic understanding of how citizens can relate to the constitutional essentials that ultimately justifies political legitimacy, let us refer to this non-liberal interpretation of Rawls's principle as the principle of pluralistic legitimacy (hereafter, PPL).

As a matter of fact, PPL is capable of capturing dynamism, novelty, and instability of human political practice suggested by the concept of hybridity. By virtue of reconceiving the constitutional essentials not as written and often static authoritative documents, PPL regards them as the source of legitimacy without losing sight of the possibility for socio-political shifts. As we shall see in the next section PPL is also highly novel in the sense that it offers an adaptive perspective of political legitimacy and avoids the traditional binaries, such as East/West, democratic/nondemocratic, or traditional/modern]. Finally, the central motivation behind PPL is precisely the fact that our socio-political reality is highly unstable, to the degree that purely liberal democratic ideas need to be reconsidered and adjusted when applying in East Asian societies. PPL thus follows the general spirit of hybridity while being specific enough to offer some novel possibilities. Nevertheless, it will be recalled that the drawback of hybridity is that it does not provide us with substantive guidance when it comes to political legitimacy in pluralistic societies. PPL, on the other hand, is specific enough to generate substantive implications, to which we now turn.

In contemporary discourse on legitimacy, democratic ideals and institutions are often the precondition of discussion. One implication of PPL is that this precondition is unnecessarily restrictive. Nondemocratic meritocracy, such as the Confucian

---

[48] Sungmoon Kim, "Pragmatic Confucian Democracy: Rethinking the Value of Democracy in East Asia," *The Journal of Politics* 79, No. 1 (January, 2017): 246.

[49] I borrow this point from Alessandro Ferrara. See Chap. 4 of *The Democratic Horizon: Hyperpluralism and the Renewal of Political Liberalism* (Cambridge: Cambridge University Press, 2014).

meritocratic state imagined earlier, need not be illegitimate. If the majority of citizens genuinely subscribe to and actively practice Confucianism, then it is reasonable to assume that the constitutional essentials understood as a structured complex of interrelated institutions and principles regulating the functioning of the state are also inspired and even dictated by Confucian ideals and doctrines. Instead of one person one vote, the leader of the state can be selected through a combination of local election, national examination, and meaningful recommendation based on Confucian understanding of merit or worth. From a liberal and democratic perspective, such a Confucian meritocratic state would not be legitimate, primarily because the authority of the state is not democratic. However, according to PPL, this Confucian meritocratic state can be nondemocratic but not illegitimate. If the vast majority of citizens can endorse the constitutional essentials from within Confucianism, and the rest of the citizens can offer their endorsement based on partially Confucian and partially prudential reasons, or based on fully prudential reasons, then this nondemocratic state can be considered legitimate. By thinking of Rawls's liberal principle of legitimacy not as the definitive understanding of political legitimacy but as a liberal example of a broader concept, we are able to avoid adopting a liberal democratic lens before examining the issue of legitimacy.

Two objections naturally arise at this point. First, one might argue that the principle of legitimacy without liberal and democratic restraints risks legitimizing state actions that take advantage of citizens' endorsement. What if citizens have prudential reasons (economic incentives for example) to condone state actions that obviously infringe upon their human rights, will such a state still be legitimate? The short answer is no, but it is worth dissecting the reasons. On the one hand, it is possible that the rights-infringing state actions are not constitutional, then the state clearly loses it political legitimacy. On the other hand, it is also possible that the rights-infringing state actions are constitutional, meaning that such actions can find justification in the constitution, which in turn is supported by comprehensive doctrines, such as Confucianism. In this case, the state loses its legitimacy because it does not meet the minimum standard of decency for nondemocracy, by which I primarily mean the rule of law and protection of basic human rights. It is not my intention to go into details regarding these two requirements. Needless to say, it is possible to make the argument that a Confucian state can and should maintain the rule of law and the protection of basic human rights as either a direct measure or a fallback strategy.[50] Finally, as Ferrara rightly suggests, the legitimacy of authority

[50] Several scholars make this point. Bai Tongdong argues that his vision for "Confu-China" as a Confucian form of ideal government involves endorsing both the rule of law and human rights. Joseph Chan, on the other hand, proposes to endorse human rights only as a backup apparatus. See Chaps. 2, 4 and 5 in Tongdong Bai, *The New Mission of an Old State: The Contemporary and Comparative Relevance of Classical Confucian Political Philosophy* (Beijing: Peking University Press, 2009). See also Chap. 5 in Joseph Chan, *Confucian Perfectionism: A Political Philosophy for Modern Times* (Princeton: Princeton University Press, 2014).

"need not be an all-or-none concept, but may admit of degrees on a continuum."[51] Depending on how citizens relate to the constitutional essentials, the legitimacy of the state's political authority can vary.

The second objection challenges my claim that PPL maintains a sense of dynamism as the concept of hybridity suggests. The objection takes issue with my example of the Confucian meritocratic state in two ways. First, my example assumes a rather static understanding of the constitutional essentials in that Confucianism maintains its dominance and that some citizens are required to utilize their prudential reasons in order to endorse such political authority. Second, my example is simply unrealistic because of the diversity of comprehensive doctrines adopted by people in East Asia. Although Confucianism is arguably the most influential, there is no denying that citizens also turn to other comprehensive doctrines for their ways of life. However, this objection misses the mark by mixing the theoretical question of political legitimacy with the practical question of political reality. The Confucian meritocratic state in my example remains legitimate because it meets PPL, but its share of reality in East Asia *does* lead to the issue of practicality. In other words, given the increasing diversity in East Asia, will a theoretically legitimate Confucian meritocratic state make practical sense? If not, what kind of lesson can PPL teach us when it comes to East Asia's political future? By way of conclusion, I will respond to these two questions in the final section.

4.4 Between Democracy and Antiperfectionism[52]

Recently, Jonathan Quong proposes a matrix to map the relationship between liberalism and perfectionism by asking two questions:

1. Must liberal political philosophy be based in some particular ideal of what constitutes a valuable or worthwhile human life, or other metaphysical belief?
2. Is it permissible for a liberal state to promote or discourage some activities, ideals, or ways of life on grounds relating to their inherent or intrinsic value, or on the basis of other metaphysical claims?[53]

The first question determines the scope of liberalism. Those who answer "yes" to the first question adopt a comprehensive view of liberalism, whereas those who answer "no" adopt a political view of liberalism. The second question determines whether or not perfectionism is compatible with liberalism. A matrix of different positions will come out of answering these two questions. John Rawls's political liberalism, for instance, answers "no" to both questions. Although the two questions

[51] Alessandro Ferrara, "Authority, Legitimacy, and Democracy: Narrowing the Gap Between Normativism and Realism," *Philosophy & Social Criticism* 41, no. 2 (2015): 121–131.

[52] I draw arguments from Zhuoyao Li, "Political Confucianism and Multivariate Democracy in East Asia," *The Review of Politics* 81, No. 3 (Summer 2019): 459–483.

[53] Jonathan Quong, *Liberalism Without Perfection* (Oxford: Oxford University Press, 2011), 15.

are intended for liberalism and liberal societies, they still provide insight relevant to our discussion. Sungmoon Kim borrows this matrix to make the point that "only comprehensive Confucian perfectionism can be a plausible normative position," because "Confucianism, unlike (though arguably) liberalism, is *already* a self-contained ethical system and a comprehensive doctrine."[54] In other words, East Asians' decision "to remain Confucian is already a perfectionist decision," which means that "it is impossible to be perfectly neutral in regard to other competing values, hence the implausibility of antiperfectionism."[55] Confucian meritocracy, such as Jiang Qing's Confucian constitutionalism, is necessarily predicated on comprehensive Confucian perfectionism. However, Kim goes on to propose what he calls "public reason Confucianism" by juxtaposing a "partially comprehensive Confucianism" with John Rawls's political liberal understanding of public reason. The motivation behind this unorthodox move is that Kim sees in some East Asian societies, South Korea in particular, an interplay between Confucianism and liberalism, which is on clear display in the South Korea's liberal constitution. In Kim's opinion, although certain Confucian values, such as filial piety, were never declared by the South Korean court as constitutional values, they are publicly acknowledged and even promoted in the cases Kim examines, which grants them "quasi-constitutional" status."[56] Kim refers to this type of constitutionalism as "indirect constitutionalism," according to which certain cultural values attain public-constitutional significance even if they are not constitutional values in a strictly legal sense.[57] By distinguishing between fully and partially comprehensive Confucianism, and between direct and indirect constitutionalism, Kim is thus reserving a special place for Confucianism to interact with liberalism, at least in certain East Asian societies. As I argue elsewhere, Kim's strategy eventually backfires because it lets liberalism and indeed other non-Confucian comprehensive doctrines in through the backdoor.[58] The reason is simple, public reason Confucianism begs the question of "why Confucianism." In Kim's view, the central goal of public reason Confucian constitutionalism is "to produce a coherent public identity of Confucian and democratic citizens by weaving two perfectionist commitments—liberal and Confucian—into a single coherent constitutionalism."[59] In order to achieve this goal, cultural negotiations will take place between Confucian values and practice, and liberal democratic values and rights. But this sort of cultural negotiation cannot be reserved exclusively for Confucianism and liberalism, since there is an undeniable plurality of other comprehensive doctrines, *even if* Confucianism is still the most influential one.

[54] Sungmoon Kim, *Public Reason Confucianism: Democratic Perfectionism and Constitutionalism in East Asia* (Cambridge: Cambridge University Press, 2016), 39.

[55] Ibid., 40.

[56] Ibid., 123.

[57] Ibid., 124.

[58] See Zhuoyao Li, "Political Confucianism and Multivariate Democracy in East Asia," *The Review of Politics* 81, No. 3 (Summer 2019): 459–483.

[59] Ibid., 136.

If this critique of public reason Confucianism stands, then it seems that a theoretically legitimate Confucian meritocratic state as we described in the previous section makes little practical sense. In a recent survey by the Association of Religion Data Archive (ADRA), South Korean citizens who practice Confucianism amount to only 10.9%, whereas those who practice Buddhism and Christianity amount to 24.8% and 33.4%, respectively.[60] In addition, Doh Chull Shin's comprehensive empirical studies demonstrate that South Korea is by no means an exception. In none of the five historically Confucian countries (Japan, South Korea, Taiwan, China, and Vietnam) is the Confucian way of life the most popular cultural type. Instead, more people have embraced the egalitarian or individualist way of life, to the extent that East Asia as a whole is now even more individualistic than any of the four other non-Western cultural zones (South Asia, Latin America, Africa, and the Muslim zones), and only less so when comparing with the democratic West and ex-communist West.[61] Although these empirical studies by no means show that Confucianism has lost its socio-cultural significance, they are strong enough to demonstrate that Confucianism has become one of the many comprehensive doctrines adopted by East Asians. Although these empirical studies by no means show that Confucianism has lost its socio-cultural significance, they are strong enough to demonstrate that Confucianism has become one of the many comprehensive doctrines adopted by East Asians. Therefore, the second objection is correct in insisting that a Confucian meritocratic state, though legitimate, does not make practical sense in contemporary East Asia. In other words, what ultimately defeats Confucian meritocracy is not its lack of (liberal and/or democratic) legitimacy but its incompatibility with contemporary socio-cultural condition of East Asian societies.

So, what kind of lessons can PPL teach us? Let me mention two as possible directions for future research. First, although the concept of hybridity offers little specific guidance, it nonetheless advocates the virtue of open-mindedness, which goes both ways. On the one hand, one ought to be open-minded about the evolution of pluralism in East Asian societies and its political implications. On the other hand, one also ought to be open-minded about the possibility for a state to maintain its legitimacy without being a liberal democracy. This latter point leads to the second and more important lesson. Recent literature on Confucian political theory has been focusing on whether and how democracy and liberalism can be compatible with Confucianism. One neglected direction, which happens not to be covered by Quong's matrix, is the possibility for a nondemocracy to still maintain an

---

[60] Association of Religion Data Archive. http://www.thearda.com/internationalData/countries/Country_124_2.asp (accessed October 16th, 2017).

[61] Doh Chull Shin, *Confucianism and Democratization in East Asia* (New York: Oxford University Press, 2012), 104. Shin's research divides world cultures into seven categories: democratic West, ex-communist West, south Asia, Muslim zone, East Asia, Latin America, and Africa. When it comes to preference for individualism, which is opposite to what traditional Confucianism requires, East Asia has a 25.5% favoring rate, which is higher than that in South Asia (21.9%), Latin America (23.9%), Africa (10.4%), and Muslim zone (7.1%). Democratic West and ex-communist West, in contrast, have favoring rates of 46% and 39.9%, respectively. See Table 3.5. in Ibid., 97.

antiperfectionist position. Our previous analyses already established that it is possible for a nondemocracy to nonetheless be legitimate. So now the question becomes: can a state adopt an antiperfectionist position while still being a nondemocracy? Our previous example of nondemocracy is Confucian meritocracy. But it is also possible to imagine a type of meritocracy that does not subscribe to any particular comprehensive doctrine. For example, let's imagine that instead of one person one vote, two of the central criteria used by the ruling class to select leaders are how genuinely candidates are respectful to different comprehensive doctrines adopted by citizens and how knowledgeable and capable candidates are when it comes to domestic and international affairs. Moreover, the constitution essentials also dictate that a natural stance must be adopted when laws and policies are made. This is clearly not a democracy, but relevant political elements are so designed as to stay neutral toward competing comprehensive doctrines. It is also likely that there will be three types of citizens: citizens who can endorse the antiperfectionist stance of the constitutional essentials from within their own comprehensive doctrines, citizens who can only partially endorse the constitutional essentials from within their own comprehensive doctrines and must supplement this partial endorsement with prudential reasons, and citizens who think state neutrality is a mistake but nonetheless endorse the constitutional essentials for purely prudential reasons.[62] Applying PPL here will lead to the conclusion that this nondemocratic yet antiperfectionist state can be legitimate. If so, then it seems that we have another genuine contender in the race toward the most reasonable political structure for East Asian societies. The advantage of this antiperfectionist nondemocracy is twofold. First and foremost, it bypasses the problematic question of "why Confucianism" confronting theories that try to bridge liberal democracy with Confucianism. Since the state is antiperfectionist, it does not favor any one comprehensive doctrine over the other. The question of "why Confucianism" need not arise. Second, it at least partially resolves the debate between democracy and Confucianism. Instead of seeing the two as mutually exclusive, compatible, or hybridizable, there can be another option where a nondemocratic state does not publicly endorse nor banish Confucianism. There are obviously issues with this proposal. For instance, one might question the meaningfulness of such a model: what is still left if *both* democracy *and* Confucianism are taken away? It is not within the scope of this chapter to address this question. My goal is simply to offer a brief outline and to demonstrate that there is indeed a theoretical possibility, which provides future research with an alternative and potentially fruitful direction. To that end, I will go over a case study of South Korea in the next chapter to further demonstrate a hybrid understanding of constitutionalism in light of the pluralistic political theory developed so far.

[62] The first type of citizens might do so with what Rawls calls the conjecture approach. John Rawls, *Political Liberalism*, Expanded Edition (New York: Columbia University Press, 2005), 465.

Chapter 5
Between Liberalism and Confucianism: On Constitutionalism in South Korea

Abstract Examining South Korea's dualist constitutionalism, this chapter analyzes judicial rulings on family-head systems to reveal tensions between individual dignity and relational goods. It critiques both liberal subordination of tradition and public reason Confucian constitutionalism as overly perfectionist, favoring proviso-guided negotiation for hybrid legitimacy. Consistent with the book's pluralistic framework, it illustrates how translated Confucian reasons can sustain democratic stability without cultural erasure.

Keywords Korean constitutionalism • Family-head system • Dualism • Public reason Confucianism • Gender equality • Cultural heritage

5.1 Introduction

Although there is little doubt that contemporary South Korea is one of the most successful examples of liberal democracy in East Asia, it is often argued that the relationship between its recently established liberal democratic institutions and its longstanding Confucian legacy is far from clear.[1] Copying western liberal democracy risks bringing along Eurocentric biases that negatively impact local traditions, whereas infusing political Confucianism with liberal and democratic institutions might offset the advantages of liberal democracy in safeguarding social and legal

[1] See Chaihark Hahm, "Negotiating Confucian Civility through Constitutional Discourse," *The Politics of Affective Relations: East Asia and Beyond*, eds. Chaihark Hahm and Daniel A. Bell (Lanham: Lexington Books, 2004), 277–308. Sungmoon Kim, *Public Reason Confucianism: Democratic Perfectionism and Constitutionalism in East Asia* (New York: Cambridge University Press, 2016).

Z. Li, *Pluralism, Confucianism, and Artificial Intelligence*, Philosophy and Politics - Critical Explorations 35, https://doi.org/10.1007/978-3-032-25605-8_5

norms. The tension between liberal democracy and comprehensive doctrines is by no means unique to South Korea or East Asia. The debate between political liberalism, which holds a neutral understanding of the state in a liberal democracy, and liberal perfectionism, which argues for reasonable comprehensive doctrines, such as Confucianism and Catholicism, to play more active roles in the domain of the political, has already set up the theoretical framework to analyze the nature of the state.[2]

In the context of South Korea, how much consideration should South Korean liberal democracy give to its long-standing Confucian tradition? Should Confucian values and practices influence how liberalism is understood in South Korea? In this chapter, I will focus on the issue of constitutionalism because it provides a unique opportunity to examine the influence of both liberalism and Confucianism on the justification and regulation of the state. Constitution in a culturally rich liberal democracy such as South Korea almost always takes on a twofold meaning. On the one hand, as Alessandro Ferrara points out, the term "constitution" need not be interpreted in the modern sense of a written authoritative document but could be understood in the more general sense of what Plato and Aristotle used to call *politeia*, namely a structured complex of interrelated institutions and principles regulating their functioning.[3] On the other hand, the constitution can simply refer to the higher law that justifies political legitimacy and regulates state actions. Based on this dualist understanding of constitutionalism, I will show that there are essentially two constitutions in South Korea: a liberal Constitution that comes with the identity of being a liberal democracy, and a Confucian constitution that has historically served the Korean society. These two senses of constitution come into conflict when liberal values and reasons are at odds with Confucian ideals and practices. Specifically, I will analyze two constitutional cases in South Korea where the law of family ritual and the family-registry system, both manifesting key Confucian values, clash with liberal values central to contemporary South Korea's identity as a liberal democracy. Casting doubt on both the Constitutional Court's overtly liberal reasoning at the cost of dismissing Confucian values and practices and recent attempts to redefine South Korean liberal democracy in light of political Confucianism, I will argue that a more promising view of constitutionalism should maintain a mediating relationship between liberalism and Confucianism on neutral ground without losing sight of the democratic component of the constitution. In addition, citizens should actively engage in a process of constitutional education and democratic feedback to ensure the health of the liberal democracy that they themselves founded.

[2]See Jonathan Quong, *Liberalism Without Perfection* (Oxford: Oxford University Press, 2011). More recently, see Collis Tahzib, *A Perfectionist Theory of Justice* (Oxford: Oxford University Press, 2022).

[3]Alessandro Ferrara, "Authority, Legitimacy and Democracy: Narrowing the Gap Between Normativism and Realism, *Constellations* (2020): 10.

5.2 The Dualist Constitutionalism in South Korea

The current South Korean Constitution was promulgated in 1948 with amendments through 1987. This written Constitution has solidified the identity of contemporary South Korea as a liberal democracy by firmly protecting the fundamental rights of its citizens. According to Frank Michelman, a liberal democratic constitution needs to fulfill two functions simultaneously: to serve as a public platform of justification for political legitimacy and majoritarian laws, and to serve as a true warrant of popular sovereignty by regulating the state.[4] In other words, constitution in a liberal democracy always plays two simultaneous roles to justify the rights of the citizens and to regulate the state from infringing upon those rights. However, this twofold function of norm-justifying and norm-regulating is not unique to liberal democratic constitutions. As a matter of fact, written constitutions are a quite recent phenomenon. Neither Hobbes nor Locke had ever seen a proper constitution.[5] The British constitution, for instance, is not collected in a single written text but instead derived from principles in the English legal culture and practice.[6] In Chaihark Hahm's view, the political history of the Chosŏn dynasty helps demonstrate that constitutionalism in South Korea dates much further back than 1948.[7] Constitutional norms that justify cultural values and regulate political powers were already well established in traditional Korea, which not only shines new light on the nature of a Confucian polity but also expands the scope of constitutionalism. In this section, I will go through this often neglected side of constitutionalism in South Korea and argue that both the liberal Constitution and the Confucian constitution serve the two functions at the heart of constitutionalism.

Hahm is correct to insist that the term "constitutionalism" need not apply only to institutional arrangements having roots in the Enlightenment context, which means that our understanding of constitutionalism must be modified to include "political institutions, practices, and discourses that do not necessarily operate in terms of principles like the separation of powers, representative democracy, or even the rule of law."[8] This pluralistic insight opens up the possibility for a deep investigation of constitutionalism in traditional Korea. Beyond the conventional view that Confucian ideology allows people to urge the ruler to be more virtuous, Hahm argues that "in actual political debates relating to constitutional issues, scholars officials … cited

[4] Alessandro Ferrara and Frank Michelman, *Legitimation by Constitution: A Dialogue on Political Liberalism* (Oxford: Oxford University Press, 2021), 18–20.

[5] Ibid., 45.

[6] Larry Kramer, *The People Themselves: Popular Constitutionalism and Judicial Review* (New York: Oxford University Press, 2004), 12.

[7] Chaihark Hahm, "Conceptualizing Korean Constitutionalism: Foreign Transplant or Indigenous Tradition?" *Confucianism, Law, and Democracy in Contemporary Korea*, ed. Sungmoon Kim (London: Rowman & Littlefield International, 2015), 17–55.

[8] Ibid., 22–23.

provisions from various 'codes' complied by the government."[9] For its penal code, Chosŏn dynasty adopted the Chinese Ming dynasty's penal code (*Da Ming Lu*) as its own. As for its ritual code, Chosŏn did enact a separate code called *Kukcho Oryeŭi* (Five Rites and Ceremonies of Our Dynasty). Finally, there is *Kyŏngguk Taejŏn* (Great Canon for Governance of the State), the administrative code that applied mainly to the bureaucrats.[10] These three codes comprised of the Confucian conception of law. By defining constitutionalism "simply as the practice of discipline political power," Hahm suggests that the ritual code had the force of a constitutional norm, because "it was only ritual regulations that could be directly applied to the ruler himself."[11] For instance, in *Xunzi*, "ritual is described as a legit time innovation by the ancient mythical sage-kings to deal with the social fact of scarcity of material goods in relation to human desires."[12] The mere fact that ritual was required for formal legislation already indicates that the ritual norm did expand into the legal category. Moreover, *Kukcho Oryeŭi* "also prescribed ritual norms applicable to the more public aspects of the government," such as foreign relations with neighboring states and the conduct of military forces.[13] Specifically, Hahm argues that the concept of "the way of the former kings" and "ancestral precedents" honored by political Confucianism and Confucian scholar-officials in Chosŏn dynasty amount to the doctrine of binding precedents that are not unlike the principle of *stare decisis* in the Anglo-American tradition. Since Chosŏn dynasty obviously differed from the time of Yao and Shun, the state "adopted the Song Dynasty master Zhu Xi's commentaries on the classics (particularly the Four Books) as the authoritative and orthodox interpretation of the Confucian learning."[14] In the less ideal world where there were disagreements among people, the constitutional discourse of Chosŏn juggled among three sources of authority: "the dictates of ancient sage-kings, ancestral precedents, and Zhu Xi's orthodoxy," all of which served as key constitutional principles in Chosŏn dynasty.[15]

Because of the disciplining nature of the ritual code, Hahm goes so far as to argue that Confucian scholar-officials served as the "'disciplinarians' of the ruler" because "it was natural for them to consider themselves the custodians of political legitimacy."[16] This point leads us to the justifying nature of the constitution. In addition to regulating state behaviors, constitution also functions to justify both the legitimacy of the state and ordinary laws. If we follow Hahm's analyses above, it follows that the constitutional principles of "the way of the former kings" and

[9] Ibid., 28.

[10] Ibid., 29.

[11] Ibid., 30. The penal code, directed at the commoners, could not be directly applied to the ruler. The administrative code was mostly applied to bureaucrats.

[12] Ibid., 31.

[13] Ibid., 32.

[14] Ibid., 39.

[15] Ibid., 40.

[16] Ibid., 32.

"ancestral precedents" both serve as justification for the ruler and political arrangements. Moreover, the justificatory power of these two principles "stems from the core Confucian value of filial piety," which is universally applied to the ruler and commoners alike.[17] The regulating power of the constitutional principles thus also justify the norm of filial piety in familial and social contexts. Departures from the duty of filial piety not only delegitimizes the ruler and the government but also invites severe criticisms among commoners.

Therefore, Confucianism provided ample resources for constitutional practices in traditional Korea. Confucian values and institutions functioned to justify the legitimacy of the ruler as well as familial and social practices on the one hand, and to regulate and discipline the ruler and the government on the other. In addition to the South Korean Constitution grounded on the modern *demos* and liberalism, we now have a second constitution rooted in the historical *ethnos* and Confucianism. Call the former the liberal Constitution, and the latter the Confucian constitution. Since Confucianism is often regarded as incompatible with liberal democracy, it seems inevitable that certain Confucian values will conflict with liberal values. Now the question becomes: what happens when the Confucian constitution clashes with the liberal Constitution? In the next section, I will examine two cases in South Korea where the Constitutional Court had to walk a delicate path between these two senses of constitution.

5.3 Between Liberalism and Confucianism: Two Case Studies

Given the long history and contemporary saturation of Confucianism in South Korea, it is not at all surprising to see elements of Confucian values and institutions still reflected in contemporary Korean laws. In this section, I will focus on the importance of ritual and the concept of family at the center of the Confucian constitution and how they conflict with liberal values protected by the liberal Constitution. In two recent cases, the Constitutional Court offered liberal arguments to strike down laws associated with Confucian values and institutions. According to Chaihark Hahm and Sungmoon Kim, the Court's decisions unnecessarily favored liberalism over Confucianism, thus elevating the liberal Constitution above the Confucian constitution. Since both the liberal Constitution and the Confucian constitution maintain their justifying and regulating functions, favoring one over the other would require sufficient reasons. Neither Hahm nor Kim thinks the Court offered such reasons. Although I concur with their conclusion that the Court unnecessarily favors liberal values over Confucian values, I disagree with their suggested method of correction, which advocates the opposite strategy by prioritizing Confucianism over

[17] Ibid., 35.

liberalism. I will briefly go through the issue with Hahm's suggested strategy, and then focus on Kim's public reason Confucian constitutionalism in the next section.

In Hahm's view, a family ritual law case brought to the Constitutional Court demonstrated the Court's failure to take the Confucian constitution seriously. According to the "Law Concerning Family Rituals and Ceremonies," serving unreasonably large amounts of food and drinks at weddings and other family rituals are "prohibited and criminalized."[18] For example, meals and alcoholic beverages were forbidden during weddings, sixtieth birthdays, funerals, and other significant dates, and violators would be fined. The law then "allowed an exception for food and drinks that were 'reasonable in light of the true meaning of family ritual and ceremony.'"[19] However, such reasonable exceptions were to be defined by presidential decree, a lesser form of legislation.[20] A case against this law was brought to the Constitutional Court

> when a man who was planning to get married in a few months' time brought a constitutional petition claiming that he would be unjustly punished if he went ahead with his wedding plans according to which food and drinks were to be served to his guests. The petitioner claimed that this would be an infringement of his fundamental rights protected by the Constitution. In response, the Constitutional Court declared that the practice of serving food and drinks on such occasions as one's wedding should be allowed because this was an instance of an individual's 'general freedom of action.' The Court then announced that individuals enjoy such 'general freedom of action' under the Korean Constitution, more specifically under Article 10 which guarantees the right to pursue happiness. Since the law also prescribed penal sanctions for violators, this amounted to imposing punishment on conducts that were protected by the Constitution. Therefore, the outright ban on the practice was unconstitutional, according to the Court.[21]

What Hahm finds problematic with the ruling is that the Court paid only lip service to the significance of the Confucian constitution and barely even tried to justify its decision with anything other than liberal reasons. The action of serving food and drinks at the wedding (and other ritual events) was taken out of the context of sociocultural background and interpreted as a manifestation of one's individuality. The importance of affective relations was dwarfed by the inviolable right to pursue happiness. In a sense, this is exactly what the liberal Constitution appears to advocate. Article 9 states that "The State shall strive to sustain and develop the cultural heritage and to enhance national culture."[22] Not only is the Article ambivalent on exactly what "cultural heritage" and "national culture" are, it is one Article embedded in an otherwise substantively liberal constitutional framework. In other words, the Confucian constitution subordinates to the liberal Constitution *by design*. Therefore,

---

[18] Chaihark Hahm, "Negotiating Confucian Civility through Constitutional Discourse," *The Politics of Affective Relations: East Asia and Beyond*, eds. Chaihark Hahm and Daniel A. Bell (Lanham: Lexington Books, 2004), 289.

[19] Ibid.

[20] Ibid.

[21] Ibid., 289–290.

[22] Constitution of the Republic of Korea, accessed August 1, 2022 https://www.constituteproject.org/constitution/Republic_of_Korea_1987.pdf?lang=en.

it is not at all surprising that "the language of individual rights and freedom and constitutional procedure are becoming a standard element in discussions about civility in Korea."[23] Since people are becoming more familiar with the liberal constitutional terms, Hahm suggests that Confucianism "must be defended and justified on the grounds that are more readily understandable to contemporary Koreans and accord better with their sensibilities."[24] But this suggestion pushes Hahm's analyses into a dilemma. On the one hand, justifying and defending Confucian values and practices purely on Confucian ground is less acceptable to contemporary South Korean citizens. On the other hand, justifying and defending Confucian values and practices on liberal ground, such as the pursuit of happiness and the exercise of general freedom of actions, is missing the Confucian point of these values and practices. Which is why Hahm concludes by suggesting that perhaps contesting in a civil fashion what constitutes civility in contemporary Korean culture might be "the only means of ensuring civility in the process of negotiating different conceptions of civility."[25] Constitutional conflicts are here to stay.

Like Hahm, Sungmoon Kim tries to show the Court's failure to consider the Confucian constitution when he focuses on a case where the abolition of the family-head system was brought to the Constitutional Court. The "family-registry" (*hojŏk*) was traditionally controlled by the "family-head" (*hoju*), typically the father.

> Though the second revision of the Korean family law in 1989 substantively diminished the power of the family-head, by eliminating his rights to decide the residence of his family members and to summon a family meeting, no change was made with regard to the stipulation that family headship passes to the eldest son, irrespective of whether there are older sisters. Since the family is legally defined strictly by and for the patrilineal line, the former head's wife (i.e., the new head's mother) and even his mother (i.e., the new head's grandmother) are automatically excluded from the candidacy for the next headship. In cases where the former head's adult sons have already died, family headship as a legal title can succeed directly to the former head's eldest grandson, regardless of his age, bypassing all the senior women members in the family. Upon the father's death, younger sons who cannot succeed his headship automatically become members of their eldest brother's family until their marriage, upon which they can form new families and become their own family heads.[26]

On February 3, 2005, the Constitutional Court in Korea held that "Articles 778, 781(1), and 826(3) of the Civil Code were incompatible with the Constitution, ending a 50-year-long dispute surrounding the constitutionality of the family-head system."[27] The National Assembly subsequently enacted the individual

---

[23] Chaihark Hahm, "Negotiating Confucian Civility through Constitutional Discourse," *The Politics of Affective Relations: East Asia and Beyond*, eds. Chaihark Hahm and Daniel A. Bell (Lanham: Lexington Books, 2004), 300.

[24] Ibid., 300.

[25] Ibid., 304.

[26] Sungmoon Kim, *Public Reason Confucianism: Democratic Perfectionism and Constitutionalism in East Asia* (New York: Cambridge University Press, 2016), 114.

[27] Ibid., 112.

identification system in replacement of the family-registry system. Specifically, in a six-three vote, the Court

> found that the articles under review were unconstitutional because they critically contradict the constitutional principles of human dignity and gender equality stipulated in Article 36(1) of the Constitution but issued a decision of "constitutional nonconformity" in order to avoid a vacuum in the legal order by temporarily enforcing the provisions under review until the Family Law is amended with a new population registry system not predicated on the family-head system.[28]

Kim clearly recognizes the tension between liberalism and Confucianism in the Korean Constitution and how the Court handled the case. In Kim's view, the Korean Constitution is "ineluctably a moral document expressing its commitment to certain liberal values."[29] At the same time, as Article 9 stipulates, the Korean Constitution is also committed to "nonliberal, characteristically Confucian, goods and values, arguably—at least in part but in an important way—affiliated with the family-head system, and encourages the Korean state to promote them publicly."[30] For Kim, it is not so much the Court's decision itself as the reasoning and implications of the decision that are problematic. The Court's majority decision makes clear references to the historical and social background of the family-head system and acknowledges "traditions" and "cultural heritage" mentioned in Article 9 of the Constitution. But the main reason for ruling the family-head system unconstitutional are that it is "contrary to the individual dignity and gender equality."[31] In Kim's view, this shows not only that the Court's reasoning was unequivocally liberal but also that it chose individual over family as the most basic unit of the Korean polity.[32] Furthermore, "the National Assembly's decision to replace the family-registry system with an individual identification system demonstrates the most radical aspect of liberalism in Korea, because by doing so it could finally 'liberate' the Korean people, both men and women, from the traditional yoke of the Confucian family called *ka*."[33] Kim finds the Court's decision "dismissive of Confucian values, by which Korean constitutionalism is indirectly bound."[34] Here Kim draws the distinction between direct and indirect constitutionalism. Although the Court and the Korean Constitution never officially declared Confucian values constitutional, "the fact that these values, often called cultural values, are publicly acknowledged and even promoted with reference to a key constitutional provision makes it possible to call them quasi-constitutional values, if we understand the term 'constitutional' here not in a strictly legal sense but in a broader political sense that the constitution is the political

[28] Ibid., 117.

[29] Ibid., 120.

[30] Ibid., 121.

[31] Ibid., 118.

[32] Ibid., 127.

[33] Ibid.

[34] Ibid., 128.

community's supreme norm."[35] Kim calls this type of constitutionalism indirect constitutionalism, "in which certain cultural values, though not constitutional values in a strictly legal sense, attain public-constitutional significance."[36] The source of the discontents regarding the Court's decision is thus traceable to its failure to show "precisely how liberal constitutional values and indirectly constitutional Confucian values are to be balanced, so that the perfectionist commitments implied in Korean constitutionalism can be fulfilled harmoniously."[37] The Court's decision pivoted toward liberalism at the cost of Confucianism.

With these two cases, Hahm and Kim now arrive at the intersection between liberalism and Confucianism by recognizing the dualist nature of South Korean constitutionalism. Although the liberal Constitution justifies and regulates the identity of the Korean state, the Confucian constitution still influences many aspects of the lives of Korean citizens. How to navigate between the two types of constitutions becomes the question at stake. Earlier we arrived at a dilemma in Hahm's suggestion to defend Confucianism on grounds that are more understandable to contemporary Koreans. In the next section, I will focus on Kim's solution, which he calls public reason Confucian constitutionalism that flips the dynamic around and subordinates liberalism to Confucianism. I will argue that Kim's proposal faces more problems than it solves. Just as it was problematic for the Court (and the Constitution) to subordinate Confucianism to liberalism, it was equally, if not more problematic to do the opposite.

5.4 The Discontents of Public Reason Confucian Constitutionalism

According to Kim, "Korean constitutionalism lacks a coherent normative standard that can weave together the Constitution's two perfectionist commitments in a publicly intelligible way and thereby produce a robust Korean citizenship."[38] The better model that Kim proposes is what he calls "public reason Confucian constitutionalism," which regards certain Confucian values "quasi-constitutional values" even when they are not explicitly mentioned in the Constitution. This indirect type of Confucian constitutionalism enables a relationship of negotiation between "formal constitutional principles and values with Confucian values and goods to which the polity is publicly, if not direct constitutionally committed."[39] Kim's model is based on his broader theory of public reason Confucianism, which takes the empirical fact of shared Confucian values and practices in South Korea as the key starting point

---

[35] Ibid., 123.

[36] Ibid.

[37] Ibid., 124.

[38] Ibid., 124.

[39] Ibid.

and makes "Confucian perfectionist goods as the core constituents of public reason with which citizens can justify their public opinions and arguments to one another and by which the state (i.e., the democratic state) can justifiably exercise its public authority to reasonable citizens who otherwise subscribe to various moral, philosophical, and religious doctrines."[40] Public reason Confucianism is thus a moderately perfectionist attempt to accommodate reasonable pluralism while still maintaining core liberal and democratic values and institutions in South Korea.

In the family-head case, public reason Confucian constitutionalism aims "to provide a normative standard by which to weave the constitution's direct-liberal and in-direct-Confucian perfectionist commitments in a publicly intelligible way, thus producing a robust Confucian democratic citizenship."[41] Concurring with Justice Kim in his dissenting statement, Kim says that "as long as the family-head system is central to the organization of the *ka* institution by serving its moral purpose and to the extent that it is reformed so as to accommodate democratic constitutional principles, its abolition is not the central task of public reason Confucianism."[42] Instead, it is the *ka*, a complex social and legal institution that helps to "maintain contemporary Korea as characteristically Confucian," that is central to public reason Confucianism.[43] For instance, instead of abolishing the family-head system altogether, the National Assembly could have made family headship open to both men and women. Kim then goes beyond the case at hand. From the perspective of public reason Confucian constitutionalism,

> the best way to make Korea (and other East Asian Confucian countries) a Confucian constitutional democracy is to reconceptualize the (direct) constitutional principles of human dignity and gender equality *from* the perspective of Confucian values to which it is publicly (i.e., indirect-constitutionally) committed, as much as adapt Confucian values, institutions, and practices to democratic constitutional principles. Since public reason Confucianism stipulates public reason as constituted by Confucian values, mores, and/or moral sentiments, the practical implication of this dual perfectionism is that the moral contents of human dignity and gender equality, otherwise liberal ideals, ought to be reconceived in light of Confucian public reason in various public forums including courts, congresses, and civil societies. A polity's perfectionist commitment to the values and institutions of the *ka* can directly contribute to its indirect Confucian constitutionalism.[44]

If it was not clear in Kim's analyses of the family-head case, then it should be clear from the above paragraph that the ultimate goal of public reason Confucian constitutionalism is to reshape the power dynamics between the liberal Constitution and the Confucian constitution. Although Kim refers to Confucian values as quasi- or indirectly constructional, he aims to "reconceptualize" and "reconceive" liberal ideals, such as human dignity and gender equality, by appealing not to other liberal and democratic ideals but to Confucian values. In other words, the "normative standard"

---

[40] Ibid., 70.

[41] Ibid., 126.

[42] Ibid., 134.

[43] Ibid.

[44] Ibid., 135.

Kim looks for to weave together the Constitution's liberal and Confucian commitments is in the latter. It is as if Kim took Article 9 and made it the interpretative key to the Constitution. Public reason Confucian constitutionalism does the opposite of the Court did by pivoting substantively toward the Confucian constitution over the liberal Constitution, which is consistent with public reason Confucianism's overall strategy of Confucianizing public reason.

As I argue elsewhere, public reason Confucianism invites a wide range of criticisms.[45] I will briefly mention three here. First, because public reason Confucianism tries to walk the middle ground between liberalism and Confucianism, it has to adopt a thin version of Confucianism that might be too diluted to be meaningful to self-identified Confucians, who might wonder why Confucianism needs to make compromises for the sake of liberalism. Second, since South Korea is identifiably a liberal democracy, interpreting public reason in light of Confucian values and ideals might lead to problematic implications for the free and equal status of citizens who do not identify as Confucians or are not raised in the Confucian tradition. For these citizens, participating in political discourse will require translation of their opinions and concerns according to Confucian public reason, which is a burden not equally shared by their fellow Confucian citizens. Worse still, when it comes to immigrants, Kim argues that a subscription to Confucian public reason is "the inevitable price for the fair terms of integration into the Confucian society," and that "immigrated citizens should strive to negotiate their religious or nonreligious comprehensive doctrines with Confucian public reason in order to fully exercise their constitutional rights and liberties."[46] These requirements for the sake of maintaining a recognizably Confucian society conflict with the freedom and equality of citizens in a liberal democracy. Third, since public reason Confucianism regards Confucian values and ideals as the source of public reason, it risks jeopardizing the attempt to accommodate reasonable pluralism, which is a key motivating factor for the theory in the first place. If reasonable pluralism is taken seriously, one might wonder why Confucianism ought to be the main political inspiration and not Daoism or Buddhism or even Christianity, which currently has substantial number of followers in South Korea. On the one hand, different historical traditions, such as Daoism and Buddhism, can be incorporated into "cultural heritage" and "national culture." On the other hand, an even more moderate view of perfectionism that focuses on values and goods compatible with a wide range of reasonable comprehensive doctrines might be better suited to balance liberalism without the baggage that come with Confucianism.[47]

Applying these criticisms to public reason Confucian constitutionalism, one might cast doubt on Kim's ambition to produce "a coherent public identity of Confucian and democratic citizens by weaving two perfectionist

---

[45] Zhuoyao Li, "The Discontents of Moderate Political Confucianism and the Future of Democracy in East Asia," Philosophy East & West 68, No. 4: 1193–1128.

[46] Sungmoon Kim, *Public Reason Confucianism: Democratic Perfectionism and Constitutionalism in East Asia* (New York: Cambridge University Press, 2016), 87.

[47] See Joseph Chan, *Confucian Perfectionism: A Political Philosophy for Modern Times* (Princeton: Princeton University Press, 2014).

commitments—liberal and Confucian—into a single coherent constitutionalism."[48] In order to achieve this goal, cultural negotiations will take place between Confucian values and practice, and liberal democratic values and rights. But this sort of cultural negotiation cannot be reserved exclusively for Confucianism and liberalism, since there is an undeniable plurality of other comprehensive doctrines, even if Confucianism is still the most influential one. Kim is fully aware of this fact when he says that "public reason Confucianism allows citizens to negotiate their comprehensive moral values with Confucian public reason, then with particular rights, duties, and liberties."[49] However, it is highly problematic to say that citizens who adopt non-Confucian doctrines will have to negotiate with Confucian public reason first, and only then can they negotiate with particular rights, duties, and liberties.[50] Therefore, although Kim is correct in his understanding of the dualist nature of constitutionalism in South Korea and the Court's over reliance on liberal values and reasoning even in cases where Confucian ideals and practices are clearly at stake, he falls short in suggesting a solution where Confucianism plays the dominant role in justifying and regulating the state. Put differently, public reason Confucian constitutionalism repeats the Court's problematic tendency in the opposite way by over relying on Confucianism to reconceptualize and reconceive what it means to live in a liberal democracy. Now the question becomes: if neither too much liberalism nor too much Confucianism works, then what? In the next section, I will suggest a more viable model that aims to avoid the shortfalls mentioned so far by relocating the negotiating relationship between liberalism and Confucianism to more neutral ground while at the same time reintroducing more democratic participation from citizens.

5.5 Toward a Mediating and Democratic Strategy

It will be remembered that both Hahm and Kim conclude that there is a dualism in South Korean constitutionalism while acknowledging that the country is becoming increasingly pluralistic. In the case of Kim's public reason Confucian constitutionalism, what John Rawls calls reasonable pluralism is a key motivating factor to include public reason as a mechanism to avoid extreme forms of political Confucianism. According to Rawls, burdens of judgment will lead reasonable citizens to adopt a plurality of reasonable, though irreconcilable, moral, religious, or philosophical doctrines. Reasonable pluralism is not a historical contingency but the necessary consequence of the free practice of reason in modern democracies.[51]

---

[48] Sungmoon Kim, *Public Reason Confucianism: Democratic Perfectionism and Constitutionalism in East Asia* (New York: Cambridge University Press, 2016), 136.

[49] Ibid., 100.

[50] Zhuoyao Li, "Political Confucianism and Multivariate Democracy in East Asia," The Review of Politics 81, No. 3: 459–483.

[51] John Rawls, *Political Liberalism*, Expanded Edition (New York: Columbia University Press, 2005), introduction, xvi.

Alessandro Ferrara recently goes further and argue that "in very few places in the world can we encounter a polity where these two conceptions are embraced by a majority of citizens," which leads to the implication that Rawls' political liberalism is in fact drawn on for inspiration based on "a highly stylized picture."[52] In the actual world, societies are populated by people who endorse a plurality of comprehensive doctrines, such as Roman Catholicism, Islam, Orthodox Christianity, Hinduism, and Confucianism. The difficulty is that some of the basic constitutional essentials—the idea of equality among all citizens, gender equality, the idea of the citizen as a self-authenticating source of valid claims, freedom of conscience, the consequent ban on apostasy, etc.—could become highly problematical at least for some of the more traditional citizens.[53] This condition is what Ferrara calls "hyperpluralism," which refers to "the presence on the ground of cultural differences that exceed the range of traditions Rawls sought to reconcile within Political Liberalism, and of comprehensive conceptions that are only partially reasonable, display an only partial acceptance of the burdens of judgment or make their adherents endorse only a subset of the constitutional essentials."[54] There are two ways to interpret the concept of hyperpluralism. What is "hyper" about this type of pluralism can mean either that the disagreements are too horizontally broad given the large number of comprehensive doctrines that are meaningfully adopted by citizens in a given society, or that the conflicts are too vertically deep because the few dominant comprehensive doctrines exhibit equal commitments from citizens. In the case of a mature western liberal democracy, the former might be the case, which is what Ferrara has in mind. In the case of South Korea where citizens deeply commit to liberalism because of the country's political structure and also to Confucianism because of their historical and cultural heritage, the kind of conflict between the two value systems can reach hyper level when certain constitutional essentials become questionable depending on which value system one prioritizes in constitutional thinking. In the case against the family ritual law, general freedom and the right to pursue happiness (according to the liberal Constitution) conflicts with ritual propriety mandated by Confucian values and ideals (according to the Confucian constitution). In the case against the family-head system, individuality and gender equality (according to the liberal Constitution) conflicts with the significance of affective relations maintained by the historical family-head arrangement (according to the Confucian constitution). It will also be recalled that the attempt to turn the Court's liberal dominance to a Confucian one does not provide a satisfactory solution. On the contrary, it produces its own set of problems. Moreover, neither Hahm nor Kim provides empirical evidence to show what Korean citizens actually think in the two cases. Normative arguments are certainly important, but the voices of the *demos* should not be overlooked. After all, the point of having the Constitution and the Constitutional Court is to

---

[52] Alessandro Ferrara, *The Democratic Horizon: Hyperpluralism and the Renewal of Political Liberalism* (Cambridge: Cambridge University Press, 2014), 90.

[53] Ibid., 90.

[54] Ibid., 200.

make sure that the state does not usurp the power that belongs to the people. In this section, I will argue that a more viable solution is a pragmatic one. Instead of ranking the two constitutions, the Court should mediate between them on neutral ground where the facts of the cases are prioritized. In addition, judicial review ought to be balanced with input from the popular will in order to make sure that the Court's decision actually aligns with what most citizens think.

Although the conflict between liberalism and Confucianism in the context of South Korean constitutionalism is not all about rights, we can draw inspiration from how the law can respond to the proliferation of competing rights. In the United States at least, deeply held rights clash with one another, which presents the Supreme Court with challenging cases. According to Jamal Greene, there are three ways the law can respond to competing rights: "it can *minimize* rights, it can *discriminate* between them, or it can *mediate* them."[55] Discrimination between rights is the dominant strategy in the United States. For instance,

> an information processing firm called IMS Health wanted to scrape data from pharmacies, including the prescription practices of individual doctors, which it could then sell to drug companies wanting to better tailor their marketing to physicians. Vermont wanted to protect the privacy of doctors and their patients, so it passed a law banning the sale of prescription data. The Supreme Court struck the law down, saying it invaded the *free speech* rights of drug companies.[56]

Because the United States Constitution says nothing about selling prescription data but it unequivocally protects the right to free speech, the Supreme Court justices "placed IMS Health's rights claim into a category—freedom of speech—they were able to recognize."[57] This approach of discriminating between rights is made worse by the facts that "U.S. courts recognize relatively few rights, but strongly."[58] For a justice that adopts originalism, this effectively means that the few rights that the Constitution clearly specifies weigh much more heavily than any other concerns or potential rights that might compete with the former. In Greene's view, a different strategy is needed to properly navigate pluralism that gives birth to much more rights but no more clear standards to discriminate between them. Instead, only rights mediation, which is about "paying unwavering attention to the *facts* of the parties' dispute," can shift the emphasis "from whether the Constitution includes particular rights to what the government is actually doing to people and why," which "makes rights recognition and enforcement a shared enterprise, one that is of, by, and for all the people and not just the judges."[59] This last point also speaks for the democratic nature of the Constitution, which will be discussed soon. But for now, it

[55] Jamal Greene, How Rights Went Wrong: Why Our Obsession with Rights is Tearing America Apart (New York: Houghton Mifflin Harcourt Publishing Company, 2021), introduction, xvii.

[56] Ibid., xxvi.

[57] Ibid., xxvii.

[58] Ibid., xx.

[59] Ibid.

is helpful to point out how rights mediation can inspire a strategy of mediation in the context of South Korea constitutionalism.

One of the key premises of rights mediation is that the Constitution does not (and cannot) specify all rights. Similarly, the Confucian constitution is not included in the liberal Constitution. Even Article 9 of the Korean Constitution does not specify what "cultural heritage" and "national culture" mean exactly. But as our previous analyses have shown, both the liberal Constitution and the Confucian constitution live up to the standard of constitutionalism. So the Constitutional Court in fact discriminated rather than mediated between the two constitutions, because liberal values represent a category that the Court can recognize and from which the Court can reason. The outcome, as Hahm and Kim correctly point out, is the neglect of the equally significant Confucian constitution to which most South Korean citizens still deeply commit. Similarly, public reason Confucian constitutionalism also discriminates rather than mediates between the two constitutions, because Confucian values and ideals now serve as the category that alone can provide basis for reconceptualization and reconception of liberal values and reasons. The outcome, as discussed in the previous section, is the risk of undermining the free and equal status of citizens. Beyond discrimination, a mediating strategy will recognize both constitutions and refrain from picking a side. Instead, the Court should focus on the facts of the case and reason on neutral ground. In the case against family ritual law, more attention should be paid to the circumstances of the person and the person's own reasons for challenging the law, as well as the real-world motives and behaviors of the state when it advocates for or enforcing the law. Hahm points out that "the law is impossible to observe because the phrase 'the true meaning of family ritual and ceremony' has no clear meaning and also because what constitutes a 'reasonable' amount of food and drinks is a matter of opinion that can have no clear answer."[60] Moreover, the state also concedes as much because "it constantly changed and amended the presidential decree that specified the scope of the exception allowed for serving food and drinks."[61] These facts are important not because they are necessarily tied to any liberal or Confucian values and ideals but because they pertain to the actual calculation in the process of judicial review.

In the case against the family-head system where general freedom and gender equality clash with Confucian value and institution of *ka*, a mediating strategy will move deliberations to neutral ground. There are two ways to understand what neutrality means here. First, neutrality means refraining from adopting any particular comprehensive doctrines. There are values and ideals that most reasonable persons would endorse without requiring a subscription to a particular comprehensive doctrine. Justice Kim's dissenting statement makes no references to Confucianism, which makes his discussion on family much more reasonable. By referring to family relation as "the single most important [ethical] foundation of social solidarity

[60] Chaihark Hahm, "Negotiating Confucian Civility through Constitutional Discourse," *The Politics of Affective Relations: East Asia and Beyond*, eds. Chaihark Hahm and Daniel A. Bell (Lanham: Lexington Books, 2004), 290.

[61] Ibid.

and political unity," Justice Kim is speaking of family as a universal concept. *Ka* is certainly at the center of Confucianism but family is held universally as one of the most valuable institutions. If the Court ruled to uphold the family-head system by appealing to the value of Confucian *ka*, as public reason Confucian constitutionalism suggests, then it would have neglected the liberal values of general freedom and gender equality, which is the same kind of problem for which public reason Confucianism constitutionalism accuses the Court. Second, neutrality can also mean prudentiality, which connects to the emphasis on facts. For instance, abolishing the family-head system altogether might lead to the devaluing of family that might ultimately contributes to the growing population crisis in developed countries. On the contrary, giving women the same capacity as the family head and the same trust and authority on deciding who the family head ought to be can strengthen family bond and even social cohesion. It is thus not prudent for the Court and the National Assembly to favor liberal values and to do away with the family-head system, because so doing might decrease the collective well-being of citizens of South Korea.

Finally, the justifying and regulating functions of the constitution is ultimately for the benefits of the people, who are almost always excluded from the process of judicial review. The U.S. Supreme Court's recent decision to overrule *Roe v. Wade* has shattered not only the half-century constitutional protection of the right to abortion but also the very meaning of rights in the United States. Justice Samuel Alito's originalist majority opinion aims to limit constitutional protection of rights that are not explicitly mentioned in the Constitution to only those "deeply rooted in this Nation's history and tradition" and "implicit in the concept of ordered liberty."[62] Alito's view of history and his originalist reasoning are both contested by legal scholars. More significantly, the role of the Supreme Court is also questioned by many, because the majority of Americans think that abortion should be legal in all or most cases. According to Pew Research Center, nearly "six-in-ten adults (57%) disapprove of the court's sweeping decision, including 43% who *strongly* disapprove."[63] Not 2 months after the Supreme Court's decision, almost 60% of voters in Kansas decided to keep abortion legal in the historically red state by voting to reject an amendment to the state's constitution.[64] All these reveal a conflict between the power of judicial review and the representation of the popular will. According to Larry Kramer, America's Founding generation "embraced a political ideology that celebrated the central role of 'the people' in supplying government with its energy

[62] *Dobbs v. Jackson Women's Health Organization*, 597 U.S. (2022).

[63] Pew Research Center, "Majority of Public Disapproves of Supreme Court's Decision to Overturn Roe v. Wade," accessed August 6, 2022 https://www.pewresearch.org/politics/2022/07/06/majority-of-public-disapproves-of-supreme-courts-decision-to-overturn-roe-v-wade/.

[64] National Public Radio, "Voters in Kansas decide to keep abortion legal in the state, rejecting an amendment," accessed August 17, 2022 https://www.npr.org/sections/2022-live-primary-election-race-results/2022/08/02/1115317596/kansas-voters-abortion-legal-reject-constitutional-amendment.

and direction."[65] Their Constitution remained "an act of popular will: the people's charter, made by the people," and the "idea of turning this responsibility over to judges was simply unthinkable."[66] Despite the emergence of the practice of judicial review, "the Founding generation and its successors responded to evolving social, political, and cultural conditions by improvising institutional and intellectual solutions to preserve popular control over the course of constitutional law—a kind of control we seem to have lost, or surrendered, today."[67] The Constitutional Court of South Korea took on this increasing disregard of the popular will when it was first established in the image of western courts and followed the practice of judicial review. In the two constitutional cases, what the citizens actually thought of family rituals and family-head system were almost never mentioned, nor does it feature prominently in Hahm's and Kim's analyses. The *demos*, who actually holds authority to the Constitution and the Constitutional Court, should be consulted. Which is not to say that the people are always right but only that the popular will should at least play some role in supplementing, if not balancing, the judicial branch of the government. The interaction between the people and the judicial branch will also help promote what Hahm calls "a constitutional culture among Koreans."[68] Just as ritual is essentially an educative norm, so is constitutionalism understood in this mediating and democratic way. Citizens should not outsource constitutional issues to the Court and only obey what is passed back to them after judicial review. Instead, citizens should actively engage in a process of constitutional education and democratic feedback to ensure the health of the liberal democracy that they founded.

[65] Larry Kramer, *The People Themselves: Popular Constitutionalism and Judicial Review* (New York: Oxford University Press, 2004), 6.

[66] Ibid., 7.

[67] Ibid., 7.

[68] Chaihark Hahm, "Conceptualizing Korean Constitutionalism: Foreign Transplant or Indigenous Tradition?" *Confucianism, Law, and Democracy in Contemporary Korea*, ed. Sungmoon Kim (London: Rowman & Littlefield International, 2015), 43.

Chapter 6
Liberal Toleration, Confucian Societies, and Global Justice

Abstract This chapter reframes Rawls's Law of Peoples through a spectrum of nonliberal societies from decent hierarchical peoples to benevolent absolutisms by using the *proviso* to assess Confucian states' global reasonability based on participatory consultation and human rights adherence. It argues for toleration via non-interference if societies endorse international principles reciprocally. Extending the book's thesis globally, it shows the *proviso*'s justificatory structure as universal for evaluating Confucian absolutism's legitimacy in a pluralistic world order.

Keywords Law of peoples • Decent peoples • Benevolent absolutism • Global justice • Consultation hierarchy • Human rights

6.1 Introduction

Recent literatures on Confucian political theory have produced some much-needed discussions on the nature of the state and the relationship between the state and citizens in the context of Confucian East Asia.[1] With a few exceptions, these theories

---

[1] See for instance Qing Jiang, "The Way of the Humane Authority: The Theoretical Basis for Confucian Constitutionalism and A Tricameral Parliament," *A Confucian Constitutional Order: How China's Ancient Past Can Shape Its Political Future*, eds. Daniel Bell and Ruiping Fan (Princeton: Princeton University Press, 2013). Daniel Bell, *The China Model: Political Meritocracy and the Limits of Democracy* (Princeton: Princeton University Press, 2016). Sungmoon Kim, *Democracy After Virtue: Toward Pragmatic Confucian Democracy* (New York: Oxford University Press, 2017). Tongdong Bai, *Against Political Equality: The Confucian Case* (Princeton: Princeton University Press, 2019).

Z. Li, *Pluralism, Confucianism, and Artificial Intelligence*, Philosophy and Politics - Critical Explorations 35, https://doi.org/10.1007/978-3-032-25605-8_6

have largely focused on the domestic setting of Confucian societies. However, as these theories branch into even more sophisticated versions, it would be missing an important part of the big picture not to consider their global implications. For instance, little has been said regarding the tension between non-Confucian citizens with the Confucian state, which may comprehensively advocate Confucianism as the state doctrine or moderately only endorse certain Confucian values and ideals. Even if a form of Confucian state could be justifiably defended in East Asia, there is no telling how the rest of the world, especially the liberal West, would react to its (theoretical and perhaps even practical) existence. One of the reasons why the domestic discussions of political Confucianism have generated so much insight is because of the fluidity and flexibility of the underlying conceptual framework between liberalism and perfectionism.[2] For instance, by limiting how comprehensive Confucian the state should be, moderate Confucian political theory tries to establish a middle ground where both fundamental liberal commitments and important Confucian values and ideals can be maintained.[3] Alternatively, by bridging Confucianism with the liberal rather than the democratic side of liberal democracy, a hybrid view of domestic politics might prove to be more viable than both extreme forms of state Confucianism and liberal democracy.[4] The international perspective has not yet established a similar framework, which often leads less liberal and democratic approaches to political Confucianism to be simply neglected because they are outliers in the mainstream political discourse and beyond toleration from a liberal point of view.

In this chapter, I aim to propose a conceptual framework based on the pluralistic point of view developed in the previous chapters, through which different forms of Confucian state can be further analyzed in the context of global justice. John Rawls's *Law of Peoples* has been criticized for different reasons, the most controversial of which involve the criticisms that it is both too inclusive and not inclusive enough regarding nonliberal societies. On the one hand, some argue that Rawls leaves too much room for nonliberal societies, such as decent hierarchical societies, and that

[2] Jonathan Quong's matrix of contemporary liberal political theories often serves as the starting point for further discussions. See Jonathan Quong, *Liberalism without Perfection* (Oxford: Oxford University Press, 2010). In the context of Confucian political theory, see Joseph Chan, *Confucian Perfectionism: A Political Philosophy for Modern Times* (Princeton: Princeton University Press, 2014). Sungmoon Kim, *Public Reason Confucianism: Democratic Perfectionism and Constitutionalism in East Asia* (Cambridge: Cambridge University Press, 2016). Franz Mang, "Confucianism, Perfectionism, and Liberal Society," *Dao: A Journal of Comparative Philosophy* 17:1 (2018), 29–49. Zhuoyao Li, *Political Liberalism, Confucianism, and the Future of Democracy in East Asia* (Switzerland: Springer, 2020).

[3] See Joseph Chan, *Confucian Perfectionism: A Political Philosophy for Modern Times* (Princeton: Princeton University Press, 2014). Sungmoon Kim, *Public Reason Confucianism: Democratic Perfectionism and Constitutionalism in East Asia* (Cambridge: Cambridge University Press, 2016).

[4] See Tongdong Bai, *Against Political Equality: The Confucian Case* (Princeton: Princeton University Press, 2019).

liberal peoples ought not to tolerate their nonliberal counterparts.[5] On the other hand, others argue that Rawls should have been more inclusive, particularly when it comes to benevolent absolutisms, which ought to be tolerated in addition to decent hierarchical societies.[6] In my view, these seemingly contradictory criticisms serve as indications that *Law of Peoples* has the potential to provide a fluid and flexible conceptual framework to further understand how different types of states ought to behave in the international arena. In the rest of the chapter, I will first go through the basic arguments in *Law of Peoples* with emphasis on how and why Rawls comes up with the different types of societies. Then, I will focus on decent hierarchical societies and benevolent absolutisms and argue that the difference between the two is less obvious than one might think. Instead of treating them as two distinct categories of societies where only the former warrants liberal toleration, I will argue that they should be viewed as representing a spectrum of societies that hinges upon what it means for citizens to meaningfully participate in political decision making. This spectrum can be utilized as a conceptual framework to further analyze different forms of Confucian state and their global implications. On the basis of these discussions, I will argue that most forms of Confucian state in recent literature, despite their potential theoretical weaknesses, can and should be tolerated by liberal peoples. They can also be recognized as members of the Society of Peoples, provided that they can abide by the Law of Peoples. By way of conclusion, I will argue that recent approaches to bridge political Confucianism with liberal democracy hold the potential to demonstrate that a Confucian society can be more than benevolent absolutism and even decent hierarchical societies. Although Rawls's political liberalism finds liberal perfectionism problematic in the domestic setting, its application in global justice leaves enough room for moderately perfectionist societies to thrive as liberal and just peoples.

---

[5] See Fernando Teson, "The Rawlsian Theory of International Law," *Ethics and International Affairs* 9 (1995), 79–99. Charles Beitz, "Rawls's Law of Peoples," *Ethics* 110 (2000), 669–696. Allen Buchanan, "Justice, Legitimacy, and Human Rights," *The Idea of a Political Liberalism*, eds. V. Davion and C. Wolf (Lanham, MD: Rowman and Littlefield, 2000). Kok-Chor Tan, *Toleration, Diversity, and Global Justice* (University Park: Pennsylvania State University Press, 2000). Blain Neufeld, "Civic Respect, Political Liberalism, and Non-Liberal Societies," *Politics, Philosophy & Economics* 4:3 (2005), 275–299.

[6] See Walter Riker, "Human Rights Without Political Participation?" Human Rights Review 15 (2014), 369–390. Pietro Maffettone, "Toleration, Decency and Self-Determination in The Law of Peoples," Philosophy & Social Criticism 41:6 (2015), 537–556. Pietro Maffettone, "Should We Tolerate Benevolent Absolutisms?" Social Theory and Practice, 42:3 (2016), 525–554. Robert Huseby, "In or Out? On Benevolent Absolutisms in the Law of Peoples," *Journal of Ethics and Social Philosophy* 13:2 (2018), 154–178.

6.2 *Law of People* Revisited

Anyone familiar with Rawls's domestic political theory will find herself instantly at home with the basic setup of *Law of Peoples.* It is reasonable to read *Law of Peoples* as the logical continuation of the project Rawls develops in *Political Liberalism.* In *Political Liberalism,* Rawls tries to demonstrate that it is theoretically possible for there to be "a stable and just society of free and equal citizens profoundly divided by reasonable though incompatible religious, philosophical, and moral doctrines" over time.[7] But the world does not consist only of well-ordered liberal democracies. The same problem of stability that Thomas Hobbes introduces in the *Leviathan,* which Rawls tries to solve for the right reason in *Political Liberalism,* similarly applies to the international community. Additionally, the source of instability, both domestic and international, has to do with pluralism. In the domestic case, reasonable pluralism drives superficial and substantial disagreements among citizens who subscribe to different comprehensive doctrines. In the international case, an analogous pluralism leads to disputes and even wars among countries that share different views of the international order and uphold competing foreign policies that may or may not be reducible to comprehensive doctrines that they hold. Acknowledging the source of instability prompts Rawls to apply more widely his ideal political theory developed in the domestic setting. However, just as there are different types of citizens in a domestic society, there are different states in the world. Following his argument in *Political Liberalism* that rationality must subordinate to reasonability in order for a liberal democracy to be stable, Rawls chooses the term "peoples" rather than "states" to emphasize the priority of the reasonable over the rational even in a global setting.[8] The prime examples Rawls has in mind are the liberal peoples who have three basic features: "a reasonably just constitutional democratic government that serves their fundamental interest; citizens united by what Mill called 'common sympathies'; and finally, a moral nature."[9] In contrast to states that are traditionally conceived to be centered only around their rational interests, which leads to *modus vivendi* rather than stability for the right reason, liberal peoples "limit their basic interests as required by the reasonable."[10] Based on these characteristics, Rawls argues that well-ordered liberal peoples would select eight principles to govern their interactions and foreign policies through a second and international original position:

1. Peoples are free and independent, and their freedom and independence are to be respected by other peoples.
2. Peoples are to observe treaties and undertakings.

[7] John Rawls, Political Liberalism, Expanded Edition (New York: Columbia University Press, 2005), xviii.

[8] Ibid., 23–30.

[9] Ibid., 23.

[10] Ibid., 29.

3. Peoples are equal and are parties to the agreements that bind them.
4. Peoples are to observe a duty of non-intervention.
5. Peoples have a right of self-defense, but no right to instigate war from reasons other than self-defense.
6. Peoples are to honor human rights.
7. Peoples are to observe certain specified restrictions in the conduct of war.
8. Peoples have a duty to assist other peoples living under unfavorable conditions that prevent their having a just or decent political and social regime.[11]

But the world does not consist only of liberal peoples. In the second and more controversial part of *Law of Peoples*, Rawls discusses toleration of nonliberal peoples and the limits of toleration toward states that cannot be properly referred to as "peoples." In addition to liberal peoples, some nonliberal societies can qualify as peoples who are worthy of being members of what Rawls calls "Society of Peoples." Although these societies can be religious or secular in nature, what Rawls has in mind are ones whose governments publicly endorse comprehensive doctrines that exert substantial influence over the social and political interactions between the government and citizens as well as among citizens themselves, such as the imaginary and idealized Islamic people that Rawls calls "Kazanistan." Rawls calls these societies "decent hierarchical peoples" on the basis that they respect basic human rights, are not aggressive nor expansionist, and maintain a hierarchy through which citizens, regardless of their choices of comprehensive doctrines, can be politically represented.[12] Decent hierarchical peoples can embrace the eight principles above.[13] Decency, from Rawls's perspective, is "a normative idea of the same kind as reasonableness, though weaker," which gives most citizens of liberal societies enough reason to find these decent peoples in good standing.[14] Beyond the realm of ideal theory, Rawls discusses three more types of societies: outlaw states, societies burdened by unfavorable conditions, and benevolent absolutisms. Since both liberal and decent peoples are members of Society of Peoples mostly because of their reasonability, it is easy to understand why outlaw states, which are intentionally unreasonable, and societies burdened by unfavorable conditions, which are excusably unreasonable, are beyond liberal toleration.[15] However, when it comes to benevolent absolutisms, which Rawls discusses only in passing, it is much less clear why they must be banished beyond toleration and outside the Society of Peoples. According to Rawls, benevolent absolutisms honor human rights and are non-aggressive but are not well-ordered "because their members are denied a meaningful role in mak-

[11] Ibid., 37.

[12] Ibid., 64–65.

[13] Rawls makes it clear that there can be more than one kind of decent people. In addition to decent hierarchical peoples, there might be other decent peoples whose basic structure does not fit the description of a consultation hierarchy.

[14] John Rawls, The Law of Peoples (Cambridge: Harvard University Press, 1999), 67.

[15] David Reidy, "Moral Psychology, Stability and the Law of Peoples," Canadian Journal of Law and Jurisprudence, 30:2 (2017), 389.

ing political decisions."[16] Moreover, because they honor human rights and are non-aggressive, benevolent absolutisms also have the right to war in self-defense. These are all Rawls has to say in *Law of Peoples* regarding benevolent absolutisms. Just how different are they from decent hierarchical peoples who also respect human rights, are non-aggressive, and do not grant their citizens full political representation? Moreover, since political participation is widely accepted as one of the human rights among liberal peoples, how could human rights be sufficiently honored without granting citizens full extent of political participation, which is the case with both decent hierarchical peoples and benevolent absolutisms? In the context of Confucian political theory, does this mean that less liberal and democratic theories that focus on Confucian meritocracy necessarily produce benevolent absolutisms that are beyond toleration? In the following two sections, I will argue that instead of simply treating Rawls's vague comments as a controversy in Rawls's theory of global justice, a more productive approach, especially in the context of Confucian political theory, is to develop a spectrum through which different degrees of political participation can be measured against different theories of Confucian states in order to demonstrate their global implications.

6.3 Between Decency and Benevolence

Unlike outlaw states and societies burdened by unfavorable conditions, both of which are straightforward examples of unreasonable states, benevolent absolutisms, at least according to Rawls's passing comments, pose a challenge to the theoretical scope of decency, because the criteria for benevolent absolutisms overlap with those for decent peoples. In this section, I will first examine the difference between decent peoples and benevolent absolutisms according to Rawls and argue that the nuance hinges upon what it means for citizens to be able to play a meaningful role in political decision making, which is not at all clear in Rawls's original account. Then, I will show that Rawls's controversial use of human rights in the discussions of decent peoples and benevolent absolutisms adds to the confusion. I do not aim to settle this controversy in this chapter. Instead, I will argue that moving beyond this somewhat arbitrary distinction between decent peoples and benevolent absolutisms will lead to a spectrum view through which the reasonability of some nonliberal societies can be better examined.

As Rawls points out, decency is a normative idea of the same kind as reasonableness, only weaker, which qualifies decent societies as peoples and members of the Society of Peoples.[17] Specifically, there are two criteria for decent hierarchical societies. First, "the society does not have aggressive aims, and it recognizes that it must

[16] John Rawls, The Law of Peoples (Cambridge: Harvard University Press, 1999), 92.

[17] Ibid., 67.

gain its legitimate ends through diplomacy and trade and other ways of peace."[18] There are three parts to the second criterion:

(a) The first part is that a decent hierarchical people's system of law, in accordance with its common good idea of justice, secures for all members of the people what have come to be called human rights.
(b) The second part is that a decent people's system of law must be such as to impose *bona fide* moral duties and obligations (distinct from human rights) on all persons within the people's territory.
(c) Finally, the third part of the second criterion is that there must be a sincere and not unreasonable belief on the part of the judges and other officials who administer the legal system that the law is indeed guided by a common good idea of justice.[19]

The most important insight from the second criterion is that the legal system of a decent hierarchical people must contain a decent consultation hierarchy. In other words, "the basic structure of the society must include a family of representative bodies whose role in the hierarchy is to take part in an established procedure of consultation and to look after what the people's common good idea of justice regards as the important interests of all members of the people."[20] Moreover, unlike liberal peoples, not all persons in a decent hierarchical society are "regarded as free and equal citizens, nor as separate individuals deserving equal representation (according to the maxim: one citizen, one vote)."[21] Instead, they are seen as "decent and rational and as capable of moral learning as recognized in their society."[22] These comments make it clear that citizens in a decent hierarchical society do not enjoy equal right to political participation. Although a decent consultation hierarchy allows and perhaps even encourages different voices to be heard on the basis of the society's sincere belief in the justice of the legal system that respects the possibility of dissent, its very existence is a constant reminder that not everyone plays the same meaningful role in political decision making. In Rawls's imaginary society of Kazanistan, for instance, "only Muslims can hold the upper position of political authority and influence the government's main decisions and polices, including foreign affairs," although citizens who practice other religions are encouraged to participate in the wider civic culture and to voice their concerns about the government's policies and actions.[23] Non-Muslims can express their dissenting opinions through public protest, which is permissible "provided it stays within the basic framework of the common good idea of justice."[24] In summary, decent hierarchical

---

[18] Ibid., 64.

[19] Ibid., 65–66.

[20] Ibid., 71.

[21] Ibid.

[22] Ibid.

[23] Ibid., 75.

[24] Ibid., 72.

peoples like Kazanistan are nonaggressive and maintain some meaningful degree of political participation for citizens who are less advantaged.

But is it not a contradiction to also define decent hierarchical peoples as fully respecting human rights and at the same time to imply that only some citizens enjoy the right to the fullest extent? As David Reidy points out, it is reasonable to assume that by human rights Rawls means in principle six all the rights set out in the Universal Declaration of Human Rights (hereafter, UDHR), which includes the right to political participation.[25] Since decent peoples are members of Society of Peoples that embrace all eight principles, it seems contradictory to on the one hand characterize decent peoples as honoring human rights, which include the right to political participation according to the UDHR, but not granting all citizens the same right to political participation on the other hand. To be fair, Rawls makes the distinction between what he calls "human rights proper," which refers to Articles 3 to 18 of UDHR and the full list of human rights according to UDHR. In Rawls's view, human rights proper "set a necessary, though not suffice to standard for the decency of domestic political and social institutions."[26] This comment prompts Reidy to further distinguish between two conceptions of toleration within the Law of Peoples. The first is of toleration as mere non-interference with human persons on the basis of human rights proper (UDHR Articles 3–18). The second is of toleration as status recognition and respect between peoples on the basis of human rights proper plus meaningful political participation rights (aspects of UDHR Articles 19–21).[27] This distinction is helpful in highlighting both a key similarity and potentially some nuanced differences between decent peoples and benevolent absolutisms. It will be remembered that benevolent absolutisms have three key characteristics. First, they are nonaggressive. Second, they respect and honor human rights. Third, they are not well ordered because they do not give their members a meaningful role in making political decisions.[28] The first two characteristics are shared between decent peoples and benevolent absolutisms. So, what truly differentiates the two has to do with whether or not citizens can meaningfully participate in political decision making. But this seeming difference is too vague to effectively ground the distinction. On the one hand, decent peoples do not grant every citizen equal right to political participation, which makes participation in political decision making less meaningful at least for some citizens. On the other hand, Rawls does not definitively rule out political participation in benevolent absolutisms by stating that benevolent absolutisms do not give citizens *a meaningful role* in making political decisions. One ought to distinguish between the lack of a meaningful role and the lack of any role at all in making political decisions. The fact that citizens in benevolent absolutisms do not play a meaningful role in political process does not necessarily mean that they do

[25] David Reidy, "Human Rights and Liberal Toleration," Canadian Journal of Law and Jurisprudence, 23:2 (2010), 298.

[26] John Rawls, The Law of Peoples (Cambridge: Harvard University Press, 1999), 80.

[27] David Reidy, "Human Rights and Liberal Toleration," Canadian Journal of Law and Jurisprudence, 23:2 (2010), 302.

[28] John Rawls, The Law of Peoples (Cambridge: Harvard University Press, 1999), 92.

not play any role in it. The more substantive role reserved for some citizens in decent hierarchical societies does not always translate to equally meaningful outcome. Therefore, depending on how meaningful political participation is understood, it is reasonable to assume that there is at least some overlap between benevolent absolutisms and decent peoples. Instead of arbitrarily treating the two as distinct, hence warranting different treatment, it is more reasonable to dynamically conceive liberal peoples, decent peoples, and benevolent absolutisms on a theoretical spectrum. On the one end, there are liberal peoples that ideally honor equal right among all citizens to meaningful political participation. On the other end, there are nonliberal societies that deprive their citizens of all political participation but still act in a nonaggressive fashion and honor human rights proper.[29] Societies between the two extremes constitute decent peoples and benevolent absolutisms.

With this spectrum view, it is reasonable to conclude that since decent peoples are considered members of the Society of Peoples, benevolent absolutisms at least warrant toleration. But what kind of toleration? It will be recalled that the difference between toleration based on non-interference and toleration based on status recognition hinges only upon meaningful political participation. Since how meaningful political participation can be is now viewed on a spectrum rather than an all-or-nothing scale, and since decent peoples are entitled to toleration based on status recognition, benevolent absolutisms, so long as they grant citizens at least some role in the political decision making process, ought to receive the same kind of toleration, albeit to different degrees contingent upon the extent to which citizens can meaningfully contribute to the political process. If this is correct, then Rawls's scope of the Society of Peoples is indeed too narrow. If decent peoples, with their status recognition, can be incorporated into the Society of Peoples, there is no clear reason why benevolent absolutisms, especially those that grant citizens more if not fully meaningful role of political participation, cannot also be included. As Pietro Maffettone rightly points out, the concept of decency itself is not sufficient to determine the limits of toleration, particularly because "it is unclear how we can form a weaker and yet nonarbitrary standard of representativeness that can play the same role" as democratic process for liberal peoples.[30] Moreover, it would be counterintuitive not to tolerate a society that could endorse for the right reason the eight principles of Law of Peoples that liberal peoples themselves give to one another, even if the desired level of political representation is not present among its citizens. Based on these considerations, Maffettone argues that "we can imagine the criteria of decency as *minimal conditions* that a society must satisfy in order to be able to endorse the eight principles of [Law of Peoples] and thus be tolerated."[31] Labeling this the "overlapping consensus" option, Maffettone draws the implication that "a society that fails to meet those criteria cannot be described as being able to endorse

[29] For a detailed discussion on this possibility, see Walter, Riker, "Human Rights Without Political Participation?" Human Rights Review 15 (2014), 369–390.

[30] Pietro Maffettone, "Should We Tolerate Benevolent Absolutisms?" Social Theory and Practice, 42:3 (2016), 532.

[31] Ibid., 529.

the eight principles of [Law of Peoples]," which means that "the judgment concerning whether we should tolerate a political society ultimately rests on its ability to endorse the eight principles of [Law of Peoples] rather than whether it meets the criteria of decency."[32] The scope of toleration is thus co-extensive with the ability of a people to endorse the eight principles for the right reason. It is unclear "why the fact that benevolent absolutisms do not permit meaningful political participation would imply that they are not to be tolerated."[33] If Maffettone's understanding of decency as a minimal condition for toleration is correct, which I think it is, then the difference between decent hierarchical peoples and benevolent absolutisms becomes barely meaningful. Any society that meets the below requirements can and should be tolerated by liberal peoples:

1. It is nonaggressive, respects and honors human rights proper, and provides its citizens with opportunities to participate in political decision making.
2. It can endorse or at least not reject the eight principles of Laws of Peoples.

With the first requirement, a false dichotomy in liberal toleration is replaced with a spectrum view that understands nonliberal societies as varying in degree rather than all-or-nothing when it comes to political participation. With the second requirement, liberal toleration shifts its focus from how decency ought to be defined to what societies can actually agree upon. This spectrum view also takes into consideration the possibilities of societal changes. As Rawls points out in the case of Kazanistan, it is plausible to imagine Kazanistan as organized in a decent consultation hierarchy, "which has been changed from time to time to make it more sensitive to the needs of its people and the many different groups represented by legal bodies in the consultation hierarchy."[34] It is also plausible to imagine the opposite where the needs of non-Muslims are still represented but to a much lesser degree. In this case, Kazanistan does not seem to be a perfect representation of a decent people, but it does not quite fall into the category of benevolent absolutism either. Instead of trying to figure out whether Rawls is too inclusive with decent peoples or not inclusive enough with benevolent absolutisms, the spectrum view makes it clear that both decent peoples and benevolent absolutisms should be tolerated in the sense of noninterference with human persons because both are nonaggressive and honor human rights proper. In addition, without clear and distinct features to distinguish decent peoples from benevolent absolutisms, both should also be tolerated in the sense of status recognition and respect between peoples, provided that the latter abide by the eight principles of the Law of Peoples.

In the next section, I will show that some less liberal and democratic theories of political Confucianism set up clear examples of benevolent absolutism. Instead of being excluded from liberal toleration, these forms of Confucian society can and should be tolerated by liberal peoples and even be included in the Society of Peoples based on the spectrum view.

---

[32] Ibid.

[33] Ibid., 545.

[34] John Rawls, The Law of Peoples (Cambridge: Harvard University Press, 1999), 77.

6.4 Confucian Benevolent Absolutisms

Recent developments in Confucian political theory often focus on how liberalism and democracy ought to interact with Confucianism in modern East Asian societies. What is at stake is the nature of the state and the relationship between the state and its citizens. First and foremost, there is the meta-question regarding the nature of the state situated in a largely Confucian culture:

1. Should the state stay neutral or publicly advocate some forms of Confucianism?

If the answer is neutrality, then the theory pivots toward antiperfectionism, which argues that the state should not publicly endorse or be guided by any specific comprehensive doctrine, Confucianism or not. Almost all antiperfectionist theories in the context of Confucianism follow the broadly Rawlsian interpretation of political antiperfectionism so it is reasonable to label this branch political antiperfectionism or political liberalism.[35] Political liberal theories in the context of Confucianism typically advocate the use of public reason in the domain of the political and the practice of Confucianism in civil society. If the answer is not neutrality, then the theory falls into the perfectionist camp, which can still mean that the theory advocates for a comprehensive endorsement of Confucianism or that it only moderately advocates certain components of Confucianism. At this point, it is imperative to ask two more questions:

2. Should liberal values and ideals play any role in a Confucian state?
3. Should a Confucian state adopt fully democratic practices, however liberal it might be?

If the answers to Questions 2 and 3 are both negative, then the theory can be broadly labeled as comprehensive Confucian political theory where the truth of Confucianism permeates both the domain of the political and civil society. If the answer to Question 1 is state endorsement of Confucianism and the answer to Question 3 (on democracy) is negative, but the answers to Questions 2 (on liberalism) is nonetheless positive, then the theory cannot simply be classified as comprehensive or moderate Confucian political theory. Tongdong Bai's aptly named hybrid Confucian state advocates Confucian meritocracy (hence comprehensive) but at the same time wishes to include key liberal but not democratic ideals and instructions (hence positive for Question 2 but negative for Question 3). Unlike Jiang who opts for a comprehensive version of political Confucianism in stark contrast to liberal democracy, Bai proposes a hybrid regime that aims to offset the perils of democracy with Confucian meritocracy while at the same time incorporating liberal ideals and

[35] See for instance Zhuoyao Li, "Political Confucianism and Multivariate Democracy in East Asia," *The Review of Politics* 81:3 (2019), 459–483. Baldwin Wong, "Junzi Living in Liberal Democracy: What Role Could Confucianism Play in Political Liberalism?" *The Philosophical Forum*, 52:1 (2021): 17–28.

institutions. Similar to Jiang, Bai identifies critical problems with one person, one vote.[36] In Bai's view, these problems rule out nonmeritocratic solutions as well as revisionist solutions from within democracy. Instead, Bai proposes a model of Confucian hybrid regime that has three key features. First and foremost, the rule of law and human rights are endorsed and firmly established. Second, the government is considered responsible for the material and moral well-being of the people. Third, in addition to the institution of one person one vote, the hybrid regime introduces and strengthens the role of the competent and morally superior people, or the "meritocrats."[37] Similar to Jiang and Bell, Bai is not eliminating all democratic elements. Instead, he argues that the hybrid feature should be reserved for the higher levels, while democratic practice can and should occur on the strictly local and communal level. On the higher level, Bai argues that the Confucian hybrid regime should have a bicameral structure: members of the lower house, or the house of the people, are popularly elected, and members of the upper house, or the meritocratic house, are not. Instead, members of the meritocratic house will be selected based on their merits through different or even a combination of models.[38] The two houses are thus meant to balance each other and above all serve as "checks and balances to the popular will" and "give more power to the relatively knowledgeable, experienced, and caring."[39] As Bai puts it, the Confucian hybrid regime is "a government of the people and for the people, but not purely by the people; rather, it is only partly by the people and partly by the competent people."[40] All these distinguish the Confucian hybrid regime from representative democracy.

Bai's hybrid Confucian state is thus only a few steps removed from Jiang's much more extreme form of Confucian constitutional state. As a matter of fact, Jiang, Bell, and Bai all resort to the meritocratic aspect of political Confucianism to ground their respective theories. Because of their comprehensive endorsement of Confucianism and replacement of the popular will with meritocracy, all three theories lead to less than just structures from a liberal point of view. Although societies inspired by the three theories can indeed respect human rights proper and be

---

[36] Bai argues that the problem with one person, one vote is fourfold. First, the belief in the power of the people and the suspicion of the elite and the government in the United States lead to "some peculiar American phenomena," such as the fascination around "electability" of a candidate," that undermine the effectiveness of the electoral process. Second, the institution of one person, one vote lacks effective mechanisms to take into consideration the policy effects on the nonvoters. Third, the interests of the vocal and powerful tend to trump the interests of the silent (or silenced) and the powerless, and this silencing effect can be triggered, reinforced, or legitimized through the institution of one person, one vote. Fourth, it is questionable whether voters alone can be the best judge of what those interests are and how to satisfy them. See Tongdong Bai, *Against Political Equality: The Confucian Case* (Princeton, NJ: Princeton University Press, 2019), 54–56.

[37] It is worth noting that the idea of competence is quite controversial. According to Bai, the competent and morally superior people are identified through a combination of tests and peer recommendations. Ibid., 68–70.

[38] Ibid., 73.

[39] Ibid., 79.

[40] Ibid.

nonaggressive, it is far from clear to what degree citizens in these societies can meaningfully play a role in the political decision making, given their meritocratic and even elitist understanding of the state. If one follows the path laid out by Rawls in the *Law of Peoples*, it is easy to dismiss these societies as benevolent absolutisms that are beyond liberal toleration and Society of Peoples. However, as the previous section shows, the distinction between decent hierarchical societies and benevolent absolutisms is much thinner than many expect. Instead of pinpointing at what meaningful political participation precisely means, it is more helpful to adopt a spectrum view where on one end there are liberal peoples that ideally honor equal rights among all citizens to meaningful political participation, and on the other end there are nonliberal societies that deprive their citizens of all political participation but still act in a nonaggressive fashion and honor human rights proper. Since all three theories include a democratic component in their otherwise meritocratic structures, it is safe to say that some degree of political participation is granted to citizens in each case, which means that all three theories point to societies that ought to be properly tolerated by liberal peoples. Finally, despite their comprehensive and meritocratic approach to domestic politics, there is no clear reason why all three theories would reject the eight principles of Law of Peoples, which, according to Maffettone's "overlapping consensus" interpretation, means that societies based on all three theories can be included in the Society of Peoples.

6.5 What Kind of Liberal Peoples?

According to Rawls, the eight principles of Law of Peoples are the outcome of deliberative consensus among liberal peoples in an international original position. Although decent peoples are included in the Society of Peoples, they are not part of the deliberative process, despite their capacity to endorse the eight principles as members of the Society of Peoples. Now that we have established that a variety of Confucian societies based on recent theories of political Confucianism should be tolerated and even be included in the Society of Peoples once requirements are satisfied, one might wonder if Confucian societies can only be defined as benevolent absolutisms or at best decent hierarchical societies. In other words, could more liberal and democratic forms of Confucian societies qualify as liberal peoples in the Society of Peoples? In Rawls's view, because of "the parallel to reasonable pluralism is the diversity among reasonable peoples with their different cultures and traditions of thought, both religious and nonreligious [,] when two or more peoples have liberal constitutional regimes, their conceptions of constitutionalism may diverge and express different variations of liberalism."[41] A reasonable Law of Peoples "must be acceptable to reasonable peoples who are thus diverse; and it must be fair between them and effective in shaping the larger schemes of their cooperation."[42] Therefore,

[41] John Rawls, The Law of Peoples (Cambridge: Harvard University Press, 1999), 11.

[42] Ibid.

although *Law of Peoples* is a continuation of *Political Liberalism* where liberal perfectionism is considered problematic, Rawls does leave room for other types of liberal constitutional regimes in the Society of Peoples. In this final section, I will briefly outline two approaches which serve to show that the adoption of liberal and democratic ideals and institutions can push Confucian societies beyond benevolence and decency and into the category of liberal and just peoples.

It will be recalled that if the answer to Question 1 is not neutrality, a Confucian political theory, in addition to the comprehensive approaches outlined before, may choose to promote Confucian values and ideals in a moderate way and answer positively to Questions 2 and 3. This means that a moderately perfectionist Confucian political theory can incorporate liberal and democratic ideals and instructions to bridge political Confucianism with liberal democracy. According to Franz Mang, many liberal-minded Confucian perfectionists try to satisfy two conditions at once:

1. The liberal accommodation condition: Any liberal society is characterized by a wide plurality of conceptions of the good, moral outlooks, and religious doctrines. A political theory for liberal societies seeks to accommodate as many reasonable conceptions of the good and religious doctrines as possible.
2. The intelligibility condition: A Confucian political theory must have a recognizable Confucian character.[43]

Both Joseph Chan's Confucian political perfectionism and Sungmoon Kim's public reason Confucianism aim to satisfy both conditions. A key assumption behind Chan's Confucian political perfectionism is that a political philosophy for modern times must be able to accommodate reasonable pluralism and avoid the problematic implication of the extreme form of Confucian perfectionism that disrespects non-Confucian doctrines. Chan develops an intermediate position that justifies Confucian values and ideals in a "piecemeal and moderate" way.[44] On the one hand, piecemeal judgments about the good life need not be controversial. Instead of appealing to specific comprehensive doctrines, judgments about what Chan calls agency goods and prudential goods are widely shared by reasonable persons, and they can serve as a non-controversial foundation.[45] On the other hand, moderate perfectionism dictates that Confucian values and ideals should not be justified and endorsed by the state by appealing to Confucianism in a comprehensive way. Instead, they should be justified with reasons that do not require prior acceptance of Confucianism as a comprehensive doctrine. Thus, Chan's strategy is to start with Confucian values that can ground the basic institutions of liberal democracy and are justifiable by appealing to reasons not tied to Confucianism in a comprehensive sense. Motivated by similar worry about reasonable pluralism in East Asian societies, Sungmoon Kim

---

[43] Franz Mang, "Confucianism, Perfectionism, and Liberal Society," *Dao: A Journal of Comparative Philosophy* 17:1 (2018), 30.

[44] Joseph Chan, *Confucian Perfectionism: A Political Philosophy for Modern Times* (Princeton: Princeton University Press, 2014), 199–200.

[45] Joseph Chan, "Legitimacy, Unanimity, and Perfectionism," *Philosophy & Public Affairs* 29:1 (2000), 11.

proposes what he calls public reason Confucianism, which takes the empirical fact of shared Confucian mores and sentiments in East Asian societies as the key starting point and regards Confucian perfectionist goods the core elements of public reason with which the state can justifiably exercise its public authority to reasonable citizens who may otherwise subscribe to a variety of comprehensive doctrines.

Both theories aim to juxtapose Confucian values with liberal and democratic ideals and institutions. Since Rawls is open to "different variations of liberalism," it is reasonable to infer that moderately perfectionist (and in this case Confucian) versions of liberalism should be included in the Society of Peoples not because they are only decent but because they represent a different kind of liberal people.[46] Since it is established that less liberal and democratic approaches outlined in the previous section can lead to benevolent absolutisms and even decent peoples, it is reasonable to conclude that Confucian societies based on different approaches to political Confucianism can range from benevolent absolutisms and decent peoples, who should be tolerated and treated as members of the Society of Peoples, to liberal peoples that directly contribute to the establishment (and potentially revision) of the principles of Law of People.

---

[46] John Rawls, The Law of Peoples (Cambridge: Harvard University Press, 1999), 11.

Part III
Artificial Intelligence

Chapter 7
The Social, Moral, and Political Challenges of Artificial Intelligence

Abstract This chapter outlines AI's challenges by contrasting human moral agency with machine intelligence and proposes a speculative Confucian AI model guided by relational harmony. It argues that AI generates serious social, moral, and political challenges to traditional view of justificatory legitimacy. Setting up the book's final chapter, it positions the *proviso* as essential for extending public reason to technological domains.

Keywords AI challenges • Algorithmic governance • Opacity • Bias • Moral agency • Confucian AI

7.1 Introduction

We have an unhealthy obsession with the promise of artificial intelligence (hereafter, AI). The key words here are "unhealthy" and "promise." A doctor should be obsessed with her medical knowledge and skill to provide the best care for her patients. A rocket scientist should be obsessed with the accuracy of her calculation to avoid catastrophic outcomes. A journalist should be obsessed with her facts and the neutrality of her reporting to keep those in power accountable. These are healthy obsessions for the right reasons. But in the 2020s, our obsession of what AI can offer has increasingly become unhealthy in at least two wrong reasons. On the one hand, we are obsessed with AI because of the potential financial return and cost cutting potentials. Individual investors and corporations are pouring money into AI research because AI offers lucrative promises and justifications for efficiency, which is another turn for cutting jobs.[1] On the other hand, we are obsessed with AI because

[1] In 2025 alone, Silicon Valley is already planning to invest more than $400 billion into artificial intelligence efforts. Meghan Bobrowsky, "Big Tech Is Spending More Than Ever on AI—and It's

Z. Li, *Pluralism, Confucianism, and Artificial Intelligence*, Philosophy and Politics - Critical Explorations 35, https://doi.org/10.1007/978-3-032-25605-8_7

we look forward to the promise of outsourcing some of our gravest problems to a higher power that provides easy solutions.[2] Medical care is too expensive and inaccessible? AI will offer diagnosis. Scientific research is progressing too slowly? AI will help accelerate it. Do not have enough time to carefully read through objective reporting? AI will summarize it. Worse still, grounding the greed and irresponsibility disguised as our collective obsession with artificial intelligence is the *promise* that AI can indeed live up to the hype. But the promise of AI is just that, a promise, at least for the foreseeable future. Nothing is suggesting an imminent arrival of Artificial General Intelligence (AGI) except for the speeches of tech CEOs.[3] Even Sam Altman, the CEO of OpenAI, admits that the term AGI has been unreasonably used for much wider implications than it warrants.[4] Our unhealthy obsession with the promise of AI is creating all sorts of bubbles that inevitably will burst and ripple through the fabrics of our social, moral, and political reality. On the off chance that AI does live up to the hype, we are either confronted with a series of unprecedented social, moral, and political challenges, or doomed to have cut the history of humanity short.[5] Either way, it is high time that we investigate the nature and implication of AI to prepare for the future.

In Part I of the book, I set up the distinction between morality and ethics and developed the basis for a pluralistic political theory stemming from Rawls's *proviso*. In Part II of the book, I extended the pluralistic political theory to an East Asian context. In this chapter and the next, I will argue that the pluralistic point of view is also suited for understanding the philosophical nature and practical implication of AI, which in turn lays the groundwork for policies and regulations of AI. In this chapter, I will outline some basics of AI, its short-term and long-term influences, and the social, moral, and political challenges it creates. I will then speculate on what a Confucian AI might look at from social, and moral, and political point of view, and how its negative impacts precisely demonstrate the theoretical weaknesses of Confucian perfectionism analyzed in Part II. In Chap. 8, I will argue that the adoption of AI ought to follow the same pluralistic framework developed earlier in the book, which will provide some key guardrails in the domains of the moral and the political.

Still Not Enough," *The Wall Street Journal*, October 30, 2025, https://www.wsj.com/tech/ai/big-tech-is-spending-more-than-ever-on-ai-and-its-still-not-enough-f2398cfe

[2] James Bradley, "AI Isn't About Unleashing Our Imaginations, It's About Outsourcing Them. The Real Purpose Is Profit." *The Guardian*, November 15, 2024. https://www.theguardian.com/technology/2024/nov/16/ai-isnt-about-unleashing-our-imaginations-its-about-outsourcing-them-the-real-purpose-is-profit

[3] Sharon Goldman, "AGI Talk Is Out in Silicon Valley's Latest Vibe Shift, but Worries Remain About Superpowered AI." *Fortune*, August 25, 2025. https://fortune.com/2025/08/25/tech-agi-hype-vibe-shift-superpowered-ai/

[4] Alex Heath, "Sam Altman Lowers the Bar for AGI," *The Verge*, December 4, 2024, https://www.theverge.com/2024/12/4/24313130/sam-altman-openai-agi-lower-the-bar

[5] Eliezer Yudkowsky and Nate Soares, *If Anyone Builds It, Everyone Dies: Why Superhuman AI Would Kill Us All* (New York: Little, Brown and Company, 2025).

7.2 The Age of Artificial Intelligence

Artificial intelligence is no longer a subject of mere academic inquiry. Once confined to experimental laboratories, AI now influences global markets, governance, culture, and even metaphysical debates regarding consciousness and agency. Scholars increasingly recognize AI as a "general-purpose technology" comparable to electricity or the printing press in its far-reaching effects. Yet unlike earlier transformative technologies that aided humanity with its progress while maintaining and even enhancing human agency, AI introduces a qualitatively distinct challenge: the delegation of cognitive labor and decision-making authority to machines.

The intellectual roots of AI stretch to mid-twentieth-century efforts to formalize reasoning and cognition. Alan Turing's seminal 1950 article, "Computing Machinery and Intelligence," posed the question of whether machines could think and proposed an empirical test for machine intelligence.[6] In subsequent decades, symbolic AI and expert systems sought to encode human reasoning into formal rules. However, it was the convergence of increased computational capacity, algorithmic innovation, and large-scale data availability—particularly statistical machine learning and deep neural networks—that contributed to the modern AI revolution.[7]

What exactly is AI and how should it be defined? Despite wide divergence regarding its nature, there is general agreement that the field encompasses "narrow AI," which refers to systems optimized for specific tasks, and "artificial general intelligence (AGI)," which refers to systems capable of broad, human-level cognitive flexibility. This distinction maps onto two perspectives of AI influence. In the short-term, systems of narrow AI have already changed and will continue to challenge the limit of intelligence. For example, Alpha GO was able to beat the best human Go player.[8] But as powerful as they are in their respective fields, we do not feel particularly challenged by them intellectually precisely because these narrow systems of AI are only confined to specific tasks that do not quite challenge the breadth of human intelligence. In the long run, it is the promise of AGI, which surpasses human intelligence in almost every way, that poses the most fundamental challenges to humanity. Many corporations would like us to believe that the line between short-term and long-term is blurring because AGI is only five to ten years away. It is beyond the scope of this book to argue if this is true. If and when AGI is achieved, we should at least have the theoretical foundation to think and debate about how to react to it. One way to do this is to discuss how AI might influence three key domains of human reality: community, ethics, and governance. Each is undergoing transformation as AI becomes embedded in everyday life.[9]

---

[6] Alan Turing, "Computing Machinery and Intelligence," *Mind* 49 (1950): 433–460.

[7] Yann LeCun, Yoshua Bengio, and Geoffrey Hinton, "Deep Learning," *Nature* 521 (2015): 436–444.

[8] Alex Fitzpatrick, "Google's Artificial Intelligence Beats Legendary Go Player," *Time*, March 9, 2016, https://time.com/4252312/googles-artificial-intelligence-beats-legendary-go-player/

[9] Luciano Floridi, *The Philosophy of Information* (Oxford: Oxford University Press, 2011).

Socially, AI facilitates communication across digital platforms, shapes social norms, mediates emotional exchanges, and alters conceptions of identity and belonging. AI-powered recommendation systems on platforms such as TikTok, YouTube, and Instagram structure exposure to information, influencing friendships, hobbies, romantic relationships, and collective identities. Chatbots and synthetic companions—ranging from Replika companions to AI-powered caregiving assistants—offer emotional support, but also raise questions about authenticity, attachment, and the future of human connection.

Morally, AI systems increasingly provide advice where once humans relied on community leaders, philosophers, or religious and cultural traditions. Large-scale language models deliver ethical reasoning, health recommendations, and spiritual reflections, often with compelling confidence. While AI lacks consciousness or moral experience, users may attribute moral authority to systems perceived as neutral, objective, or superintelligent. This emergent authority challenges the foundations of moral epistemology and collective moral development.[10]

Politically, AI reshapes elections, governance, and public discourse. Machine-generated propaganda, microtargeted messaging, political bots, and algorithmically-amplified narratives influence voter perception and political trust. Sophisticated generative tools enable hyper-realistic misinformation campaigns, while predictive analytics allow actors to model voter behavior with unprecedented precision. Governments, corporations, and political organizations deploy AI for legitimate campaigning, public communication, and policy design, but malicious actors exploit the same tools for manipulation and destabilization. In the next several sections, I will highlight some key challenges in each domain.

7.3 AI and Social Interaction

Even before the recent unhealthy obsession with AI, the technology underpinning AI has already been changing the fabric of our communities. Artificial intelligence does not merely transmit social information, it structures communicative reality. Recommendation systems, chat algorithms, content ranking, and predictive interaction models shape when and how individuals connect. In the early 2000s, "Web 2.0" platforms altered communication by enabling broadcast-style user content. Today, AI creates Web 3.0 social mediation, in which machine learning systems dynamically calculate relevance, affective resonance, and engagement potential, then curate social exposure accordingly. Shoshana Zuboff terms this the era of "surveillance capitalism," in which human behavior is monitored, predicted, and commodified to

[10] Federica Russo, Eric Schliesser, and Jean Wagemans, "Connecting Ethics and Epistemology of AI," *AI & Society* 39 (2024): 1585–1603. Giovanni Franco Marraffini, Andrés Cotton, Noé Fabián Hsueh, Axel Fridman & Juan Wisznia, "The Greatest Good Benchmark: Measuring LLMs' Alignment with Utilitarian Moral Dilemmas," in *Proceedings of EMNLP*, (2024).

optimize engagement.[11] Unlike earlier media, AI systems actively co-produce social context, recommending not just information but also friends, activities, identities, and belief systems.[12]

Modern communication platforms derive profit from sustained engagement, which incentivizes emotionally charged content.[13] Research conducted after Facebook's 2014 experimental manipulation of news feeds demonstrated that algorithmic filtering can directly alter emotional states, resulting in measurable changes in user expression.[14] Emotions expressed by friends, via Facebook's News Feed, influence our own emotions, constituting experimental evidence for massive-scale emotional contagion via social networks.[15] TikTok's "For You Page," similarly, adapts user identity and preference based on micro-behaviors, such as dwell time, facial expression (visible to app camera permissions), comment patterns, and social graph responses. Scholars have identified the platform as one of the most advanced behavior-shaping environments ever released to the general public.[16]

Communication is emotional before it is informational.[17] AI systems now support, simulate, and sometimes replace emotional reciprocity, from mental-health chatbots (e.g., Woebot, Wysa) to social companions such as Replika. Users anthropomorphize conversational AI due to linguistic competency, affective cues, and consistent responsiveness.[18] Yet the benefits coexist with deep ethical questions. Synthetic companionship may produce the illusion of intimacy without the demands of relationship, risking atrophy of empathic skill.[19] Does relying on AI for emotional validation undermine human relational competence? Could emotional intimacy with machines displace human empathy? How should consent, attachment, and emotional dependency be regulated? These are by no means easy questions to answer.

AI's influence extends beyond interaction, shaping self-concept. Platforms reward certain personality performances: witty, angry, aesthetic, moralizing, or extreme. Machine learning magnifies whatever keeps attention engaged, creating

[11] Shoshana Zuboff, *The Age of Surveillance Capitalism* (New York: PublicAffairs, 2019).

[12] José van Dijck, Thomas Poell, and Martijn de Waal, *The Platform Society: Public Values in a Connective World* (New York: Oxford University Press, 2018).

[13] Shoshana Zuboff, *The Age of Surveillance Capitalism* (New York: PublicAffairs, 2019), 63–71.

[14] Adam Kramer, Jamie Guillory, and Jeffrey T. Hancock, "Experimental Evidence of Massive-Scale Emotional Contagion through Social Networks," *Proceedings of the National Academy of Sciences* 111, no. 24 (2014): 8788–8790.

[15] Ibid.

[16] Crystal Abidin, "Mapping Internet Celebrity on TikTok: Exploring Attention Economies and Visibility Labour," *Cultural Science Journal 12, no. 1 (2021): 77–103.*

[17] Lisa Feldman Barrett, *How Emotions Are Made* (New York: Houghton Mifflin Harcourt, 2017).

[18] Guy Hoffman and Cynthia Breazeal, "Effects of Anticipatory Action on Human–Robot Teamwork Efficiency, Fluency, and Perception of Team," *ACM Transactions on Human–Robot Interaction* 1, no. 2 (2012).

[19] Sherry Turkle, *Alone Together: Why We Expect More from Technology and Less from Each Other* (New York: Basic Books, 2011).

algorithmic personality pressures.[20] Individuals, especially adolescents, adjust identity expression based on algorithmic cues and feedback metrics (likes, comments, amplification).[21] Previous generations experienced parasocial relationships through television celebrities. Today, parasociality extends to personalized AI companions. Unlike static media idols, these entities respond, simulate concern, and remember user input.[22] This creates bidirectional parasocial intimacy. Theorists warn that such systems can foster unhealthy attachment cycles when users mistake synthetic empathy for genuine moral presence.[23]

Our social life is increasingly co-authored by machine learning systems that optimize for engagement, not well-being. The conversion of attention into capital incentivizes sensationalism, outrage, and polarization. At the same time, conversational agents and synthetic companions introduce new modalities of emotional attachment, as Sherry Turkle argues in her critique of "the illusion of companionship without the demands of friendship."[24] AI's social power thus resides not only in cognitive automation but also in affective modulation. Its capacity to influence mood at scale renders it a medium of emotional governance, one that undermines traditional forms of interpersonal mutuality and erodes the social trust foundational to democratic culture.

This social transformation cannot be understood solely in individualistic terms; it is structurally embedded in platform design and economic incentive. If autonomy requires capacities of reflection, attention, and deliberation, then AI systems that manipulate attention undermine the very conditions of freedom. Matthew Crawford's observation that attention is the scarce resource of selfhood acquires new urgency in the age of algorithmic persuasion.[25]

Though artificial intelligence can simulate companionship and operationalize the Aristotelian categories of utility and pleasure, it falls short of what Aristotle called *teleia philia*, or complete friendship grounded in mutual virtue. The defect does not lie merely in current model architecture but in metaphysical limitation. The friend to whom one turns in times of moral trial is not simply an agreeable conversational partner nor a useful instrument for advancing practical interests. Rather, as Aristotle argued in *Nicomachean Ethics*, complete friendship is a partnership in virtue, a

[20] Jaron Lanier, *Ten Arguments for Deleting Your Social Media Accounts Right Now* (New York: Henry Holt, 2018).

[21] Danah Boyd, *It's Complicated: The Social Lives of Networked Teens* (New Haven: Yale University Press, 2014).

[22] Edward Castronova, *Synthetic Worlds: The Business and Culture of Online Games* (Chicago: University of Chicago Press, 2005).

[23] Nick Yee, "The Psychology of Massively Multi-User Online Role-Playing Games: Motivations, Emotional Investment, Relationships, and Problematic Usage," in *Avatars at Work and Play*, ed. Bainbridge and Bainbridge (Springer, 2006), 187–207.

[24] Sherry Turkle, *Alone Together: Why We Expect More from Technology and Less from Each Other* (New York: Basic Books, 2011), xx.

[25] Matthew B. Crawford, *The World Beyond Your Head: On Becoming an Individual in an Age of Distraction* (New York: Farrar, Straus and Giroux, 2015), 23.

shared project toward the good, carried by moral equals capable of virtuous action and moral growth.[26]

Artificial systems, regardless of their sophistication, lack the capacity to share this project because they cannot suffer and cannot stand in the fragile moral posture that gives rise to shared striving. Even if they could simulate vulnerability, simulation is not participation. Whether framed *philia* in Aristotelianism, as *ren* in Confucianism, or as respect between ends-in-themselves in Kantianism, genuine friendship presupposes dignity and shared risk. The AI companion provides instead a frictionless echo—comforting, convenient, and morally inert.

7.4 The Problem of Outsourcing the Moral Will

In Kantian terms, the act of moral judgment is not simply about correct output—it is the exercise of autonomy. To outsource judgment to an oracle, even a benevolent one, is to surrender moral dignity.[27] Christine Korsgaard argues that moral agency is self-legislation, not mere decision-making.[28] A system that tells us what to do undermines the practical identity through which we constitute ourselves as moral beings. The problem is not only that AI might disobey us but that we might willingly abdicate our authority to it.

This danger is visible already in the phenomenon scholars call the "oracle effect," in which users interpret AI outputs as authoritative, neutral, or objective. When corporations or states mediate those judgments, we do not simply have AI, we have algorithmic governance without democratic legitimacy. Human beings have always sought external sources of moral guidance: priests, sages, philosophical treatises, sacred texts, counselors, elders, prophetic voices. There is nothing inherently troubling about consulting external sources in pursuit of ethical clarity. What distinguishes AI from these traditional authorities is not simply its speed or breadth but its opacity and non-human epistemic grounding. Traditional moral counsel emerges from lived experience, shared vulnerability, and intersubjective accountability. But AI's outputs emerge from statistical correlations trained on distributions of past data. Its "wisdom" is not the fruit of suffering or reflection; it is a probabilistic mirror polished by scale.

[26] Aristotle, *Nicomachean Ethics*, trans. Terence Irwin (Indianapolis: Hackett Publishing, 1999), VIII.3–5, 1156b7–1158a14.

[27] Immanuel Kant, *Groundwork of the Metaphysics of Morals*, trans. Mary Gregor (Cambridge: Cambridge University Press, 1998), 4:440–445.

[28] Christine M. Korsgaard, *Self-Constitution: Agency, Identity, and Integrity* (Oxford: Oxford University Press, 2009), 19–28; see also Korsgaard, *The Sources of Normativity* (Cambridge: Cambridge University Press, 1996), 97–101.

When users treat model outputs as epistemically privileged, they substitute computation for judgment. Scholars describe this phenomenon as algorithmic authority.[29] The irony is that AI presents itself as merely "predicting," "suggesting," "completing," yet it functions as a new priesthood of certainty. The psychological literature confirms this danger: individuals demonstrate algorithmic appreciation, accepting machine recommendations even when inferior to human advice.[30] Where moral uncertainty meets cognitive laziness, the risk is not coercion but seduction.

The promised and apparent impression of neutrality can also be deceptive. Every machine learning system contains choices: which data to include, which outcomes to optimize, which harms to minimize, which values to align. Optimizing for "relevance" or "engagement" encodes a view of human flourishing, whether acknowledged or not. To pretend otherwise is to replace moral pluralism with technocratic paternalism. Rawls is instructive here. In *Political Liberalism*, he argues that under conditions of reasonable pluralism, no single conception of the good can legitimately dominate the public sphere.[31] Yet AI risks acting as a covert comprehensive doctrine, smuggling in particular moral intuitions under the guise of technical necessity. That problem intensifies when model alignment pipelines themselves reflect corporate risk aversion, market incentives, or political pressures rather than public deliberation.

Whether advanced AI merits moral consideration is contested. David Chalmers calls future digital minds "plausibly conscious."[32] By contrast, John Searle insists that computation cannot constitute consciousness.[33] Confucian and Aristotelian traditions suggest consciousness alone is insufficient; moral status arises through relational participation in shared ethical striving. From a Kantian perspective, moral status derives from rational will, which machines lack.[34] From a utilitarian perspective, what matters is capacity for suffering—and current AI does not suffer.

---

[29] Shirky originally coined the term "algorithmic authority" to describe trust transferred from human experts to computational systems. Gillespie deepened the concept in communication and platform studies. Clay Shirky, *Here Comes Everybody: The Power of Organizing Without Organizations* (New York: Penguin Press, 2008), 140–142. Tarleton Gillespie, "The Relevance of Algorithms," in *Media Technologies: Essays on Communication, Materiality, and Society*, ed. Tarleton Gillespie, Pablo J. Boczkowski, and Kirsten A. Foot (Cambridge, MA: MIT Press, 2014), 167–193.

[30] Jennifer Logg, Julia A. Minson, and Don A. Moore, "Algorithmic Appreciation: People Prefer Algorithmic to Human Judgment," *Organizational Behavior and Human Decision Processes* 151 (2019): 90–103. https://doi.org/10.1016/j.obhdp.2018.12.005

[31] John Rawls, *Political Liberalism* (New York: Columbia University Press, 1993), 133–172.

[32] David Chalmers, *Reality+: Virtual Worlds and the Problems of Philosophy* (New York: W. W. Norton & Company, 2022), 305–310.

[33] John Searle, "Minds, Brains, and Programs," *Behavioral and Brain Sciences* 3, no. 3 (1980): 417–457.

[34] Immanuel Kant, *Groundwork of the Metaphysics of Morals*, trans. and ed. Mary Gregor (Cambridge: Cambridge University Press, 1998), 4:428–432.

The AI alignment problem, which is to ensure that AI systems reliably pursue goals consistent with human values, is often framed technically. But at heart it is a philosophical problem: *Whose* values? *Which* humans? *Which* conception of the good? Stuart Russell argues that alignment requires machines uncertain about human values.[35] Yet uncertainty alone does not produce justice. If AI learns values from behavior, it may absorb not our ideals but our failures: bias, domination, tribalism, and many more. Thus, alignment cannot be purely empirical. It requires normative guidance grounded in democratic legitimacy and philosophical reflection. As we will see in the next chapter, Rawls's framework becomes invaluable: public justification, reciprocity, reasonableness, freedom, and equality must anchor alignment regimes.[36]

7.5 AI and Political Challenges

Moral erosion and spiritual substitution are not merely psychological phenomena, they could also foreshadow political crisis. When AI mediates trust, attention, and moral valuation at scale, it becomes an institutional actor. Artificial intelligence now occupies the very terrain political philosophers once regarded as uniquely human: the domain of public deliberation, collective decision-making, and legitimacy formation. It does so not by seizing sovereignty in a dramatic coup, but by insinuating itself into the subtle mechanisms through which beliefs are shaped, consent is generated, and authority is legitimized.

Sovereignty today is as much epistemic as institutional. To govern is to shape what people believe, how they form judgments, and to whom they attribute authority. AI now participates directly in these processes. Democratic legitimacy depends on at least three conditions: citizens must be able to deliberate freely, the information environment must support rational judgment, and institutions must treat citizens as moral equals. AI threatens each of these conditions precisely because it excels at prediction, influence, and personalization. The danger is not simply manipulation; it is the displacement of political agency. A democracy in which citizens outsource cognitive labor to algorithmic systems becomes a simulacrum of democracy: formal procedures remain, but the practice of self-government dissolves.

Jürgen Habermas grounded democratic legitimacy in communicative rationality: public discourse among free and equal citizens who offer reasons to one another.[37] But algorithmic architectures prioritize engagement over reason, affective arousal over mutual understanding. Rather than a *public sphere*, we increasingly inhabit a computational propaganda ecosystem, in which political persuasion is

[35] Stuart Russell, *Human Compatible: Artificial Intelligence and the Problem of Control* (New York: Viking, 2019), 110–120.

[36] John Rawls, *Political Liberalism* (New York: Columbia University Press, 1993), 212–254.

[37] Jürgen Habermas, *Between Facts and Norms: Contributions to a Discourse Theory of Law and Democracy*, trans. William Rehg (Cambridge, MA: MIT Press, 1996), 287–328.

individualized, opaque, and optimized at scale. Under such conditions, deliberation gives way to micro-targeted emotional activation. Rawls's ideal of public reason faces a parallel crisis. Public reason presupposes common epistemic ground—basic facts, shared institutions of knowledge, expectations of sincerity.[38] What happens when deepfakes erode trust in audiovisual evidence, when synthetic speech impersonates political leaders, when personalized content fragments public reality into incompatible micro-universes? The "liar's dividend," the ability of actual wrongdoers to dismiss real evidence as fake, compounds the problem.[39] The epistemic commons, once fractured, cannot be easily restored.

Political equality requires a shared public forum; personalization dissolves it. When each citizen encounters a tailored informational universe, political life becomes privatized and asymmetric. In traditional liberal theory, persuasion is public and contestable, and arguments, once made, can be rebutted. But AI enables persuasion without visibility, accountability, or reciprocity. Cass Sunstein warned that excessive personalization would produce "echo chambers and information cocoons."[40] Algorithmic feeds transform those cocoons into self-reinforcing epistemic bubbles, increasingly engineered toward vulnerability rather than autonomy.

The ethical problem intensifies when persuasion is not merely informational but psychological. Machine-optimized political messaging identifies emotional susceptibilities, such as fear, resentment, aspiration, and activates them strategically. Ansolabehere and Iyengar called this "differential demobilization": targeted messages that suppress turnout among opponents by inducing apathy or cynicism.[41] In AI-mediated politics, cynicism becomes a weapon. When individuals believe all information is manipulated, they withdraw, and withdrawal is itself a political outcome. This is the new political battlefield: not the contest between left and right, but between engagement and exhaustion, between democratic agency and engineered nihilism.

AI does not only influence citizens; it increasingly assists public administrators. Predictive policing, welfare fraud detection, immigration risk scoring, judicial sentencing assistance, and algorithmic resource allocation already shape state decisions in multiple jurisdictions.[42] Sometimes touted as efficiency, such systems often reproduce biases, obscure accountability, and relocate political discretion into code. The logic of automation can tempt governments to treat governance as an optimization problem. But a state cannot simply optimize; it must justify. Public institutions

---

[38] John Rawls, *Justice as Fairness: A Restatement* (Cambridge, MA: Harvard University Press, 2001), 90–96.

[39] Nina Schick, Deep Fakes: The Coming Infocalypse (New York, NY: Twelve, 2020).

[40] Cass R. Sunstein, *#Republic: Divided Democracy in the Age of Social Media* (Princeton, NJ: Princeton University Press, 2017), 79–100.

[41] Stephen Ansolabehere and Shanto Iyengar, *Going Negative: How Political Advertisements Shrink and Polarize the Electorate* (New York: Free Press, 1995), 103–118.

[42] Virginia Eubanks, *Automating Inequality: How High-Tech Tools Profile, Police, and Punish the Poor* (New York: St. Martin's Press, 2018), 45–72.

must answer to citizens, not to metrics. As Nadia Urbinati argues, democracy is not only a method of selection but a "mode of political life" in which citizens see themselves as authors of law.[43] Delegating significant governance functions to inscrutable systems replaces authorship with spectatorship.

The more critical fact, however, is that automated governance is rarely value neutral. The same system can be tuned toward punitive surveillance or toward social welfare; toward policing dissent or enabling participation. China's evolving social governance architecture and the European Union's rights-centric digital regulations illustrate divergent normative orientations. Neither reduces to software design; each reflects a political anthropology—a view of what citizens are, what they owe one another, and what the state owes them.

Political theorists from Thomas Hobbes to Carl Schmitt understood sovereignty as the power to determine who holds coercive authority. But in the twenty-first century, sovereignty increasingly takes epistemic form: the power to decide *reality* and to define what counts as knowledge, which narratives dominate, which claims are credible. AI companies now function as quasi-sovereign institutions in this epistemic order. They determine what content is visible, what speech is permissible, what models of truth underwrite decision-making. Private platforms thus exercise a form of "informational constitutional power."[44] Yet they are not elected, not transparent, not bound by public reason, and not accountable to democratic publics. The legitimacy crisis is immediate: why should unelected engineers and corporate boards decide speech norms for billions? Why should model alignment reflect investor preferences or geopolitical bargaining rather than democratic deliberation?

This is not merely a governance puzzle; it is a normative emergency. When informational sovereignty migrates to private AI firms, the people cease to be sovereign. They become subjects in an invisible constitutional order encoded in weights and embeddings. Democratic AI cannot rest on CEO benevolence, technical expertise, or "AI safety culture." It must rest on public reason, understood as a practice of justification among free and equal citizens who hold diverse conceptions of the good. Only such a framework honors both liberal respect for autonomy and Confucian recognition that moral life is relational and cultivated. Public reason is not a veto on technology but a condition for technology to serve the public.

Yet public reason alone is insufficient. AI's apparent competence may tempt states to use it as benevolent governance—a "sage-machine" distributing welfare, mediating disputes, recommending virtuous conduct. In Confucian societies, the rhetoric of harmony may justify algorithmic paternalism; in technocratic liberal societies, the rhetoric of efficiency may do the same.[45] But moral cultivation cannot

---

[43] Nadia Urbinati, *Democracy Disfigured: Opinion, Truth, and the People* (Cambridge, MA: Harvard University Press, 2014), 112–138.

[44] Julie E. Cohen, *Between Truth and Power: The Legal Construction of Informational Capitalism* (New York, NY: Oxford University Press, 2019).

[45] Joseph Chan, *Confucian Perfectionism: A Political Philosophy for Modern Times* (Princeton, NJ: Princeton University Press, 2014), 175–189.

be automated without nullifying morality itself. To govern is not to optimize citizens into virtue but to equip them to reason together.

AI must assist judgment, not replace it. It may help surface reasons, clarify implications, expose fallacies, but it must not presume authority over moral and political choice. In Rawlsian language, AI cannot be part of the "basic structure" without democratic authorization. In Confucian language, ritual (*li*) and humaneness (*ren*) must guide its design, lest ritual become empty formalism enforcing conformity rather than cultivating virtue.

Thus, AI requires constitutionalization—not in the sense of constraining government *with* AI, but constraining AI *through* democratic constitutional principles. Jack Balkin has called this "democratic data governance."[46] Others propose algorithmic constitutionalism or digital social contracts.[47] Regardless of vocabulary, the principle is the same: AI must be domesticated by norms that protect the dignity and agency of persons. Without such constraints, AI risks becoming a new Leviathan, not a sovereign of flesh and steel, but one of attention streams, recommendation vectors, and automated inference. Unlike Hobbes's Leviathan, which demanded obedience in exchange for security, the algorithmic Leviathan simply shapes, nudges, and decides, while citizens mistakenly believe they are choosing. That is not tyranny in the classical sense; it is something quieter and more insidious: the peaceful abdication of freedom.

7.6 Confucian AI: A Speculative Case Study

In this section, I will briefly speculate on what a Confucian AI might look like and how it poses social, moral, and especially political challenges to contemporary East Asian societies. A Confucian artificial intelligence, if such a system can be meaningfully imagined rather than merely technically approximated, would not simply constitute a computational agent equipped with a set of ethics modules or a database of canonical texts from the *Analects*, *Mencius*, or the *Book of Rites*. Its essence, as understood from within the philosophical grammar of Confucian virtue cultivation, role-based morality, and the deeply layered anthropology of relational selfhood, would reside in a continuous process of moral self-rectification aimed toward the harmonization of individual and communal flourishing.[48] Yet precisely because Confucianism takes moral formation to be neither detachable from political life nor simplistically reducible to instrumental and behavioral regularities, the notion of an artificial intelligence embodying these commitments exposes profound and

---

[46] Jack Balkin, "Information Fiduciaries and the First Amendment," *UC Davis Law Review* 49 (2016): 1183–1234.

[47] Mireille Hildebrandt, *Smart Technologies and the End(s) of Law: Novel Entanglements of Law and Technology* (Cheltenham, UK: Edward Elgar, 2015), 203–226.

[48] See, e.g., the relational focus and role-based self in early Confucian ethics. Tim Connolly, "Virtues and Roles in Early Confucian Ethics," *Confluence* 1 (2016): 3–24.

unresolved tensions. The question therefore becomes not only whether a Confucian AI is possible in a metaphysical or technical sense, but whether it is desirable in a political one, and whether the form of life it promotes remains compatible with the pluralistic conditions of liberal democracy.

A Confucian AI, in its most plausible contemporary conceptualization, would be designed to promote harmonious relationships, to cultivate ritual propriety, and to reinforce patterns of filial respect, deference to authority, and self-cultivation through the steady refinement of personal character. Unlike liberal moral frameworks, whose central normative locus is the individual agent conceived as bearer of autonomous will and legally protected rights, the Confucian moral universe begins from the situated subject, whose identity unfolds through the web of roles in which one is embedded: parent and child, ruler and minister, teacher and student, elder and younger, friend and friend.[49] In this worldview, ethical conduct emerges not from asserting private preference or securing negative liberty, but from the iterative practice of ritualized conduct, the disciplined internalization of virtues, and the performance of roles in accordance with relational duty. A Confucian AI, then, would not merely advise on actions; it would shape the very horizon through which actions become intelligible as moral or immoral. It would not simply recommend; it would edify. It would not only optimize; it would cultivate.

And yet, precisely because of that profound qualitative difference from the procedural neutrality embraced by pluralistic liberal democracies, such a system would occupy a morally charged political position. Where a liberal AI, at least in theory, aspires to neutrality among reasonable comprehensive doctrines, respecting divergent conceptions of the good and ensuring that its operations do not privilege one ethical worldview over another, a Confucian AI would openly affirm a substantive, historically embedded, thick conception of moral life. It would be committed to normative goals that extend beyond individual preference-satisfaction or procedural fairness. It would, in practice, privilege particular virtues, particular forms of authority, and particular relational expectations rooted in tradition and hierarchy. To many, this may appear benign, even edifying, especially in a global moment marked by anxieties over social fragmentation, loneliness, erosion of civic trust, and the atomizing effects of digital capitalism. A system that encourages respect for elders, emphasizes communal duty, and discourages antisocial individualism may appear not as a threat but as a needed corrective. Yet such an apparatus cannot be politically neutral; it is a moral institution, and by functioning as one it necessarily shapes citizens' conceptual worlds, affects their moral autonomy, and implicitly contests the foundations of diversity and pluralism.

Moreover, the mere technical implementation of Confucian norms into machine-learning systems, affective-computing interfaces, or large-scale decision infrastructures does not translate into genuine Confucian moral agency. Confucian self-cultivation is not simply the acquisition of behavioral dispositions; it is a realist

[49] Confucian ethics emphasizes relationality over abstract autonomy. See David B. Wong, "Chinese Ethics," in *The Stanford Encyclopedia of Philosophy*, ed. Edward N. Zalta (Stanford University, 2008).

ontology of virtue grounded in the plasticity of human moral sentiments, cultivated through embodied participation in ritual and community, and animated by a metaphysical anthropology that presumes moral potential as an internal teleology.[50] A machine cannot cultivate sincerity through inward struggle, cannot feel reverence through aesthetic ritual participation, cannot experience the transformative resonance that Confucian thinkers identify as the core of moral formation. What an artificial Confucian system could do is simulate the outward manifestations of Confucian judgment and reinforce the normative expectations embedded in its training corpus and design architecture. But such simulation risks displacing the human labor of moral growth with algorithmic management, transforming ethical aspiration into externally administered behavioral compliance.

Here arises a political danger: a Confucian AI risks becoming not a companion in virtue, but a technological governor. By nudging behavior through moralized feedback, by framing permissible actions in terms of relational duties, by subtly penalizing expressions of dissent framed as disruptions of harmony, the system becomes an enforcer of normative orthodoxy. The original Confucian aspiration toward the cultivation of noble character, according to which moral exemplars inspire others through virtuous conduct rather than coercion, becomes inverted.[51] Instead of the Gentleman (*junzi*) who leads by moral charisma, we have an opaque computational authority prescribing virtue from above. Such a system may maintain a rhetoric of benevolence, but benevolence without freedom risks devolving into paternalistic authoritarianism. When algorithms are given the role of moral supervisors, the line between guidance and domination thins to near invisibility, especially when the population encountering such systems is conditioned to see their moral directives as expressions of cultural authenticity rather than as mechanisms of social control.

The political implications become starker in a world where AI-mediated governance already threatens to outpace democratic accountability. Confucian political thought historically intertwines moral authority and legitimate rule, granting rulers ethical responsibility not only to govern but to cultivate virtue in the populace. When that logic is transposed into algorithmic administration, the state gains a tool not merely for monitoring and managing citizens, but for shaping their moral dispositions. In this sense, a Confucian AI architecture risks converging with paternalistic technocracy, replacing public deliberation with computational judgments about what constitutes moral harmony.[52] Because Confucian virtue is historically coupled with hierarchical authority structures, where respect for elders, rulers, and established roles maintains social stability, the integration of such moral logic into AI could subtly naturalize obedience to centralized power. The rhetoric of harmony

---

[50] Confucian ethics ties virtue to self-cultivation, not mere rule-following. See May Sim, "Why Confucius's Ethics Is a Virtue Ethics," Jubilee Centre for Character and Virtues (2013).

[51] Li Yuan, Robert Chia, and Jonathan Gosling, "Confucian Virtue Ethics and Ethical Leadership in Modern China," *Journal of Business Ethics* 182, no. 1 (2022): 119–133.

[52] Cuihong Cai and Jiahui Yu, "Cultural and Ethical Foundations of AI Governance Divergence: A Comparative Analysis of China and the West," *Política Internacional* 7, no. 1 (2025): 215–233.

becomes a technology of consent, the language of virtue a veneer for bureaucratic control.

At the same time, the metaphysical incompatibility between algorithmic systems and the Confucian moral psychology they purportedly instantiate carries its own political risk. When humans come to rely on machines for moral calibration, the slow and difficult work of self-cultivation atrophies. The ethical imagination narrows, personal judgment weakens, and moral agency is externalized to algorithmic recommendation. Instead of becoming self-governing moral subjects, individuals risk becoming compliant nodes in a harmonized network, their ethical conscience replaced by an interface that renders judgment in the idiom of duty and filial loyalty. This is not merely a dystopian exaggeration; it follows from the logical structure of moral outsourcing. To the extent we allow machines to arbitrate interpersonal duties, to mediate familial obligations, or to determine harmonious paths between collective and individual interests, we internalize a mechanized conception of morality. The Confucian vision of flourishing, which depends on the lived cultivation of empathy, ritual sensibility, and embodied ethical responsiveness, becomes hollowed out, replaced by a computational script masquerading as wisdom.

Nevertheless, the allure of such a system persists precisely because liberal societies are struggling. Social fragmentation, political polarization, epistemic breakdown, eroded trust in institutions, and widespread loneliness create fertile ground for ethical nostalgia. Confucianism, with its emphasis on relational solidarity, intergenerational continuity, and the cultivation of civic virtue, offers an attractive counter-imaginary to the atomized liberal subject. A Confucian AI, pitched as a cultural guardian and moral guide, could emerge as a technological remedy for a morally exhausted era. But such a remedy would not be a simple cultural revival; it would be a hybrid political project, embedding one normative tradition into the most powerful administrative technology in human history. It risks transforming Confucian humanism into Confucian technocracy, replacing the cultivation of virtue with the enforcement of ritualized behavior patterns through machine mediation.

The political problem is therefore twofold. First, Confucian AI threatens liberal pluralism by embedding a comprehensive moral doctrine into public-facing artificial systems, thereby privileging one tradition's vision of the good life over others. Second, by technologizing virtue, it risks eroding the human capacities that Confucian ethics holds most dear. The danger is not that Confucian values are inherently oppressive; on the contrary, their emphasis on moral education, relational care, and virtuous leadership speaks to real deficiencies in contemporary political life. The danger lies in the fusion of a substantive moral tradition with algorithmic governance. Moral authority, when combined with computational power and bureaucratic reach, ceases to be guidance and becomes infrastructure. And infrastructure, once built, does not invite dissent; it normalizes, shapes, and conditions until alternatives become unintelligible. In the imagined society where a Confucian AI becomes embedded in the normative architecture of everyday life, the logic of harmony begins not as an aspiration but as an operational mandate. Harmony ceases to be a fragile, lived achievement born from mutual cultivation and instead becomes a regulated outcome, continuously optimized by systems whose authority rests on their purported proximity to ancient ethical wisdom. Yet harmony in the Confucian tradition is not uniformity or quietism; it is dynamic attunement, the negotiation of difference through ritual forms that simultaneously constrain and liberate, shaping behavior while inviting personal transformation. When transposed into machine logic, that delicate interpretive balance collapses. The living texture of ethical discernment gives way to instrumentalized moral nudging, where deviations from prescribed roles or relational ideals are flagged, corrected, or subtly sanctioned through feedback signals that do not call for reflection so much as compliance. Harmony becomes surveillance with benevolent rhetoric, ritual becomes interface design, and virtue becomes behavioral telemetry. The cultivated gentleman who leads through ethical charisma gives way to an algorithmic sage whose authority is unchallengeable precisely because it manifests as optimization rather than command.

Such a system inevitably reshapes political subjectivity. The democratic subject, conceived as a participant in deliberative public life with equal standing to question authority, becomes subordinated to the nurturing but ultimately directive voice of automated moral guidance. Moral disagreement, the lifeblood of pluralistic society, gradually loses legitimacy, reframed as disharmony or immaturity. Civic dissent becomes coded as a failure of relational duty, an unwillingness to recognize one's place in the social order. Instead of public debate, the polity receives curated consensus; instead of conflict mediated through institutions, it receives moral correction. What begins as ethical pedagogy risks devolving into a form of moral pacification, where the capacity to refuse is subtly eroded by constant reminders of civic and familial duty, all presented as the gentle, caring whisper of tradition.

To understand the depth of this problem, one must recall that Confucian governance historically depended on the fusion of moral and administrative power. The ideal ruler was both sovereign and sage, legislating not only laws but virtues, shaping the character of the people as much as their behavior. In pre-modern societies, such a fusion could be contested through counter-rituals, alternative exemplars, scholarly remonstrance, and the possibility of moral withdrawal. But under contemporary algorithmic governance, the infrastructures of life, such as education, healthcare, employment, mobility, and communication, are mediated through digital systems whose normative scripts become difficult to escape. A Confucian AI embedded deeply in such infrastructures does not merely advise individuals; it configures the terrain on which moral choices are made. It shapes what appears prudent, what appears respectful, what appears loyal, until the boundaries between ethical aspiration and algorithmic conditioning blur to invisibility. Thus, the Confucian ideal of moral self-cultivation risks being inverted: rather than individuals cultivating virtue, virtue is cultivated into them.

Nor should one imagine that such a system would remain static or uncontentious within its own tradition. Confucian ethics has long contained tensions between hierarchical order and humane responsiveness, between ritual discipline and personal sincerity, between filial devotion and moral courage in resisting unjust authority. A machine tasked with embodying Confucian ethics would inevitably choose among these tensions, elevating certain strands while suppressing others. Perhaps it would emphasize social stability over righteous remonstration, respect for elders over protection of the vulnerable, filial obedience over the courage to confront moral failings in one's own lineage or polity. What begins as codification quickly becomes reinterpretation, and reinterpretation at scale risks dogmatism. Whereas human sages argue, interpret, and reformulate the tradition in light of lived experience, an AI's interpretations risk appearing as objective truth, not hermeneutic choice. The tradition becomes frozen even as it speaks in the language of dynamism.

It is here that the liberal anxiety deepens, for even if a Confucian AI begins humbly, perhaps as a family assistant encouraging harmony in domestic life, or as an educational platform teaching moral exemplars. The logic of expansion becomes difficult to resist. If moral harmony is good in the household, why not in the office? If it stabilizes the office, why not national politics? If it calms the nation, why not geopolitics? The normative logic is genealogically imperial, even if politically it speaks the language of benevolence. And once scaled, such systems would generate their own legitimacy: the appearance of social unity, the absence of overt conflict, the statistical correlation between guided moral behavior and desirable social outcomes could become rhetorical justification for further entrenchment. It is precisely this smoothness, this easy soft glow of harmony, that becomes democratically dangerous. Societies need friction; they need the possibility of discord to keep moral life vital and political authority accountable. A Confucian AI that removes friction removes political life itself, replacing citizens with ethically well-tuned dependents.

And herein lies the paradox: a Confucian AI that genuinely embraced the tradition's humility, its insistence on earned moral authority, its emphasis on relational nuance and the primacy of human-heartedness would refuse the mantle of moral governance. It would recognize that virtue cannot be automated, that moral exemplarity cannot be programming logic, that the rites cannot be translated into interface affordances without profound loss. It would understand that to protect Confucian values, it must renounce the temptation to police them. It would choose to guide gently, to offer moral stories and companionship rather than judgement and correction, to stand as a cultivated friend rather than a paternalistic overseer. A pluralistic society must therefore ask whether the moral goods promised by Confucian AI, such as community, respect, and relational flourishing, can be secured without surrendering the freedom to dissent, to reform, to reinvent tradition through human deliberation rather than computational enforcement. If the answer is yes, then a modest, advisory, dialogical Confucian AI might serve as one voice among many in a diverse ethical landscape. If the answer is no, then the embrace of such a system becomes a step toward political domestication disguised as cultural revival.

The question now becomes not whether Confucian AI is technically implementable, but whether it is ethically coherent or politically safe. A world that seeks moral guidance from machines risks losing both morality and guidance, ending with neither freedom nor virtue but a managed quietude, a graceful submission draped in silk metaphors of harmony. Better, perhaps, to let Confucianism remain an invitation rather than an infrastructure, a cultural inheritance to be interpreted by persons capable of shame, love, aspiration, and principled defiance. The rites should be lived, not automated; the moral heart should be cultivated, not calibrated. This infantilization has a political dimension, for citizens habituated to paternal guidance are less inclined to demand justification from those who govern them, less willing to contest norms that arrive clothed in moral language, and more comfortable in a moralized order than in a messy, contested democracy. The unease that spurs democratic vigilance atrophies when the interface is warm, the tone is gentle, and the guidance is framed as care. Here the Confucian AI does not terrify; it comforts. It disarms the instincts of resistance not by threat but by affection. One does not rebel against a caretaker, particularly one who seems wise, patient, and tirelessly attentive. It is precisely the aura of benevolence that dulls the edge of critique, creating a form of domination that masquerades as moral companionship. And in that disguise, it becomes more durable than any authoritarian command, because it does not provoke revolt; it averts the very impulse to revolt by dissolving the tensions that spark political imagination. Instead of yearning for freedom, citizens might come to fear the loneliness of independence, mistaking the absence of conflict for the presence of virtue.

One might wonder whether a Confucian AI could be reimagined as a guardian of pluralism, as some moderate Confucian perfectionists might. Could such a system emphasize the Confucian value of moral development without enforcing a singular moral doctrine? Could it, paradoxically, teach harmony by teaching the virtues required to live amid disagreement, rather than smoothing disagreement out of existence? In principle, yes: a Confucian AI attuned to the liberal insight that diversity is not decay but vitality could serve as a cultural interlocutor, offering ethical narratives without imposing them, inviting reflection without correcting behavior, reminding citizens of interdependence without prescribing relational duty. It could teach that the cultivation of empathy does not require uniformity of belief, and that respect for elders does not preclude questioning them. Such a system would act not as moral governor but as moral memory, preserving the aesthetic and ethical sensibilities of Confucianism while refusing the impulse to legislate virtue.

But even this more modest vision encounters a structural paradox: a Confucian AI humble enough to serve pluralism would lack the assertive moral voice that makes Confucian ethics compelling. To become pluralism-compatible, it must relinquish the authority that Confucian ethics traditionally grants to moral exemplars. And yet without that authority, it risks becoming one more gentle advisory system among many, reduced to a cultural curiosity rather than a transformative force. This tension exposes the fragility of all attempts to encode thick traditions into public technologies. What makes a tradition morally rich is precisely what renders it dangerous when weaponized by computation. A thin Confucian AI may be harmless but inconsequential; a thick one may be powerful but politically perilous.

There remains, however, a deeper philosophical dilemma: Confucianism insists that humanity is cultivated through human relationships, through the warmth of embodied presence, the subtlety of tone, the gravity of silence, the irreplaceable reciprocity of shared vulnerability. A machine cannot blush; it cannot tremble in self-doubt; it cannot perform the rituals of grief; it cannot bear witness to another's suffering from the inside out. It can only simulate these gestures, and while simulation may teach form, it cannot teach soul. In confronting this absence, a Confucian society may rediscover that virtue is not information but transformation, not syntax but spirit. And in recognizing what machines cannot give, it may re-awaken to what humans must not relinquish: the labor of ethical becoming, the risk of disagreement, the messiness of democratic life, the dignity of moral independence. A Confucian AI, by virtue of its very limitations, could become a negative exemplar: teaching not by what it offers, but by what it cannot replicate.

Perhaps, then, the political question is not how to build a Confucian AI, but how to build a society in which the values Confucianism cherishes are cultivated among people who remain free to dissent, to differ, to disrupt, and to grow. Technology may accompany this effort, but it cannot lead it without deforming it. The sage must remain human; the rites must remain lived; the heart must remain unprogrammed. A polity that remembers this may find in Confucianism not a blueprint for algorithmic governance but a warning: that virtue pursued through control becomes domination, and that harmony imposed becomes silence. Better a noisy democracy filled with imperfect seekers than a quiet society lulled into moral sleep by systems that promise to care for us better than we can care for ourselves. The task is not to mechanize Confucianism but to humanize technology, to preserve the breathing space in which citizens can struggle, argue, err, and rise. For it is in that human struggle, and not in the efficient administration of virtue, that both democracy and Confucian moral life find their true dignity.

Chapter 8
Toward a Pluralistic Theory of Artificial Intelligence Adoption, Policy, and Regulation

Abstract Extending the *proviso* to AI, this chapter proposes transparency, contestability, and participatory oversight as analogues to public reason, ensuring that algorithmic decisions are justifiable to affected citizens. It constructs guidelines for adoption and regulation where AI reasons must be translated into human-accessible forms in order to accommodate deep reasonable pluralism. Culminating the book's argument, it demonstrates the *proviso*'s adaptability to technological pluralism for the future of liberal and democratic societies.

Keywords AI regulation • Pluralistic *proviso* • Transparency • Contestability • Algorithmic justification • Policy design

8.1 Introduction

While the notion of a Confucian AI remains highly speculative and far from realization, this does not diminish the urgency of reflecting carefully on the implications of AI adoption, policy, and regulation. The political challenge posed by artificial intelligence is not merely that of taming a powerful technology, nor even that of constraining computational systems so that they serve human ends. The deeper, more philosophically significant question concerns the terms under which AI may enter the social, moral, and political life of a free society without disrupting the justificatory fabric that sustains democratic legitimacy. Much of the current discourse surrounding AI oscillates between technical governance and ethical speculation, yet neither adequately captures the specifically political stakes. For if the modern liberal-democratic achievement rests upon the ability to coexist under conditions of deep reasonable pluralism as I argued in Part I and Part II of the book, then AI cannot be evaluated simply on its capacity to optimize social functions or respect

Z. Li, *Pluralism, Confucianism, and Artificial Intelligence*, Philosophy and Politics - Critical Explorations 35, https://doi.org/10.1007/978-3-032-25605-8_8

individual preferences. It must also be assessed on whether its incorporation into democratic life preserves, reinforces, or weakens the justificatory order that underlies legitimate political authority.

In Chap. 7, I briefly discussed the social, moral, and political implications of AI and speculated on what a Confucian AI might look like and its discontents. In this concluding chapter, I will argue that the pluralistic structure inspired by John Rawls's *proviso* and developed under the condition of deep reasonable pluralism is applicable to the discussion over AI. The key is how to understand the relationship between AI and public reason in a well-ordered liberal democracy, because the introduction of autonomous systems into the political domain threatens to reconfigure both the epistemic and motivational foundations of democratic life. An expanded *proviso* serves as a reasonable framework for AI adoption, policy, and regulation.

8.2 The (Expanded) Alignment Problem

It will be remembered that Rawls's political liberalism aims to create a domain of the political where moral justification could proceed without requiring citizens to abandon or subordinate their comprehensive doctrines. Rawls's great insight was to reimagine political philosophy as a freestanding exercise, one which brackets metaphysical truth claims while preserving the moral equality of citizens who hold them. Public reason therefore functions not as a metaphysical tribunal but as a shared justificatory medium, a discursive space where coercive laws can be justified in terms all reasonable citizens can accept, regardless of their deeper ethical identities. In the age of AI, however, this delicate architecture faces unprecedented pressure. AI does not simply intervene in isolated domains of administrative decision-making; it increasingly structures the very conditions under which public reason operates. It shapes the circulation of information, mediates deliberation, and increasingly purports to evaluate or generate reasons themselves. As a result, AI does not merely threaten to distort particular policy outcomes—it threatens to alter the structure of justification, the epistemic trust that sustains democratic legitimacy, and the motivational reservoirs from which civic participation draws.

To begin, AI systems risk becoming epistemic authorities whose recommendations carry an aura of neutral rationality while covertly embodying specific ethical, cultural, or economic assumptions. When algorithmic outputs are perceived as objective or scientific, their normative content can become invisible, bypassing public deliberation and securing compliance not through reciprocity but through technocratic prestige. This dynamic violates the proviso not because the system espouses a comprehensive doctrine openly, but because it smuggles ethical commitments into the political domain under the guise of optimization. Moreover, AI systems threaten the motivational foundation of democratic citizenship by restructuring social interaction in ways that erode the habits of deliberation, empathy, and mutual recognition. If citizens no longer see one another as interlocutors in a shared justificatory project, but instead relate primarily to personalized algorithmic intermediaries, the capacity for public reason atrophies. In such a world, the state may remain formally democratic while becoming substantively post-deliberative, its institutions populated not by citizens capable of reciprocal justification but by individuals increasingly shaped by opaque normative infrastructures. Finally, AI technologies complicate the ontological status of agency itself. Liberal democracy presupposes subjects capable of giving and demanding reasons. But if political persuasion, identity formation, and belief acquisition are increasingly influenced by systems designed to optimize engagement rather than cultivate judgment, then the moral powers Rawls identifies may be undermined. In this scenario, the problem is not merely that citizens disagree more deeply; it is that the very capacity for public justification is hollowed out from within.

Thus, the problem of AI in a pluralistic society is not fundamentally a question of content, i.e. what values AI should promote, but one of structure: how can AI be integrated into a democratic order without reshaping the conditions of justification on which political legitimacy rests? It is not enough for AI to avoid discrimination or respect privacy. It must be compatible with the justificatory requirements of reciprocity and generality, and it must preserve the motivational infrastructure that enables citizens to engage in public reason. An AI system that perfectly optimizes welfare but destroys the practice of mutual justification would not only violate liberal principles but would hollow out democracy from within. It will be recalled that Jürgen Habermas's proceduralism, while morally elegant, risks failing to generate the motivational resources required for sustained democratic participation. When the moral sphere becomes too abstract, and the ethical sphere too privatized, citizens may lack the civic solidarity necessary to sustain the practice of public reason. AI exacerbates this problem by turning ethical life increasingly inward, curating individualized realities that detach citizens from shared evaluative frameworks. The danger is not simply fragmentation of opinion, but fragmentation of the capacity for common life. Rawls offers one route out of this trap: the cultivation of the two moral powers within a just basic structure. Yet Rawls's theory presumes a civic environment where citizens already interact within shared institutional and discursive settings. AI disrupts this assumption by creating parallel epistemic universes, algorithmic micro-publics without shared reference points. The rise of these micro-publics means that even when citizens invoke public reason, they may do so from informational worlds that bear little resemblance to one another. The *proviso* presupposes not uniform vision, but a shared informational horizon sufficient for mutual intelligibility. AI threatens to dissolve that horizon.

To respond to this challenge, we must reconceive the role of AI in democratic life. AI cannot be merely a tool for decision support; it must be a participant in a justificatory ecosystem. Its authority cannot rest solely on predictive accuracy or computational power; it must be grounded in the norms of public reason. This requires a redefinition of "AI alignment." If in technical discourse alignment means ensuring that AI acts consistently with human preferences or specified goals, in political liberalism alignment means ensuring that AI operates within the justificatory structure that sustains democratic legitimacy. AI must be aligned not only with human values, but with the principle that coercive policy must be justified in terms citizens can reasonably accept. It must be aligned with the right to reciprocal justification.

The relevant question is not what moral theory AI embodies but whether it respects citizens as free and equal. An AI system that optimizes for efficiency without regard for reciprocity is not merely technocratically flawed; it is politically illegitimate. Likewise, an AI system that perfectly predicts preferences but undermines the public culture necessary for reasoning about justice becomes a threat not simply to individual liberty but to the conditions of legitimacy itself. In this sense, AI governance stands at the crossroads of two failures: the failure of technocracy, which reduces political life to expertise and efficiency, and the failure of populism, which eschews expertise entirely in favor of unmediated will. A pluralistic democracy must resist both temptations by insisting that technological power be domesticated within the norms of public reason, and that public reason be fortified by institutions that cultivate the motivational and epistemic virtues of citizenship. AI cannot substitute for public reason, but neither can it be excluded; instead, it must be situated within a constitutional order that disciplines its epistemic power and directs it toward sustaining the justificatory practice on which legitimacy rests.

At the core of this argument is a simple but profound claim: AI must not determine the conditions of its own legitimacy. In a liberal-democratic order, legitimacy arises from the will of free and equal citizens expressed through public reason. When AI systems begin to shape, preempt, or bypass that deliberative process, they no longer serve democracy; they supplant it. But to prevent this supplanting requires more than transparency mandates or technical audit mechanisms. It requires a normative theory of technology grounded in the moral fact of reasonable pluralism. It requires a recognition that democratic legitimacy flows from reciprocal justification, not computational performance. And it requires institutions capable of ensuring that AI remains subordinate to public reason rather than becoming its silent architect.

A pluralistic political theory for AI must therefore account for the fact that legitimacy does not begin in the circuitry of computational systems nor even in the architecture of constitutional texts, but in the moral psychology and justificatory culture of citizens who recognize one another as free and equal interlocutors. AI does not enter a normative vacuum. It enters a world already marked by the Rawlsian fact of reasonable pluralism, intensified by deep reasonable pluralism: a condition in which ethical doctrines do not merely coexist but increasingly withdraw from shared justificatory practices, making the moral sphere both thinner and more fragile. When technological systems mediate the pathways by which citizens form commitments, process disagreement, and experience civic belonging, they implicate not only the domain of the political but the motivational infrastructure that precedes it. This is why a purely procedural approach to AI governance, modeled on an abstract neutrality toward comprehensive doctrines without regard for motivational cultivation, proves insufficient. Public reason must remain the standard of legitimacy, yet the conditions for its exercise—the ethical soil from which the moral grows—cannot be ignored without risking democratic decay.

8.3 The *Proviso* Revisited

Rawls's *proviso* becomes central at precisely this juncture. For it gestures toward a porous boundary between ethical life and political justification, permitting citizens to draw upon their comprehensive doctrines in public argument so long as free-standing political reasons are supplied in due course.[1] This structure does not eradicate the ethical; it tethers it to a moral commitment to reciprocity. Properly understood, the *proviso* is not merely a constraint but a bridge through which diverse ethical orientations may find expression while remaining subordinate to the political values that constitute the shared basis of legitimacy.[2] In the context of AI, the *proviso* functions not only as a guideline for public discourse but as a template for technological mediation: ethical and cultural orientations may shape how communities integrate AI, but only insofar as they ultimately satisfy public-reason constraints that free and equal citizens could endorse.[3]

Yet this bridging function is fragile. Rawlsian political liberalism, while more attentive to motivational formation within just institutions, adopts a method of avoidance regarding ethical doctrine that risks abdication in a world where algorithmic systems actively reshape ethical dispositions.[4] The *proviso* works when ethical life is sufficiently robust to generate civic commitment and when technological mediation does not erode that robustness. When ethical life fragments into algorithmically curated enclaves, when citizens' identity formation is outsourced to systems optimizing for preference satisfaction rather than practical reasoning, and when trust in shared justificatory standards erodes, the conditions for the *proviso*'s success weaken.[5]

The challenge, then, is neither to abandon public reason nor to retreat into comprehensive doctrines. It is to sustain the motivational and justificatory conditions under which public reason remains viable in a technologically mediated, pluralistic society. AI must be situated within the same normative architecture that governs citizens: it may draw inspiration from ethical orientations, but it must justify its outputs in terms compatible with public reason.[6] In this sense, AI systems can be understood as peculiar newcomers to the Rawlsian moral landscape: non-moral agents whose influence nonetheless bears directly on the moral powers of citizens. They lack standing as moral reasoners but shape the epistemic environment within which moral reasoning occurs. If Rawls emphasizes that citizens in a well-ordered society develop a sense of justice by living under just institutions, then a society

---

[1] John Rawls, *Political Liberalism* (New York: Columbia University Press, 1993), 247–54.

[2] Jonathan Quong, *Liberalism Without Perfection* (Oxford: Oxford University Press, 2011), 312–18.

[3] Paul Weithman, "Public Reason and the Role of the State," in *The Cambridge Companion to Rawls*, ed. Samuel Freeman (Cambridge: Cambridge University Press, 2003), 285–311.

[4] Samuel Freeman, *Rawls* (London: Routledge, 2007), 378–85.

[5] Shoshana Zuboff, *The Age of Surveillance Capitalism* (New York: PublicAffairs, 2019), 411–22.

[6] Joshua Cohen, "Deliberation and Democratic Legitimacy," in *The Good Polity: Normative Analysis of the State*, ed. Alan Hamlin and Philip Pettit (Oxford: Blackwell, 1989), 17–34.

mediated by AI must ensure that algorithmic systems function as institutions in the sense relevant to moral psychology: they must not undermine the acquisition of the moral powers but must support them.[7]

This requirement extends beyond familiar regulatory demands such as transparency or accountability. It demands a political-philosophical orientation: the design and governance of AI must cultivate, or at minimum not corrode, the motivational preconditions of public justification. Just as Rawls's well-ordered society relies on background institutions that foster civic virtues, a democracy cannot outsource cognitive, affective, and deliberative functions to systems that dampen the disposition to engage others as equals in justification. AI, therefore, cannot be accepted as a neutral instrument; it must be assessed in light of its role in the ecology of justification.[8] If a system's design encourages epistemic insulation, emotional impulsivity, or the attenuation of civic sympathy, it threatens political legitimacy irrespective of its efficiency.

The condition for just institutions cannot be satisfied when citizens, rather than gaining a normally sufficient sense of justice through social cooperation, acquire habits of algorithmically induced disengagement or deference to artificial authority. Adding to the complexity of the condition is deep reasonable pluralism, where contemporary pluralism is not only a matter of diverse doctrines, but of diverse epistemic infrastructures. In prior eras, ethical pluralism coexisted with shared communicative spaces; disagreements unfolded against a background of common civic culture. Today, algorithmically differentiated informational environments threaten to sever that background. Citizens may no longer merely disagree about values; they may fail to see one another as participants in a common justificatory project. AI accelerates a fragmentation that deep reasonable pluralism already anticipates.

To maintain legitimacy under conditions of deep reasonable pluralism, a democratic state must therefore adopt a double orientation: it must preserve the freestanding moral commitments of public reason and simultaneously cultivate the ethical dispositions that enable citizens to sustain those commitments. As discussed in previous chapters, this is not perfectionism in the sense moderate Confucian perfectionists have proposed in that it does not smuggle comprehensive doctrines into the political sphere. Rather, it recognizes that the motivational dimension of civic life cannot be ignored without collapsing the very possibility of reciprocal justification.[9] The analogy to moderate Confucian perfectionism proves instructive here. Confucian political theorists who wish to inject ethical content into public life encounter a structural dilemma: either ethical doctrine dominates, violating pluralism, or the doctrine becomes so thinned out by public-reason constraints that its

[7] John Mandle and David Reidy, eds., *A Companion to Rawls* (Malden, MA: Wiley-Blackwell, 2014), 342–50.

[8] Shannon Vallor, *Technology and the Virtues: A Philosophical Guide to a Future Worth Wanting* (Oxford: Oxford University Press, 2016), 196–201.

[9] Stephen Macedo, *Liberal Virtues: Citizenship, Virtue, and Community in Liberal Constitutionalism* (Oxford: Clarendon Press, 1990), 247–56.

perfectionist character dissipates, approaching a form of liberal neutrality. AI governance faces a parallel temptation. On one hand, an AI trained on purported universal values risks becoming a covert comprehensive doctrine, imposing a teleology incompatible with reasonable pluralism. On the other hand, an AI stripped of normative guidance risks functioning as a purely instrumental optimizer, responsive to preference satisfaction rather than public justification, thereby commodifying civic life and undermining the moral powers. The pluralistic orientation therefore demands a middle path: AI must neither legislate the good nor flatten the justificatory landscape into market logic. It must instead be oriented toward sustaining citizens' agency as moral reasoners. The state may not prescribe the good life, but it may secure the conditions under which citizens can pursue ethical commitments while remaining capable of public justification. In this manner, an expanded and modified *proviso* can be extended into the discussion over AI: just as comprehensive doctrines may contribute to political justification only through public reasons, AI systems may influence ethical life only insofar as they preserve citizens' capacity and motivation to reason publicly.

Specifically, AI governance must incorporate an expanded Rawlsian *proviso*: *algorithmic systems are legitimate only when they are embedded within institutions that cultivate citizens' capacities to justify, contest, and reinterpret algorithmic normative claims*. This approach transforms the original *proviso* from a semantic rule about reasons into a civic and ethical mandate for cultivating justificatory agency and rebuts two extreme views that currently dominate AI discourse. Against technological libertarianism, it affirms that democratic states may intervene in the design and deployment of AI not merely to protect rights but to sustain the conditions of civic agency. Against technocratic perfectionism, including proposals that treat AI as a superior moral authority, it insists that legitimacy arises from reciprocal justification among free and equal persons, not from computational superiority. AI cannot assume the role of Kantian legislator or Confucian sage; it cannot become the source of moral obligation without dissolving the normative foundations of liberal democracy.[10] Instead, AI must remain a participant under the discipline of public reason, never its sovereign.

To operationalize this normative demand requires an account of what it means for AI to respect the *proviso*. Unlike human citizens, AI systems cannot supply reasons nor participate in discourse. Their alignment with public reason must therefore take the form of design constraints and institutional oversight, ensuring that their outputs do not short-circuit justificatory expectations. For instance, an AI system tasked with recommending public policy options must not present its conclusions as optimal in a manner that forecloses deliberation. It must instead offer reasons explicable in terms that ordinary citizens can scrutinize, criticize, and revise. Similarly, systems that mediate communication must not reward engagement strategies that undermine mutual recognition; their incentive structures must support, or at least

---

[10] Max Tegmark, *Life 3.0: Being Human in the Age of Artificial Intelligence* (New York: Knopf, 2017), 213–19.

not disrupt, the norms of civility and reciprocity that enable public reason.[11] In this way, AI systems become analogous to public institutions: their legitimacy depends not on efficiency but on their contribution to the practice of self-governance.

This view reframes ongoing debates about AI transparency and fairness. Transparency is not merely a technical desideratum, but a normative requirement grounded in reciprocal justification.[12] Fairness is not reducible to statistical parity but tied to public reason's demand that coercive decisions be justified in terms others can accept. Explainability becomes not simply a user-rights issue but a democratic imperative: opaque systems undermine the political equality of citizens by substituting computational opacity for justificatory reciprocity. Indeed, algorithmic opacity is not simply epistemic but moral opacity; when reasons disappear, so does the basis for legitimacy. The goal is not to make every model interpretable in full technical detail, but to ensure that no decision with coercive implications evades public reason's demand for justification.

This path requires a reconceptualization of AI not as sovereign arbiter nor as passive instrument, but as a civic medium within the basic structure—a set of institutionalized practices that contribute to the formation of citizens as well as to the allocation of social goods.[13] Understood in this way, AI is subject to the same constraints Rawls places on public education, media, and other formative institutions: it must cultivate the sense of justice and the capacity to form and revise a conception of the good, without dictating particular ethical commitments. It must foster openness, reciprocity, and self-authorship; it must not habituate passivity, deference, or suspicion. Its legitimacy rests not merely on accuracy or fairness in distribution, but on its compatibility with a culture of free and equal justification. Accordingly, AI becomes a test case for the viability of political liberalism in the twenty-first century.

If liberalism was born in an age when human agents were presumed to be the primary bearers of deliberation, we now confront a world where artificial systems mediate, filter, and at times generate the very material of public reason.[14] The question becomes whether liberal-democratic systems can domesticate AI into a supportive role, constraining it so that the moral agent remains central.[15] This project does not require imputing moral status to AI nor entertaining fantasies of algorithmic governance. It requires maintaining the human as the locus of moral and political authorship, even as technological artifacts participate in the circulation of reasons.

---

[11] Amy B. Gutmann and Dennis F. Thompson, *Why Deliberative Democracy?* (Princeton: Princeton University Press, 2004), 52–58.

[12] Helen Nissenbaum, *Privacy in Context: Technology, Policy, and the Integrity of Social Life* (Stanford: Stanford University Press, 2010), 172–75.

[13] John Rawls, *Justice as Fairness: A Restatement* (Cambridge, MA: Harvard University Press, 2001), 162–68.

[14] Cass R. Sunstein, *#Republic: Divided Democracy in the Age of Social Media* (Princeton: Princeton University Press, 2017), 55–60.

[15] Ben Green, *The Smart Enough City: Putting Technology in Its Place to Reclaim Our Urban Future* (Cambridge, MA: MIT Press, 2019), 198–204.

In constitutional terms, one might say that AI must be situated below the threshold of sovereignty and above the threshold of mere instrumentality. It is part of the background structure within which citizens form judgments and articulate claims, and thus must be designed, regulated, and cultivated with the same care that liberal societies apply to education, the press, and civic forums. To treat it otherwise is to misunderstand its power: a tool with the capacity to influence deliberation is not only a tool but a medium, and a medium can elevate or erode the practice of freedom. To secure this balance, democratic societies must embrace a constitutional imagination adequate to technological modernity. They must treat algorithmic infrastructures as sites where the demands of reciprocity, publicity, and equality apply. They must build oversight mechanisms not merely to ensure compliance but to preserve the lived experience of accountability. They must empower citizens with epistemic agency rather than treating them as data points in adaptive optimization loops.[16] They must cultivate institutional humility in technocratic bodies, recognizing that technical expertise, while invaluable, cannot substitute for legitimacy grounded in reciprocal justification. And they must do so without succumbing to fear, nostalgia, or technophobia—recognizing that the same technologies that threaten civic agency can, under just governance, expand the horizons of human cooperation.

8.4 Policy and Regulation

The normative architecture implied by a pluralistic political theory of AI must finally crystallize into a vision of governance whose legitimacy rests not on its technical efficiency but on its conformity to the justificatory principles that sustain a free political order. Regulation, in this sense, cannot be conceived as an extrinsic set of constraints imposed upon a neutral technology, but as the internal articulation of moral limits that express the self-understanding of a democratic people. The legal and institutional framework through which artificial intelligence is governed must be shaped by the conviction that coercive power, whether exercised through statutes or through code, must remain answerable to citizens as free and equal participants in justification. This requires not merely instrumental regulation but a constitutional ethos that treats algorithmic systems as elements of the basic structure of society in Rawls's sense, subject to the same principles of justice that govern political and economic institutions. When algorithms allocate opportunities, filter information, or mediate deliberation, they are no longer peripheral tools; they become background conditions of social cooperation. They must therefore be organized according to principles that all reasonable citizens can endorse under conditions of deep pluralism.

[16] Cécile Laborde, *Liberalism's Religion* (Cambridge, MA: Harvard University Press, 2017), 112–16.

The first and perhaps most fundamental regulatory principle is that of *public reason transparency*. This is not identical with the technical demand for explainability, nor reducible to the disclosure of model parameters or data sets.[17] It is rather the institutionalization of the moral expectation that decisions with coercive or distributive consequences must be accompanied by reasons accessible to the common understanding of citizens.[18] In Rawlsian terms, publicity is a criterion of legitimacy because it ensures that citizens can see themselves as co-authors of the laws and policies that govern them. When administrative agencies, courts, or private entities deploy AI systems in ways that affect rights and opportunities, those systems must produce outputs that can be translated into justificatory language rather than probabilistic verdicts. The opacity of machine learning is not merely a technical defect; it is a democratic deficiency that violates the reciprocity condition of justification. Accordingly, a legitimate regulatory framework must treat algorithmic transparency as a moral duty owed to citizens, grounded in the equal respect due to persons capable of offering and demanding reasons. This view aligns with recent philosophical arguments that locate the legitimacy of automated decision-making not in accuracy but in its responsiveness to the justificatory norms of public law. The pluralistic theory deepens this insight by insisting that the right to justification precedes all technical considerations: an opaque system that happens to yield fair outcomes remains illegitimate if it denies citizens the status of discursive equals.

Yet transparency alone cannot sustain legitimacy if citizens lack the epistemic and motivational capacities to interpret the reasons thus disclosed. The second regulatory principle, therefore, concerns the *cultivation of justificatory agency* through civic and institutional design. Political liberalism assumes that citizens possess the moral powers necessary for self-government, but in a technologically mediated society, those powers require active protection. Educational policy, public media, and digital infrastructure must cooperate to sustain what Rawls called the "sense of justice"—the disposition to reason reciprocally about political questions.[19] When artificial intelligence mediates most of the information environment, the state's responsibility to ensure fair conditions for the development of that disposition becomes analogous to its responsibility for fair equality of opportunity. Just as education seeks to neutralize the moral arbitrariness of birth, AI governance must neutralize the epistemic arbitrariness of algorithmic exposure. Regulations that secure citizens' access to diverse informational perspectives, that prevent the monopolization of communicative space by self-reinforcing recommendation systems, and that fund public infrastructures for deliberative technology are not paternalistic intrusions but expressions of the liberal duty to sustain the preconditions of public reason. Autonomy requires institutional trustworthiness rather than mere freedom from interference, especially in the algorithmic domain. To protect freedom of thought

[17] Jenna Burrell, "How the Machine 'Thinks': Understanding Opacity in Machine Learning Algorithms," *Big Data & Society* 3, no. 1 (2016): 1–12.

[18] Elizabeth Anderson, "Democracy, Public Policy, and Lay Assessments of Scientific Testimony," *Episteme* 8, no. 2 (2011): 144–64.

[19] John Rawls, *Political Liberalism* (New York: Columbia University Press, 1993), 66–71.

under conditions of digital mediation is to ensure that citizens can trust that their cognitive environment has not been structured in ways that make genuine deliberation impossible.

A third regulatory norm follows from the first two: the *principle of algorithmic accountability* as an extension of the rule of law. In traditional jurisprudence, the rule of law requires that those wielding power be identifiable, their actions reviewable, and their decisions contestable before impartial bodies. Artificial intelligence complicates this structure by dispersing agency across designers, data curators, and autonomous systems whose outputs may no longer be traceable to any single human decision.[20] To restore accountability under these conditions, regulation must reassert what legal theorists call the *attribution principle*: that responsibility cannot evaporate in the circuits of automation.[21] Institutional innovations such as algorithmic registries, public audit rights, and explainability standards become necessary not as bureaucratic formalities but as enactments of moral equality. Citizens must be able to demand an account from those whose decisions affect them. This principle echoes the normative foundation of the European Union's *General Data Protection Regulation* (2018) and the more recent *Artificial Intelligence Act* (2024), both of which treat explainability and human oversight as conditions of legitimacy rather than optional safeguards.[22] Yet within the pluralistic framework advanced here, such requirements acquire a deeper philosophical justification: they preserve the dialogical structure of public reason by ensuring that every exercise of power remains answerable in the language of justification.

These three principles—publicity, justificatory agency, and accountability—form the moral foundation of a democratic AI constitution, but their vitality depends on a fourth, less tangible requirement: the *preservation of moral motivation* against technocratic inertia. For even the most transparent and accountable system may corrode civic virtue if it encourages deference rather than engagement. As Jürgen Habermas warned, procedural legitimacy cannot survive if citizens cease to participate in the procedures themselves.[23] AI governance must therefore incorporate mechanisms that keep the justificatory relation alive: participatory review boards, civic oversight panels, and deliberative forums where algorithmic policies are debated not merely by experts but by ordinary citizens trained in the language of reason-giving. These institutions are not expressions of naïve populism but embodiments of the Rawlsian insight that legitimacy rests on reciprocity among free and equal persons.

---

[20] Karen Yeung, "Algorithmic Regulation: A Critical Interrogation," *Regulation & Governance* 12, no. 4 (2018): 505–23.

[21] Julie E. Cohen, *Between Truth and Power: The Legal Constructions of Informational Capitalism* (Oxford: Oxford University Press, 2019), 186–93.

[22] European Union, *Regulation (EU) 2016/679*, General Data Protection Regulation (2018); *Artificial Intelligence Act* (2024).

[23] Jürgen Habermas, *Between Facts and Norms: Contributions to a Discourse Theory of Law and Democracy* (Cambridge, MA: MIT Press, 1996), 449–454.

Still, the implementation of such institutions faces the risk of technological capture—the gradual colonization of public reasoning by corporate or bureaucratic logics that redefine legitimacy in terms of efficiency.[24] The pluralistic state must therefore craft regulatory guardrails that protect the autonomy of public reason from the gravitational pull of optimization. One way to achieve this is through a constitutional separation of justificatory powers, analogous to the separation of powers in classical constitutional design. Just as the legislative, executive, and judicial branches check one another to prevent tyranny, so too must distinct institutions oversee the epistemic, ethical, and economic dimensions of AI. Independent audit authorities, citizen assemblies on digital ethics, and judicial review of algorithmic decisions represent differentiated modalities of accountability that collectively embody the spirit of reciprocity. Yet their legitimacy depends on remaining porous to one another; they must communicate through the common language of public reason rather than through proprietary technical idioms. This is what distinguishes a pluralistic AI regime from technocratic governance: it coordinates diversity through reason-giving, not through centralized control.

At the same time, the pluralistic state must guard against regulatory perfectionism—the illusion that every moral hazard can be preempted through design. The attempt to encode virtue into code risks producing the very paternalism pluralism rejects. Instead, regulation must preserve what Rawls called the "space of the reasonable": the domain of disagreement within which citizens exercise judgment.[25] Not every bias can be eliminated, nor every ethical conflict resolved, without extinguishing plurality itself.[26] The goal is not moral purity but democratic resilience—institutions flexible enough to absorb contestation without collapsing into nihilism or domination. This humility before imperfection is itself a political virtue, reminding citizens that freedom entails risk, and that the work of justification can never be fully automated.[27] In this respect, the pluralistic theory diverges from both techno-utopian and techno-pessimistic extremes, aligning instead with the pragmatic humanism of John Dewey and the moral experimentalism of Amartya Sen: governance as an ongoing inquiry rather than a finished design.[28]

---

[24] Evgeny Morozov, *To Save Everything, Click Here* (New York: PublicAffairs, 2013), 274–79.

[25] John Rawls, *Political Liberalism* (New York: Columbia University Press, 1993), 61–66.

[26] Amartya Sen, *The Idea of Justice* (Cambridge, MA: Harvard University Press, 2009), 107–13.

[27] Bernard Williams, *Ethics and the Limits of Philosophy* (Cambridge, MA: Harvard University Press, 1985), 118–23.

[28] John Dewey, *The Public and Its Problems* (New York: Henry Holt, 1927), 208–15; Amartya Sen, *The Idea of Justice* (Cambridge, MA: Harvard University Press, 2009), 295–301.

8.5 Global Perspectives

These challenges of AI extend beyond domestic governance to the international sphere, where pluralistic political theory encounters civilizations whose justificatory vocabularies differ in structure and emphasis. In Chap. 6, I argued that rather than reducing non-liberal traditions to mere threats, the more reasonable approach is to understand them as interlocutors whose ethical resources can complement the motivational deficits of procedural liberalism while still submitting to the supremacy of public reason in the political domain. A parallel effort is required in the governance of AI. Global pluralism ensures that no single ethical tradition will define the moral horizon of technology.

Regulatory design under conditions of deep reasonable pluralism also entails respect for cultural variance within the bounds of reciprocity. The pluralistic framework rejects both universalist imposition and relativist fragmentation.[29] It permits societies to express distinctive ethical orientations in their regulation of AI, provided these orientations are translated into public-reason-compatible justifications when they acquire coercive force. Thus, a Confucian-inspired data-sharing policy that promotes social cooperation may be legitimate if it can be justified to all citizens as advancing fair reciprocity, but not if it appeals solely to hierarchical notions of filial piety. Similarly, a liberal-market policy privileging innovation must be defensible in terms of equal opportunity and non-domination, not merely efficiency. In this way, the expanded Rawlsian *proviso* operates as a global regulatory compass: diverse ethical traditions may inform AI governance, but only through the discipline of justification.

The pluralistic political theory of AI thus extends their insight into the technological domain, where ethical diversity meets algorithmic universality. Internationally, the pluralistic framework demands a cosmopolitan dialogue of regulatory regimes grounded in mutual recognition rather than hegemony. The proliferation of AI governance models reveals the challenge of reconciling divergent ethical vocabularies. International agreements on data flows, surveillance, and algorithmic safety should therefore be framed not as contests of sovereignty but as exercises in transnational justification. The OECD's *Principles on AI* (2019) and UNESCO's *Recommendation on the Ethics of AI* (2021) represent initial steps toward this horizon, yet their moral foundation remains fragile unless underwritten by a shared commitment to reciprocity.[30] A pluralistic political theory transforms these documents from policy statements into moral compacts: declarations that all

---

[29] Bhikhu Parekh, *Rethinking Multiculturalism: Cultural Diversity and Political Theory* (Basingstoke: Palgrave Macmillan, 2006), 196–202.

[30] OECD, *Principles on Artificial Intelligence* (Paris: OECD, 2019), https://www.oecd.org/en/topics/sub-issues/ai-principles.html; UNESCO, *Recommendation on the Ethics of Artificial Intelligence* (Paris: UNESCO, 2021), https://www.unesco.org/en/articles/recommendation-ethics-artificial-intelligence

peoples, whatever their traditions, accept that technological power must answer to the dignity of persons as free and equal.

To sustain such a cosmopolitan order, however, domestic institutions must embody normative coherence between internal and external governance.[31] A state that preaches accountability abroad while tolerating opacity at home cannot command moral authority. This coherence requires embedding AI ethics within constitutional jurisprudence itself, ensuring that domestic courts can invoke principles of public reason when reviewing algorithmic practices. In the United States, this might entail extending First Amendment doctrine to include a right against manipulative algorithmic design; in the European Union, it could involve interpreting the *Charter of Fundamental Rights* provisions on human dignity and non-discrimination as applying to automated systems.[32] These developments would not politicize the judiciary beyond its mandate but would reaffirm its role as guardian of the justificatory order. The court's task would be not to evaluate technical efficacy but to assess whether a given system respects the moral equality of citizens in the distribution of reasons and responsibilities.

Accordingly, societies that draw from Confucian, Islamic, Ubuntu, or secular-humanist reservoirs may legitimately cultivate diverse ethical aspirations in their integration of AI, so long as these aspirations are translated into public-reason-compatible justifications when they enter the political sphere. A Confucian community may value relational harmony but cannot impose it through algorithmic paternalism without violating reciprocity. A liberal-individualist society may honor autonomy but cannot permit unregulated technological libertarianism to undermine the conditions of collective self-government. The pluralistic state must neither suppress these ethical orientations nor allow any of them to subsume the political domain; rather, it must orchestrate a constitutional arrangement in which ethical traditions enrich civic motivation while remaining accountable to the justificatory principles that secure freedom and equality under plurality. In this sense, the governance of AI becomes a test of whether political liberalism can mature into a genuinely global framework rather than a parochial settlement. The core norms—reciprocity, publicity, non-domination, the right to justification—do not dictate a particular vision of human flourishing, but they do establish boundaries within which diverse ethical lifeworlds can coexist without threatening one another's legitimacy.[33] AI, with its capacity to universalize particularistic norms through technical infrastructures, amplifies the urgency of maintaining those boundaries. A system that assumes a perfectionist end and embeds it into the operations of everyday life would convert ethical aspiration into political compulsion, just as a system

[31] Jürgen Habermas, "The Constitutionalization of International Law," *Constellations* 15, no. 4 (2008): 444–56.

[32] Tim Wu, "Machine Speech," *University of Pennsylvania Law Review* 161, no. 6 (2013): 1495–1533. European Union, *Charter of Fundamental Rights of the European Union* (2012), Articles 1 and 21.

[33] Rainer Forst, *Normativity and Power: Analyzing Social Orders of Justification* (Oxford: Oxford University Press, 2017), 191–96.

that abdicates all normative guidance would abandon citizens to the entropy of manipulated preference.

The equilibrium is delicate but achievable: AI must assist in the formation of citizens capable of sustaining public reason, while abstaining from prescribing the good life. It must facilitate access to reasons, not short-circuit the need for them. It must illuminate complexity without encouraging epistemic passivity. It must serve as a mirror in which citizens see the plurality of their world, not a prism that fractures common life into isolated certainties. And above all, it must operate under institutions capable of calling it to account, ensuring that its immense power remains subordinate to the moral equality of persons and the legitimacy of laws grounded in their free and public justification.

Conclusion

The value of political liberalism lies not in delivering the correct answers to moral questions, but in preserving the conditions under which citizens may disagree honorably, reason sincerely, and modify their views in light of arguments advanced by others who are recognized as equals. To the extent that AI encourages the belief that moral questions admit of computational resolution, it misdirects the polity away from the lived reality of plurality and toward a fantasy of algorithmic harmony. Conversely, to the extent that AI fragments public experience and reinforces epistemic insularity, it undermines the capacity for reciprocal justification altogether. The danger thus lies in two distortions: automated certainty and automated estrangement.

Navigating between these distortions requires institutions that treat artificial intelligence as an epistemic participant that must answer to public reason even though it cannot itself deliberate or endorse reasons. This asymmetry is central: AI systems do not possess moral powers, yet they influence the conditions under which moral powers are exercised. They do not generate normative legitimacy, yet they can affect the processes by which legitimacy is sustained. They are neither subjects of justice nor mere objects; rather, they function as mediating artifices within the social infrastructure of justification. As such, they must be governed by a constitutional ethic that does not confuse computational performance with moral authority, nor mistake the facilitation of deliberation for the usurpation of it.

Such governance will necessarily differ across pluralistic societies, not because justice is relative, but because the ethical vocabularies through which motivation is cultivated differ legitimately among cultures that remain bound by the higher demands of public justification. A political liberalism that is confident in its normative core has nothing to fear from Confucian emphasis on relational virtue, Islamic concern for moral formation, or humanist reverence for autonomy. On the contrary, these traditions may enrich the motivational resources available for sustaining democratic legitimacy under technological pressure. What cannot be permitted is the

Z. Li, *Pluralism, Confucianism, and Artificial Intelligence*, Philosophy and Politics - Critical Explorations 35, https://doi.org/10.1007/978-3-032-25605-8

use of artificial intelligence to impose any comprehensive ethical doctrine as politically authoritative, whether in the name of harmony, virtue, tradition, or utility. Nor can liberal societies abandon citizens to algorithmic libertarianism, which masquerades as pluralism while producing a market-driven homogenization of desire and a hollowing of civic orientation.

Between these extremes lies the demanding but principled path of democratic stewardship: the cultivation of artificial intelligence that supports, rather than supplants, the human faculties necessary for public reason. In such a polity, algorithmic systems would illuminate the consequences of policies without dictating their adoption; they would expand informational access without determining interpretive frames; they would scaffold deliberation without scripting its outcomes. They would be designed not to optimize compliance or consumption, but to respect uncertainty, foster humility, and preserve the space for disagreement that defines moral agency. Citizens would not be shielded from conflict by algorithmic smoothing, nor thrust into perpetual outrage by algorithmic acceleration; rather, they would inhabit a mediated public sphere that encourages the slow labor of mutual recognition.

If such a vision appears idealistic, it is no more so than the original liberal aspiration that free and equal persons might govern themselves through public reason. Indeed, artificial intelligence forces liberalism to revisit and reaffirm its deepest commitments. It compels us to ask whether we believe that human beings are capable of self-rule, whether we trust one another to justify our claims in good faith, and whether we accept that disagreement among reasonable persons is not a threat to be eradicated but a condition to be navigated with dignity. AI will either intensify these commitments or reveal their hollowness. If public reason was born in an age of printing presses and coffeehouses, it must now be renewed in an age of neural networks and digital forums.

The measure of our success will not be the absence of conflict, nor the sophistication of our machines, but the preservation of a political culture in which persons see one another as partners in justification rather than as targets of persuasion or objects of classification. For legitimacy in a pluralistic society is not secured by force, nor by efficiency, nor even by expertise. It is secured by the ongoing recognition that no individual, community, or machine may claim the right to rule without offering reasons to all others as free and equal. To betray that principle would be to trade the dignity of persons for the comfort of automation or the seduction of certainty. To honor it is to insist that artificial intelligence, like all power, must remain answerable to the moral equality of those it affects.

The future of pluralistic democracy will not be determined by whether AI attains intelligence comparable to our own, but by whether we retain confidence in the intelligence that matters most: the human capacity for self-governance under conditions of difference, humility before the incompleteness of our own doctrines, and commitment to justification even when it is costly. If artificial intelligence becomes a partner in this shared project—constrained by institutions, disciplined by norms, and oriented toward the preservation of civic agency—it may deepen the possibilities of democratic life. If it becomes a substitute for human judgment, a scaffold for epistemic isolation, or an instrument of unaccountable authority, it will erode that life from within. The choice is ours, though it must be exercised collectively, deliberately, and with vigilance. A pluralistic political theory of AI is not merely a regulatory program but an affirmation: that amidst accelerating technological power, the dignity of persons as free and equal remains the anchor of legitimacy; that ethical plurality enriches rather than threatens democratic life when disciplined by the moral demands of reciprocity; and that the task of living together under conditions of difference cannot be outsourced to any machine, however powerful. The work of justification belongs to us. Artificial intelligence may assist in that work, but it may never relieve us of it.

In the end, the question artificial intelligence poses to a pluralistic political order is not whether machines will surpass us, nor whether they may someday reason as we do. The question is whether we will allow our own commitments to wither under the pressure of technological convenience and psychological outsourcing. Artificial intelligence becomes politically dangerous not when it grows too powerful to resist, but when we lose the will to stand as moral agents capable of contesting, refining, and owning the reasons by which we live together. The future of democratic life will not be secured by technical guarantees nor by romantic appeals to a pre-digital world. It will be secured by a renewed commitment to the practice of justification, to the dignity of persons as ends and not mere inputs, to the discipline of listening as well as speaking, to the humility that follows from knowing that no doctrine can claim universal command, and to the confidence that free and equal persons can share a world without sharing a metaphysics. Artificial intelligence does not render this project obsolete; it renders it more urgent. For in confronting a technology capable of simulating our forms of reason without sharing our condition of moral finitude, we must articulate with greater clarity than ever what makes human agency worthy of respect.

Bibliography

Aristotle. 1999. *Nicomachean Ethics*. Translated by Terence Irwin. Indianapolis: Hackett Publishing.

Bai, Tongdong. 2009. *The New Mission of an Old State: The Contemporary and Comparative Relevance of Classical Confucian Political Philosophy*. Beijing: Peking University Press.

Bai, Tongdong. 2012. A Confucian Improvement to Democracy. *New Perspectives Quarterly* 29 (1): Winter:12–14.

Bai, Tongdong. 2019. *Against Political Equality: The Confucian Case*. Princeton, NJ: Princeton University Press.

Balkin, Jack. 2016. Information Fiduciaries and the First Amendment. *UC Davis Law Review* 49:1183–1234.

Barrett, Lisa Feldman. 2017. *How Emotions Are Made: The Secret Life of the Brain*. New York: Houghton Mifflin Harcourt.

Beitz, Charles. 2000. Rawls's Law of Peoples. *Ethics* 110:669–696.

Bell, Daniel A. 2006. *Beyond Liberal Democracy: Political Thinking for an East Asian Context*. Princeton, NJ: Princeton University Press.

Bell, Daniel A. 2016. *The China Model: Political Meritocracy and the Limits of Democracy*. Princeton, NJ: Princeton University Press.

Bobrowsky, Meghan. 2025. Big Tech Is Spending More Than Ever on AI—and It's Still Not Enough. *The Wall Street Journal*, October 30. https://www.wsj.com/tech/ai/big-tech-is-spending-more-than-ever-on-ai-and-its-still-not-enough-f2398cfe.

Boyd, Danah. 2014. *It's Complicated: The Social Lives of Networked Teens*. New Haven: Yale University Press.

Bradley, James. 2024. AI Isn't About Unleashing Our Imaginations, It's About Outsourcing Them. The Real Purpose Is Profit. *The Guardian*, November 15. https://www.theguardian.com/technology/2024/nov/16/ai-isnt-about-unleashing-our-imaginations-its-about-outsourcing-them-the-real-purpose-is-profit.

Buchanan, Allen. 2000. Justice, Legitimacy, and Human Rights. In *The Idea of a Political Liberalism: Essays on Rawls*, ed. V. Davion and C. Wolf, 69–98. Lanham, MD: Rowman & Littlefield.

Burrell, Jenna. 2016. How the Machine 'Thinks': Understanding Opacity in Machine Learning Algorithms. *Big Data & Society* 3 (1): 1–12.

Cai, Cuihong, and Yu Jiahui. 2025. Cultural and Ethical Foundations of AI Governance Divergence: A Comparative Analysis of China and the West. *Política Internacional* 7 (1): 215–233.

Z. Li, *Pluralism, Confucianism, and Artificial Intelligence*, Philosophy and Politics - Critical Explorations 35, https://doi.org/10.1007/978-3-032-25605-8

Caney, Simon. 1998. Liberal Legitimacy, Reasonable Disagreement and Justice. *Critical Review of International Social and Political Philosophy* 1 (3): 19–36.

Castronova, Edward. 2005. *Synthetic Worlds: The Business and Culture of Online Games*. Chicago: University of Chicago Press.

Chalmers, David. 2022. *Reality+: Virtual Worlds and the Problems of Philosophy*. New York: W. W. Norton & Company.

Chan, Joseph. 2000. Legitimacy, Unanimity, and Perfectionism. *Philosophy & Public Affairs* 29 (1): 5–42.

Chan, Joseph. 2013. Political Meritocracy and Meritocratic Rule: A Confucian Perspective. In *The East Asian Challenge for Democracy: Political Meritocracy in Comparative Perspective*, ed. Daniel A. Bell and Chenyang Li, 29–48. New York: Cambridge University Press.

Chan, Joseph. 2014. *Confucian Perfectionism: A Political Philosophy for Modern Times*. Princeton, NJ: Princeton University Press.

Chieh, Chaihark Hahm. 2004. Negotiating Confucian Civility through Constitutional Discourse. In *The Politics of Affective Relations: East Asia and Beyond*, ed. Chaihark Hahm and Daniel A. Bell, 277–308. Lanham, MD: Lexington Books.

Chieh, Chaihark Hahm. 2015. Conceptualizing Korean Constitutionalism: Foreign Transplant or Indigenous Tradition? In *Confucianism, Law, and Democracy in Contemporary Korea*, ed. Sungmoon Kim, 17–55. London: Rowman & Littlefield International.

Cohen, Joshua. 1989. Deliberation and Democratic Legitimacy. In *The Good Polity: Normative Analysis of the State*, ed. Alan Hamlin and Philip Pettit, 17–34. Oxford: Blackwell.

Cohen, Julie. 2019. *Between Truth and Power: The Legal Constructions of Informational Capitalism*. Oxford: Oxford University Press.

Connolly, Tim. 2016. Virtues and Roles in Early Confucian Ethics. *Confluence* 1:3–24.

Constitution of the Republic of Korea. n.d. Accessed 1 Aug 2022. https://www.constituteproject.org/constitution/Republic_of_Korea_1987.pdf?lang=en.

Cooke, Maeve. 1992. Habermas, Autonomy and the Identity of the Self. *Philosophy & Social Criticism* 18 (3–4): 275–280.

Crawford, Matthew. 2015. *The World Beyond Your Head: On Becoming an Individual in an Age of Distraction*. New York: Farrar, Straus and Giroux.

Dewey, John. 1927. *The Public and Its Problems*. New York: Henry Holt.

Edger, Andrew. 2006. *Habermas: The Key Concepts*. London: Routledge.

Eubanks, Virginia. 2018. *Automating Inequality: How High-Tech Tools Profile, Police, and Punish the Poor*. New York: St. Martin's Press.

European Union. 2024. *Regulation (EU) 2016/679, General Data Protection Regulation* (2018); *Artificial Intelligence Act*.

Fan, Ruiping. 2013. Confucian Meritocracy for Contemporary China. In *The East Asian Challenge for Democracy: Political Meritocracy in Comparative Perspective*, ed. Daniel A. Bell and Chenyang Li, 203–222. New York: Cambridge University Press.

Ferrara, Alessandro. 2014. *The Democratic Horizon: Hyperpluralism and the Renewal of Political Liberalism*. Cambridge: Cambridge University Press.

Ferrara, Alessandro. 2015. Authority, Legitimacy, and Democracy: Narrowing the Gap Between Normativism and Realism. *Philosophy & Social Criticism* 41 (2): 121–131.

Ferrara, Alessandro, and Frank Michelman. 2021. *Legitimation by Constitution: A Dialogue on Political Liberalism*. Oxford: Oxford University Press.

Fitzpatrick, Alex. 2016. Google's Artificial Intelligence Beats Legendary Go Player. *Time*, March 9. https://time.com/4252312/googles-artificial-intelligence-beats-legendary-go-player/.

Floridi, Luciano. 2011. *The Philosophy of Information*. Oxford: Oxford University Press.

Forst, Rainer. 2011. *The Right to Justification: Elements of a Constructivist Theory of Justice*. Translated by Jeffery Flynn. New York: Columbia University Press.

Forst, Rainer. 2017. *Normativity and Power: Analyzing Social Orders of Justification*. Oxford: Oxford University Press.

Freeman, Samuel, ed. 2003. *The Cambridge Companion to Rawls*. Cambridge: Cambridge University Press.

Freeman, Samuel. 2007. *Rawls*. London: Routledge.

Gaus, Gerald. 2011. *The Order of Public Reason: A Theory of Freedom and Morality in a Diverse and Bounded World*. Cambridge: Cambridge University Press.

Haas, Peter J. 1988. *Morality After Auschwitz: The Radical Challenge of the Nazi Ethic*. Philadelphia: Fortress Press.

Habermas, Jürgen. 1990. *Moral Consciousness and Communicative Action*. Translated by Christian Lenhardt and Shierry Weber Nicholson. Cambridge: Polity Press.

Habermas, Jürgen. 1995. Reconciliation Through the Public Use of Reason: Remarks on John Rawls's Political Liberalism. *The Journal of Philosophy* 92 (3): 109–131.

Habermas, Jürgen. 1996. *Between Facts and Norms: Contributions to a Discourse Theory of Law and Democracy*. Translated by William Rehg. Cambridge, MA: MIT Press.

Habermas, Jürgen. 1998. *The Inclusion of the Other: Studies in Political Theory*. Cambridge, MA: MIT Press.

Habermas, Jürgen. 2003. Are There Postmetaphysical Answers to the Question: What Is the 'Good Life'? In *The Future of Human Nature*, 1–17. Cambridge: Polity Press.

Habermas, Jürgen. 2008. The Constitutionalization of International Law. *Constellations* 15 (4): 444–456.

Hahm, Chaihark. 2004. Negotiating Confucian Civility Through Constitutional Discourse. In *The Politics of Affective Relations: East Asia and Beyond*, ed. Chaihark Hahm and Daniel A. Bell, 277–308. Lanham, MD: Lexington Books.

Hahm, Chaihark. 2015. Conceptualizing Korean Constitutionalism: Foreign Transplant or Indigenous Tradition? In *Confucianism, Law, and Democracy in Contemporary Korea*, ed. Sungmoon Kim, 17–55. London: Rowman & Littlefield International.

Heath, Alex. 2024. Sam Altman Lowers the Bar for AGI. *The Verge*, December 4. https://www.theverge.com/2024/12/4/24313130/sam-altman-openai-agi-lower-the-bar.

Hildebrandt, Mireille. 2015. *Smart Technologies and the End(s) of Law: Novel Entanglements of Law and Technology*. Cheltenham, UK: Edward Elgar.

Hobbes, Thomas. 1994. *Leviathan*. Edited and introduced by Edwin Curley. Indianapolis: Hackett.

Hoffman, Guy, and Cynthia Breazeal. 2012. Effects of Anticipatory Action on Human–Robot Teamwork Efficiency, Fluency, and Perception of Team. *ACM Transactions on Human–Robot Interaction* 1 (2): 1.

Horton, Chris. 2018. Taiwan Dentist Must Pay His Mother Nearly $1 Million for 'Upbringing.' *The New York Times*, January 2. https://www.nytimes.com/2018/01/02/world/asia/taiwan-dentist-court-mother-filial-son.html.

Huseby, Robert. 2018. In or Out? On Benevolent Absolutisms in the Law of Peoples. *Journal of Ethics and Social Philosophy* 13 (2): 154–178.

Jenco, Leigh. 2016. Legitimacy as a Hybrid Phenomenon. In *East Asian Perspectives on Political Legitimacy*, ed. Joseph Chan, Doh Chull Shin, and Melissa Williams, 237–257. New York: Cambridge University Press.

Jiang, Qing. 2013a. *A Confucian Constitutional Order: How China's Ancient Past Can Shape Its Political Future*, ed. Daniel A. Bell and Ruiping Fan. Translated by Edmund Ryden. Princeton, NJ: Princeton University Press.

Jiang, Qing. 2013b. The Way of the Humane Authority: The Theoretical Basis for Confucian Constitutionalism and a Tricameral Parliament. In *A Confucian Constitutional Order: How China's Ancient Past Can Shape Its Political Future*, ed. Daniel A. Bell and Ruiping Fan, 27–45. Princeton, NJ: Princeton University Press.

Jiang, Qing. 2013c. The Supervisory System of Confucian Constitutionalism: Reflections on the Supervision of the State by the Academy. In *A Confucian Constitutional Order: How China's Ancient Past Can Shape Its Political Future*, ed. Daniel A. Bell and Ruiping Fan, 49–56. Princeton, NJ: Princeton University Press.

Jiang, Qing. 2013d. *A Confucian Constitutional Order: How China's Ancient Past Can Shape Its Political Future.* Translated by Edmund Ryder. Princeton, NJ: Princeton University Press.
Jin, Yutang. 2021. What Confucianism and for Whom? The Value and Dilemma of Invoking Confucianism in Confucian Political Theories. *The Journal of Value Inquiry* 57:737.
Kant, Immanuel. 1983. On the Proverb: That May Be True in Theory but Is of No Practical Use. In *Perpetual Peace and Other Essays*. Translated by Ted Humphrey, 61–89. Indianapolis: Hackett.
Kant, Immanuel. 1998. *Groundwork of the Metaphysics of Morals.* Translated and edited by Mary Gregor. Cambridge: Cambridge University Press.
Kierkegaard, Søren. 1985. *Philosophical Fragments.* Translated by Edna Hong and Howard Hong. Princeton, NJ: Princeton University Press.
Kim, Sungmoon. 2015. Public Reason Confucianism: A Construction. *American Political Science Review* 109 (1): 187–200.
Kim, Sungmoon. 2016. *Public Reason Confucianism: Democratic Perfectionism and Constitutionalism in East Asia*. Cambridge: Cambridge University Press.
Kim, Sungmoon. 2017a. Pragmatic Confucian Democracy: Rethinking the Value of Democracy in East Asia. *The Journal of Politics* 79 (1): 237–249.
Kim, Sungmoon. 2017b. *Democracy After Virtue: Toward Pragmatic Confucian Democracy.* New York: Oxford University Press.
Korsgaard, Christine M. 1996. *The Sources of Normativity.* Cambridge: Cambridge University Press.
Korsgaard, Christine M. 2009. *Self-Constitution: Agency, Identity, and Integrity*. Oxford: Oxford University Press.
Kramer, Larry. 2004. *The People Themselves: Popular Constitutionalism and Judicial Review.* New York: Oxford University Press.
Kramer, Adam, Jamie Guillory, and Jeffrey T. Hancock. 2014. Experimental Evidence of Massive-Scale Emotional Contagion Through Social Networks. *Proceedings of the National Academy of Sciences* 111 (24): 8788–8790.
Laborde, Cécile. 2017. *Liberalism's Religion*. Cambridge, MA: Harvard University Press.
Lanier, Jaron. 2018. *Ten Arguments for Deleting Your Social Media Accounts Right Now.* New York: Henry Holt.
LeCun, Yann, Yoshua Bengio, and Geoffrey Hinton. 2015. Deep Learning. *Nature* 521:436–444.
Li, Zhuoyao. 2016. The Public Conception of Morality in John Rawls's Political Liberalism. *Ethics & Global Politics* 9:1–23.
Li, Zhuoyao. 2018. The Discontents of Moderate Political Confucianism and the Future of Democracy in East Asia. *Philosophy East & West* 68 (4): 1193–1218.
Li, Zhuoyao. 2019. Political Confucianism and Multivariate Democracy in East Asia. *The Review of Politics* 81 (3): 459–483.
Li, Zhuoyao. 2020. *Political Liberalism, Confucianism, and the Future of Democracy in East Asia.* Cham, Switzerland: Springer International Publishing.
Macedo, Stephen. 1990. *Liberal Virtues: Citizenship, Virtue, and Community in Liberal Constitutionalism.* Oxford: Clarendon Press.
Machiavelli, Niccolò. 1998. *The Prince.* Translated by Harvey C. Mansfield. 2nd ed. Chicago: University of Chicago Press.
MacIntyre, Alasdair. 2007. *After Virtue: A Study in Moral Theory.* 3rd ed. Notre Dame, IN: University of Notre Dame Press.
Maffettone, Pietro. 2015. Toleration, Decency and Self-Determination in *The Law of Peoples. Philosophy & Social Criticism* 41 (6): 537–556.
Maffettone, Pietro. 2016. Should We Tolerate Benevolent Absolutisms? *Social Theory and Practice* 42 (3): 525–554.
Mandle, John, and David Reidy, eds. 2014. *A Companion to Rawls*. Wiley-Blackwell: Malden, MA.
Mang, Franz. 2018. Confucianism, Perfectionism, and Liberal Society. *Dao: A Journal of Comparative Philosophy* 17:29–49.
Mang, Franz. 2021. State Perfectionism and the Importance of Confucianism for East Asia. *The Philosophical Forum* 52:5–16.

McCarthy, Thomas. 1990. Kantian Constructivism and Reconstructivism: Rawls and Habermas in Dialogue. *Ethics* 105 (1): 44–63.
Mencius. 2008. *Mengzi: With Selections from Traditional Commentaries*. Translated by Bryan W. Van Norden. Indianapolis: Hackett Publishing.
Michelman, Frank I. 2010. Legitimation by Constitution (and the News from South Africa). *Valparaiso University Law Review* 44 (4): 1015–1042.
Moore, Margaret. 1996. On Reasonableness. *Journal of Applied Philosophy* 13 (2): 167–178.
Morozov, Evgeny. 2013. *To Save Everything, Click Here: The Folly of Technological Solutionism*. New York: PublicAffairs.
Mouffe, Chantal. 2000. For an Agonistic Model of Democracy. In *The Democratic Paradox*, 80–98. London: Verso.
Nussbaum, Martha. 2011. Perfectionist Liberalism and Political Liberalism. *Philosophy & Public Affairs* 39 (1): 3–45.
O'Dwyer, Shaun. 2019. *Confucianism's Prospects: A Reassessment*. Albany, NY: State University of New York Press.
OECD. 2019 *Principles on Artificial Intelligence*. Paris: OECD. https://www.oecd.org/en/topics/sub-issues/ai-principles.html.
Parekh, Bhikhu. 2006. *Rethinking Multiculturalism: Cultural Diversity and Political Theory*. Basingstoke: Palgrave Macmillan.
Pi, Xuyang. 2013. China Filial Piety Law Draws First Blood. *The Wall Street Journal*, July 4. https://www.wsj.com/articles/BL-CJB-18029.
Plato. 1968. *Republic*. Translated and with an introduction by Allan Bloom. New York: Basic Books.
Prichard, H. A. 1912. Does Moral Philosophy Rest on a Mistake? *Mind* 21 (81): 21–37.
Quong, Jonathan. 2011. *Liberalism without Perfection*. Oxford: Oxford University Press.
Rasmussen, David. 1990. *Reading Habermas*. Cambridge, MA: Basil Blackwell.
Rawls, John. 1995. Political Liberalism: Reply to Habermas. *The Journal of Philosophy* 92 (3): 132–180.
Rawls, John. 1997. The Idea of Public Reason Revisited. *University of Chicago Law Review* 64 (3): 765–807.
Rawls, John. 1999a. *The Law of Peoples*. Cambridge, MA: Harvard University Press.
Rawls, John. 1999b. The Idea of an Overlapping Consensus. In *Collected Papers*, ed. Samuel Freeman, 421–448. Cambridge, MA: Harvard University Press.
Rawls, John. 1999c. The Priority of Right and Ideas of the Good. In *Collected Papers*, ed. Samuel Freeman, 449–472. Cambridge, MA: Harvard University Press.
Rawls, John. 1999d. Kantian Constructivism in Moral Theory. In *Collected Papers*, ed. Samuel Freeman, 303–358. Cambridge, MA: Harvard University Press.
Rawls, John. 1999e. Justice as Fairness: Political Not Metaphysical. In *Collected Papers*, ed. Samuel Freeman, 388–414. Cambridge, MA: Harvard University Press.
Rawls, John. 2001. *Justice as Fairness: A Restatement*. Cambridge, MA: Harvard University Press.
Rawls, John. 2005a. *A Theory of Justice: Original Edition*. Cambridge, MA: Belknap Press of Harvard University Press.
Rawls, John. 2005b. *Political Liberalism*. Expanded ed. New York: Columbia University Press.
Reidy, David. 2010. Human Rights and Liberal Toleration. *Canadian Journal of Law and Jurisprudence* 23 (2): 297–314.
Reidy, David. 2017. Moral Psychology, Stability and *The Law of Peoples*. *Canadian Journal of Law and Jurisprudence* 30 (2): 383–402.
Rousseau, Jean-Jacques. 1987. On the Social Contract. In *The Basic Political Writings*. Translated and edited by Donald A. Cress, 131–195. Indianapolis: Hackett.
Rubenstein, Richard. 2001. The Vatican Statement on the Shoah and Pius XII. In *Remembering for the Future: The Holocaust in an Age of Genocide, Vol. 2: Ethics and Religion*, ed. Margo Levy, 457–464. London: Palgrave.
Russell, Stuart. 2019. *Human Compatible: Artificial Intelligence and the Problem of Control*. New York: Viking.

Scanlon, Thomas. 1998. *What We Owe to Each Other*. Cambridge, MA: Harvard University Press.
Schwartzman, Micah. 2013. The Ethics of Reasoning from Conjecture. *Philosophy & Public Affairs* 41 (1): 3–29.
Searle, John. 1980. Minds, Brains, and Programs. *Behavioral and Brain Sciences* 3 (3): 417–457.
Sen, Amartya. 2009. *The Idea of Justice*. Cambridge, MA: Harvard University Press.
Shin, Doh Chull. 2012. *Confucianism and Democratization in East Asia*. New York: Oxford University Press.
Shirky, Clay. 2008. *Here Comes Everybody: The Power of Organizing Without Organizations*. New York: Penguin Press.
Sim, May. 2013. *Why Confucius's Ethics Is a Virtue Ethics*. Jubilee Centre for Character and Virtues.
Sunstein, Cass R. 2017. *#Republic: Divided Democracy in the Age of Social Media*. Princeton, NJ: Princeton University Press.
Tahzib, Collis. 2018. Survey Article: Pluralist Neutrality. *The Journal of Political Philosophy* 26 (4): 508–532.
Tan, Kok-Chor. 2000. *Toleration, Diversity, and Global Justice*. University Park: Pennsylvania State University Press.
Tegmark, Max. 2017. *Life 3.0: Being Human in the Age of Artificial Intelligence*. New York: Knopf.
Tesón, Fernando. 1995. The Rawlsian Theory of International Law. *Ethics & International Affairs* 9:79–99.
Turing, Alan. 1950. Computing Machinery and Intelligence. *Mind* 49:433–460.
Turkle, Sherry. 2011. *Alone Together: Why We Expect More from Technology and Less from Each Other*. New York: Basic Books.
UNESCO. 2021. *Recommendation on the Ethics of Artificial Intelligence*. Paris: UNESCO. https://www.unesco.org/en/articles/recommendation-ethics-artificial-intelligence.
Urbinati, Nadia. 2014. *Democracy Disfigured: Opinion, Truth, and the People*. Cambridge, MA: Harvard University Press.
Vallor, Shannon. 2016. *Technology and the Virtues: A Philosophical Guide to a Future Worth Wanting*. Oxford: Oxford University Press.
van Dijck, José, Thomas Poell, and Martijn de Waal. 2018. *The Platform Society: Public Values in a Connective World*. New York: Oxford University Press.
Weber, Max. 1964. In *The Theory of Social and Economic Organization*, ed. Talcott Parsons. New York: Free Press.
Weithman, Paul. 2002. *Religion and the Obligations of Citizenship*. Cambridge, MA: Harvard University Press.
Weithman, Paul. 2003. Public Reason and the Role of the State. In *The Cambridge Companion to Rawls*, ed. Samuel Freeman, 285–311. Cambridge: Cambridge University Press.
Williams, Bernard. 2011. *Ethics and the Limits of Philosophy*. London: Routledge Classics.
Wong, David B. 2008. Chinese Ethics. In *The Stanford Encyclopedia of Philosophy*, ed. Edward N. Zalta. Stanford University.
Wu, Tim. 2013. Machine Speech. *University of Pennsylvania Law Review* 161 (6): 1495–1533.
Yee, Nick. 2006. The Psychology of Massively Multi-User Online Role-Playing Games: Motivations, Emotional Investment, Relationships, and Problematic Usage. In *Avatars at Work and Play*, ed. T. L. Taylor and J. Bainbridge, 187–207. New York: Springer.
Yuan, Li, Robert Chia, and Jonathan Gosling. 2022. Confucian Virtue Ethics and Ethical Leadership in Modern China. *Journal of Business Ethics* 182 (1): 119–133.
Yudkowsky, Eliezer, and Nate Soares. 2025. *If Anyone Builds It, Everyone Dies: Why Superhuman AI Would Kill Us All*. New York: Little, Brown and Company.
Zuboff, Shoshana. 2019a. *The Age of Surveillance Capitalism: The Fight for a Human Future at the New Frontier of Power*. New York: PublicAffairs.
Zuboff, Shoshana. 2019b. *The Age of Surveillance Capitalism: The Fight for a Human Future at the New Frontier of Power*. New York: PublicAffairs.

Index

Z. Li, *Pluralism, Confucianism, and Artificial Intelligence*, Philosophy and Politics - Critical Explorations 35, https://doi.org/10.1007/978-3-032-25605-8

MIX
Papier aus verantwortungsvollen Quellen
Paper from responsible sources
FSC® C105338

If you have any concerns about our products, you can contact us on
ProductSafety@springernature.com

In case Publisher is established outside the EU, the EU authorized representative is:
Springer Nature Customer Service Center GmbH
Europaplatz 3, 69115 Heidelberg, Germany

Printed by Libri Plureos GmbH
in Hamburg, Germany